adopting
older
children

adopting older children

A PRACTICAL GUIDE TO ADOPTING AND PARENTING CHILDREN OVER AGE FOUR

Stephanie Bosco-Ruggiero, MA,
Gloria Russo Wassell, MS, LMHC,
and Victor Groza, PhD

NEW HORIZON PRESS
Far Hills, New Jersey

Requests for permission should be addressed to:
New Horizon Press
P. O. Box 669
Far Hills, NJ 07931

Stephanie Bosco-Ruggiero, MA, Gloria Russo Wassell, MS, LMHC,
and Victor Groza, PhD
    Adopting Older Children:
    A Practical Guide to Adopting and Parenting Children Over Age Four

Cover design: Charley Nasta
Interior design: Scribe Inc.

Library of Congress Control Number: 2014938451

ISBN-13 (paperback): 978–0-88282–482–6
ISBN-13 (eBook): 978–0-88282–483–3

New Horizon Press

Manufactured in the U.S.A.

18   17   16   15   14   1   2   3   4   5

DEDICATION

Dedicated to all the children waiting for their forever families.
—SBR

Dedicated to my parents, Edmondo and Assunta Russo,
for opening their hearts to any child in need beyond their own.
Through their example they taught me the value of caring for all children.
—GRW

Dedicated to Adoption Partners families who teach us about
older child adoptions and to the staff who work with me and our
families, Becky Bernstein and Holli Camelio Rizenthaler.
—VG

AUTHORS' NOTE

This book is based on the authors' research, personal experiences, interviews and real life experiences. In order to protect privacy, names have been changed and identifying characteristics have been altered except for contributing experts.

For purposes of simplifying usage, the pronouns his/her and s/he are sometimes used interchangeably. The information contained herein is not meant to be a substitute for professional evaluation and therapy with mental health professionals.

ACKNOWLEDGMENTS

The authors would like to express their appreciation to the following individuals for their time and effort in reviewing all or parts of this book:

Diane E. Lang, PhD,
Director of Instructional Support Services, Orange-Ulster
BOCES, New York

Beth Brindo, MSSA, LISW,
Case Western Reserve University, Mandel School of Applied
Social Sciences

Susan Hansen, PhD,
Consultant, National Center for Social Work Trauma Education
and Workforce Development, Fordham University Graduate
School of Social Service

Dianne M. Jandrasits, PsyD,
Matilda Theiss Child Development Center,
Western Psychiatric Institute and Clinic of University of
Pittsburgh Medical Center

Tonia M. Safford-McClure,
 MAEd in School Psychology, PsyD in Educational Psychology,
 School Psychologist in California

Lenore Strocchia-Rivera, PhD,
 Founder, Learning Insights, and Visiting Adjunct Assistant
 Professor, Teachers College, Columbia University

Judy S. Schwartz, LMSW,
 Adoption Specialist

I would like to thank my parents for all the support they have given me throughout my life; I wish every child could be blessed with such loving parents. I also would like to thank my husband, Joe, for supporting me in so many ways during the writing of this book and my son, Michael, for letting Mommy write while he watched his shows. I am thankful to Dr. Virginia Strand for bringing me into the field of child welfare and child trauma research. Finally, thanks to all the incredible adoptive families who took time out of their busy lives to talk to us about their experiences and to New Horizon Press for publishing our book on older child adoption.—SBR

Table of Contents

Introduction

Every child deserves to have at least one constant caregiver who loves him or her fully. Unfortunately, for millions of children, this is the stuff of fairytales. Many children wait and wait for a family but sometimes that family never appears. According to the Department of Health and Human Services, in 2012 in the United States, more than 56,000 children were adopted from foster care, but another 23,000 aged out of the system, never having been adopted.[1] Those who age out of foster care are at a higher risk for low educational attainment, premature or single parenthood, unemployment/underemployment and/or homelessness. Children who grow up and age out of orphanages in low-resource countries face even bleaker futures.

Children's lives are on the line. This is why we decided to write this book. About a quarter of the 400,000 American children in foster care are legally free to be adopted and UNICEF estimates that there are millions of orphans in the world who need permanent families and homes.[2]

While many families are more than willing to adopt an infant domestically or internationally, many prospective adoptive parents still hesitate to adopt an older child or sibling group, according to Harris Interactive.[3] In addition to a lack of comprehensive information about older child adoption and sibling groups, there also is a lot of misinformation and fear regarding older child adoption. This guide aims to provide you and your family with a broad span of knowledge about older child adoption and parenting.

Older child adoption is being considered by an increasing number of families. One reason for this trend is that the number of infants being placed for adoption in high-resource countries has been decreasing, due in part to the fact that single parenthood is no longer stigmatized in many of those countries, so there is more support for single parents. Furthermore, many low-resource countries are trying to manage intercountry adoption and build domestic programs; this has the consequence of limiting the number of infants who can be adopted internationally except in those countries where child trafficking safeguards are not in place. Some countries only allow foreigners to adopt children with special needs, which includes an increasing number of older children. A recent upswing in media attention, both good and bad, about older child adoption also may be inspiring interest.

In the United States, there are some indications that the number of people who consider older child adoption far surpasses the number who actually adopt older children.[4] Factors that prevent people from following through on their interest in adopting an older child include misinformation, fear and a lack of responsiveness from public agencies.

Sensational stories in the media also give people a distorted view of older child adoption. The public hears stories about children being sent back to their countries of origin or "rehomed" by desperate adoptive parents, or they read stories about violent behavior by older adoptees. But what the public does not grasp is that these stories represent outlier cases. These stories do not characterize the nature of older child adoption in general. Most parents who adopt older children experience neither fairytales nor nightmares. Rather, they experience some of the expected challenges of raising children who have suffered trauma but ultimately they succeed in helping their children heal.

The vast majority of parents who adopt older children feel positive about their experience and in hindsight would do it again. Adoption generally has a strongly positive effect on children who have endured early adversity and, in fact, a majority of adopted children end up falling within the normal range of development and behavioral functioning, Susan Smith reported for the Evan B. Donaldson Adoption Institute.[5]

Older child adoption is not always easy. It demands a high level of commitment, patience and dedication and it is not a good choice for everyone. Adoptive parents of older children are not starting from scratch. They inherit the pain and hurt inflicted by others on their child. It is no easy task to raise a hurt child and remain unhurt yourself. The preparation is different as well. Instead of learning about diapers and baby food, parents of children adopted at an older age need to learn about attachment, trauma, grief, loss and disrupted development.

Despite inherent challenges, the rewards of older child adoption exceed many parents' expectations. As you prepare for your adoption journey, take time to learn from other adoptive families that have successfully built a tapestry of love and support for their children. Every day, resilient adoptive parents are raising their children beyond pain and toward healing and wholeness. The perseverance, commitment, strength and dedication of many adoptive parents is truly remarkable and inspiring.

Adoptive parents of older children carry heavy burdens and they deserve our utmost respect, understanding and support. As they heal their hurt children they also are healing our communities. Adoptive families need the best information possible to help them in their journeys. It is our hope that this guide will be a starting point for many prospective pre-adoptive parents looking for accurate, comprehensive information about older child adoption. We also hope that prospective parents get a sense of the special community of parents they will be a part of after they adopt.

This guide is focused on prospective, pre-adoptive and adoptive parents of children adopted after the age of four. While there are many guides and resources for parents who adopt infants and toddlers, there are not enough books about adopting and raising older children and teens. However, parents of children adopted at birth may also find this guide useful, because as their children grow, the children may also need help with loss and grief, identity formation and navigating relationships with biological family members. While there is some great information about older child adoption online and we refer to it throughout the book, it is helpful to have all the information you need in one handy guide.

This guide was written for you—the adoptive parent—because you will have the greatest impact on your child. It will help you learn the language of older child adoption, understand many of the challenges your child may face and direct you to additional quality information should you need it. Interwoven throughout the book are stories about—and advice from—real adoptive parents who are navigating parenthood every day with grace and flexibility.

If you are pressed for time, as most parents are, first read those chapters most relevant to you and your adoption journey. Return to the book as often as you need, mark it up, tab the pages and always keep it within arm's reach when the going gets tough.

This book is divided into four parts and includes an appendix of useful adoption resources organized by chapter. Part I is aimed at prospective adoptive parents who are in the process of deciding whether to adopt an older child. It includes detailed information about waiting children, adoptive parents and the process of adopting either domestically, internationally or through the tribal child welfare system. At the end of Part I, we look at what post-adoption services may be available to adoptive families.

Part II explores families that have adopted an older child. First, we focus on the changes and challenges older child adoption brings to families. Then we look at family dynamics, especially sibling relationships, how to help your child navigate his past and biological family relationships. We also look at multicultural and multiracial adoptive families, including their strengths, potential challenges and how parents can celebrate their adopted child's cultural heritage.

Part III focuses on understanding the older adopted child. Each adopted child is a unique individual. Some older adopted children will have needs that are quite complex and difficult to understand while others will have few special needs (even though they have carried the label of "special needs adoption"). Part III looks at how adoption can shape a child's emerging sense of self. Then it reveals how past trauma may impact the older adoptee. For some children, the past has left serious mental and/or physical scars, while for others the past has made them stronger and more resilient. Some children need a therapeutic family milieu and long-term professional help while others are able to heal in a short period of time. This section also looks at grief and loss in older adopted children and attachment issues. In Part III, we seek to give parents an understanding of the complex factors that may shape their child's development and functioning so they are better able to get help for their child if he or she needs it.

Part IV of this book concentrates on the adoptive parent. It examines the unique strength, resilience and adaptability of many adoptive parents. It looks at the adoptive parent's need for social support, community and understanding and how you can build a support network that meets your needs. Finally, we discuss the importance of self-care and of getting professional help for yourself and respite care for your child when you are having trouble coping with the daily demands of adopting and parenting an older child.

Thank you for all that you do for your children and for our communities. We hope this book helps you to find the world of support and understanding available to you whenever you need it. Best wishes for a fulfilling, love-filled parenting journey.

PART I

the adoption process

CHAPTER 1

Deciding to Adopt an Older Child

Deciding to build a family, whether through birth or adoption, is one of the most important and impactful decisions you will make in your life. Any experienced parent will tell you that having or adopting a child is an event that turns your life upside down and that parenting is one of the toughest jobs on earth. Deciding to have or adopt a child is not a decision that should be made lightly. Most certainly, the decision to adopt an older child is no exception.

The reasons people are interested in domestic or international older child adoption vary, but may include:

- Infertility
- They want children but decide to adopt for health or other reasons
- To provide a loving home to a child in need
- Older child adoption fits better with the prospective parent(s)' age and/or life-stage
- A religious or spiritual calling
- They were adopted and thus understand the importance of adoption
- They are fostering a child or children and want him/her/them to become a permanent part of the family

- They know someone who has adopted an older child and see how life-changing it has been for the child and the adoptive family
- Their children are grown and they want to raise more children
- They have a talent for working with challenged children or teens

There may be multiple reasons you are drawn to older child adoption. As you prepare to make your decision about adoption you may feel a natural amount of anxiety that comes with making such a life-changing decision. This is perfectly normal and acceptable. What is not acceptable, however, is making a decision without being well-informed. You must become educated about the challenges older adoptees have experienced in their lives and some of the issues they may encounter after adoption. Also read about the process of adopting an older child and what post-adoption services and support may be available to you. As you learn more about older child adoption, ask yourself these questions:

- Is adopting an older child right for me and my family?
- Is adoption about my needs or the needs of the child?
- Do I know enough about older child adoption to make an informed decision?
- Do I have realistic expectations about adopting an older child?
- Will I be thoroughly committed to my adoptive child, even when his or her behavior sometimes makes me dislike him or her?
- Do I have patience for a child whose behaviors may be the result of someone else's abuse and/or neglect?

If you have done your research and spoken to other adoptive parents and still have doubts about adopting an older child, discuss your feelings with an adoption professional, trusted family member, friend, clergyman or therapist. If you and your partner do not seem to be on the same page on adoption, don't force a decision on a person who is hesitant. In the end you will make the right decision. If you are confident you can be committed to an older adopted child through good times and bad, embark on a journey that may be the most rewarding of your life!

BETH'S STORY

Beth and her husband adopted four siblings who came into their care at the ages of six and a half, five, three-and-a-half and two, through their state's Department of Family and Protective Services. They always had a desire to adopt.

Beth explained, "I nannied for years and realized early in life that I don't particularly enjoy the infant years. I knew I wanted to be a mother but I didn't necessarily want to have a baby. [In adopting from the foster care system] I was able to give [four children] a safe and loving home, while living the dream I have had since I was thirteen of having a large family."

Beth feels some of the adoptive parents she has met in support groups simply weren't ready to adopt. She said, "We quickly realized that, as a family who came to adoption as a "plan A," we were in the minority. I have discovered that many adopt children as a "plan B" after exhausting every known medical option to conceive. Many of these parents, before bringing a wounded child into their life, did not grieve or heal fully after "plan A" was no longer viable. I listened to the expectations and disappointments of well-meaning parents played out in group therapy more times than I can count. The parents were venting with nodding support instead of being told they need to deal with their issues and not project them onto their children. It is a serious problem in this emerging adoption culture."

Beth's advice to people who are considering older child adoption is to "enter into a therapeutic discussion (with yourself, your partner, your therapist, whomever...) about the impacts of your decision." She also recommends that people do thorough research about older child adoption. Prior to adopting, Beth says that she and her husband spent a long time asking questions and looking into the process before they actually took their first steps.

EDUCATING YOURSELF ABOUT OLDER CHILD ADOPTION

The decision to adopt and parent an older child should be informed by love, hope and knowledge. Lois Wright and Cynthia Flynn asked fifty-eight adoptive parents of teens what advice they had for people considering teen adoption and the dominant piece of advice was get as much information as possible about older child adoption and the specific child you are adopting.[1]

There are many uncertainties with older child adoption, but one thing is certain—it is *not* a fairytale and it takes a lot of hard work. Unlike infants, older adoptees join their families with prior life experiences that have shaped their psychological, behavioral, physical, social and emotional development. They join your family with hope, joy and love but also with hidden pain. Prospective parents of older adoptees must open their hearts and minds to the promises and difficulties of older child adoption.

Your family's adoption journey will not be the same as anyone else's. There is no magic formula or crystal ball that will predict what your experience will be like. Your adopted child may struggle with many issues or adjust surprisingly well to her new family. And just like any child, your adopted child will have her own strengths and weaknesses.

Often the media covers sensational stories about adoption that are not representative of the average adoption experience. It is up to you to get a more accurate picture of what older child adoption is like. When you speak to parents who are raising children adopted at an older age, note the range of experiences. Some families will describe nightmare scenarios, while others will say they had no problems at all, but these are outlier experiences. Most families you talk to will describe an older child adoption journey that fits somewhere in the middle of these two extremes; their child and family have faced a number of challenges and setbacks but ultimately, through love and commitment, have persevered. Many adoptive parents you will speak to will say older child adoption has been the most rewarding experience of their lives. Undoubtedly their families too have experienced good times and bad, but these parents understand the difference they have made in the life of a child.

Prior to deciding whether to adopt an older child, educate yourself:

- Attend adoptive parent support group meetings to hear from parents about their family's challenges and how they cope.
- Find an adoption navigator, recruiter or mentor who works with prospective and pre-adoptive parents of older adoptees.

- Visit online discussion forums for adoptive parents of older children.
- Read books and articles about older child adoption and visit adoption websites.
- Have frank conversations with adoption professionals about your expectations, hopes and needs.
- Learn how adoption has changed the lives of older children and teens by listening to or reading their stories.

There are numerous resources listed throughout this guide that will help you learn more about the many aspects of older child adoptions including the process, how to access post-adoption services, common issues older adoptees and adoptive families face and parenting support.

ADVICE TO PROSPECTIVE PARENTS FROM THOSE WHO HAVE ADOPTED OLDER CHILDREN

We asked a group of adoptive parents what advice they have for people contemplating older child adoption. Their answers reflect the importance of prospective parents being educated about the needs of adopted children, having realistic expectations and understanding that healing will not happen overnight. The parents we talked to believe love is an essential ingredient in raising children who have experienced early challenges in their lives, but they agree that love may not be enough to heal these children. They advise parents to become educated about the needs of older adopted children so they will understand their child's behavior and seek professional help as needed.

To prepare for difficult behaviors, a parent who adopted a nine-year-old from the American foster care system advised prospective parents: "Read up on the impact of trauma and attachment disorders. Consider the worst-case scenario—severe mental illness, violent outbursts, near constant disrespect and defiance, the child pushing you away at every turn. Hopefully healing will happen, but can you stay committed to your child if it doesn't?"

A parent who adopted three children with special medical needs—a twenty-month-old from Belarus, a seven-month-old from Guatemala and

a six-year-old from Ukraine—said prospective parents "need to be prepared as much as possible, they need to research as much as possible, be
prepared for grief, anger, defiance and moodiness. Prepare for the worst
and hope and pray for the best!"

A parent who adopted a four-year-old from Ukraine added, "Make
sure you are prepared and understand the true needs of an older child
coming from a hurt place. Really be educated on the emotions, challenges,
behaviors, attachment issues and loyalty issues (to biological family, country of birth) an older child may have when adopted. Make sure you know
the delays a child may have even if the child is considered typical."

ADOPTIVE FAMILIES DESCRIBE WHAT
SUCCESS MEANS TO THEM

Parents who were interviewed in conjunction with several studies described what success meant to them in terms of their older child or teen's
adoption and what factors they believed contributed to the adoption's
success. Compare your notions of success about adoption with what these
families had to say.

A slight majority of parents who adopted teenagers interviewed for
a study conducted by Wright and Flynn published in 2006 characterized
success as having a sense of normalcy in family life. These parents said
they do the same things any family does (e.g. activities, celebrations).
Many parents in the same study also described success as having a sense
of emotional connectedness and love in their family.

For Wright and Flynn's study and another conducted by the Children's
Bureau, parents were asked what factors contributed to the success of their
older child or teen's adoption. Common themes included:

- Commitment to the parent-child relationship[2]
- Having realistic expectations about the adoption[3]
- Viewing parenting as rewarding[4]
- Their parenting style (exhibiting flexibility and a sense
  of humor)[5]

Forty-four percent of the parents from the Wright and Flynn study said that they experienced emotional drain, tension and stress as a result of the adoption, but a majority reporting stress did not regret their decision to adopt.[6]

Many of the teens surveyed for the Wright and Flynn study considered their adoption a success because there was a feeling of family normalcy.[7] Like the parents interviewed for the study, many of the teens also attributed success to their commitment to the parent-child relationship. In this study, 95 percent of the teens interviewed said that, in retrospect, adoption was the right choice. Eighty-six percent of the teens rated their adoption between seven and ten on a scale of one to ten, with ten being the highest ranking.

Wright and Flynn asked the teens to describe the worst aspect of adoption and many said missing biological family members and conflicts with their adoptive parents about rules and punishment. When asked what advice they would give other teens considering adoption, several recommended that others carefully consider their compatibility with a prospective adoptive parent or parents.

We asked several adoptive parents what the most rewarding aspect of adoption had been for them. One mother of three children with special medical needs said, "It is amazing to give a real life to children who otherwise will never have one—real siblings, love and nutrition."

A parent of a girl with blindness and other special needs adopted at the age of four from Ukraine replied, "Seeing our girl grow and heal... and just the honor of being her parents."

A third parent who, with her spouse, adopted an eight-year-old boy from foster care, replied: "The most rewarding part [of adopting] is seeing how far he's come. He was in thirteen homes before ours, including three pre-adoptive homes which he had to leave due to his behavior. One former foster mom who we are still in contact with says she is still his "Nana" and tells me frequently that she can't believe how well he is doing. She is a very experienced foster parent (having parented over one hundred kids), so that means a lot. "I would adopt my son again—it was worth all the hard work we put in to see how he is now and the awesome young man he is becoming."

YOU'VE DECIDED TO ADOPT AN OLDER CHILD; NOW WHAT?

After you've done your research and have decided older child adoption is right for you and your family, you need to decide whether to adopt domestically or internationally, what type of agency you want to work with and what type of child (age, needs, background, nationality) you want to adopt. There are some factors to help you decide whether US or international adoption is best for you.

DOMESTIC OLDER CHILD ADOPTION	INTERNATIONAL OLDER CHILD ADOPTION
Very inexpensive, public subsidies available	Agency fees are higher and no public subsidies from county or state
Possible contact with biological family	Most likely no contact with biological family
Adequate information about child's biological family and family history	May not receive accurate (or any) information about child's biological family or family history
Easy to get information about US child welfare system	Foreign child welfare systems confusing; must work with foreign agencies
Follow-up visits from agency to see how family is adjusting	May not receive follow-up visits or adequate post-adoption support from agency
Adequate background information about child's medical history	Often cannot obtain accurate birth records or information about child's medical history
You may be able to adopt a child from the same racial or ethnic background as you	All adoptions will be transcultural and/or transracial

DOMESTIC OLDER CHILD ADOPTION	INTERNATIONAL OLDER CHILD ADOPTION
May adopt from home county or state	Will need to travel a great distance to adopt your child, will need to pay travel costs and take time off from work to process the adoption abroad
Post-adoption services available through county or state	Agency may not offer adequate post-adoption services for families adopting internationally
No post-adoption self-reporting requirements	May need to submit follow-up reports to foreign agency or government
Waiting time for pre-adoptive training and home study may be lengthy	Agency may be more parent-friendly; waiting time for training and home study is minimal

CHAPTER 2

Who Can Adopt an Older Child?

In the United States, older children, especially those over the age of ten who are legally free for adoption, may wait for years to find a forever family and, sadly, many of those waiting will never find one. Special needs children from abroad, those who are older or who have health problems also may wait years to find a family to love them. This is why it is so important for prospective adoptive parents to understand how welcome they are to adopt an older child and just how much they are needed. The beauty of older child adoption is that parents from varying backgrounds, ages, ethnicities and sexual orientations are welcome to adopt. While prospective older parents, single parents or those with limited financial means may face challenges adopting an infant, they will encounter fewer problems adopting older children. Likewise, gays and lesbians may face challenges adopting an infant in the United States but are welcome by many public agencies to adopt an older child. Their ease in adopting an older child will depend, however, on agency culture and state laws. For gays and lesbians, adopting internationally is a different story which we will discuss later.

Waiting children, particularly older ones, will be asked by their caseworkers what type of family situation might work best for them in terms of family structure and location. A teen may be interested in being adopted by a married couple rather than a single parent or by adoptive parents who do not have any other children; sibling groups may only want to be adopted together. Furthermore, a child may prefer prospective parents in a particular geographic location so they can maintain contact with biological family members, their foster family or friends.

Laws regarding the age above which a legally free child must consent to be adopted by particular prospective parents vary state by state. There is the chance that after visits with a prospective family, or even living with them for several months, a child will decline to be adopted.

PROSPECTIVE OLDER ADOPTIVE PARENTS

Adoptions through the American child welfare system by older adults have increased over the past decades. As Americans live longer, middle age and beyond is no longer considered too late for parenting. Members of the baby-boomer generation are more active in their senior years than most generations that have come before them. They are starting new careers, going to school and developing new businesses, so why not start a new family?

Older adults may be more emotionally and financially ready to parent compared to when they were in their twenties and thirties. Adults over the age of fifty may even be interested in raising adopted children after their biological children are grown and have left home. Some, never having had biological children, may fulfill their dreams of raising children long after their childbearing years have passed. The child welfare system provides older adults an opportunity to become parents, whereas the private system of infant adoption is no longer an option due to age requirements set by most private agencies.

There are upper age limits on infant adoption, because private agencies want to ensure adoptive parents are healthy enough to parent a young child. Generally there are no maximum age requirements for domestic older child adoption because agencies want to expand their pool of prospective parents. Also, older parents may have years of parenting experience behind them, making them excellent applicants for raising children who have experienced early adversity.

PROSPECTIVE SINGLE ADOPTIVE PARENTS

Adoption by single adults has increased over the past few decades as well. In 2011, close to one-third of adoptions from foster care were by single adults, according to the US Department of Health and Human Services.[1] Since the 1980s it has become more culturally acceptable for single parents to raise children on their own.

Women in particular have become increasingly willing and interested in raising children alone, though single fatherhood is on the rise as well. Children may come to single women biologically, through relationships with partners, surrogate partners, artificial insemination or through adoption. Older child adoption may appeal particularly to single women who are in a later stage of life when raising an infant is not an option. Single women who have a strong support system may adopt with the hope they will later find a partner with whom to raise the child. Others may not be as concerned about finding a partner and are willing and expecting to take on the burden of parenting largely on their own. Lesbians and gay men may need to adopt as single parents, even if they have a partner, due to restrictions on gay couples adopting in their states.

While there are more single women interested in adoption, the pool of prospective single male adoptive parents is growing. Single men may have concerns similar to single women including feeling that, as older single men, they are more prepared to parent an older child than an infant. Some single men who adopt may be gay and do not yet have a partner or are restricted to adopting as a single man due to state laws against same-sex second parent adoption. While the number of single adoptive fathers is increasing, single adoptive mothers greatly outnumber single adoptive fathers by a ratio of thirteen to one.[2]

KINSHIP CARE AND ADOPTION

Kinship care or kinship adoption refers to the care or adoption of a child by a relative such as a grandparent, aunt or uncle. Some states have a broader definition of kin that includes non-related persons such as close friends of the family. Kinship care arrangements are made in families every day without the involvement of the courts or the child welfare system. Parents may be unable to care for their children due to military deployment or sudden illness. In certain cultures, informal care of children by kin is not uncommon. In Native American cultures, for example, members of the extended family and even unrelated members of the tribe are expected to care for children in need. Quite often, Native American children whose parents are unable to care for them are raised by grandparents or other older relatives.

Custody or guardianship agreements may be preferred to formal care or adoption by relative caregivers, because it does not result in termination of parental rights but gives the caregivers authority to make decisions for the child.

The Fostering Connections to Success and Increasing Adoptions Act of 2008 placed a major emphasis on kinship care and adoption. The Act encouraged states to enact policies requiring child welfare agencies to do a diligent search for all extended family members of a child removed from the home and to notify those family members of the child's removal within thirty days. It also made funding available to states for programs that emphasize and support kinship care and adoption. Kinship navigator programs help kin caregivers access services vital to successfully raising the child(ren) in their care. Since the Act was passed, kinship care and adoption have grown. From 2000 to 2008 the percentage of children adopted out of child protective care by relatives increased from 21 to 30 percent.[3]

In a majority of states, related family members are given preference in the care of a child removed from the home. Relatives who are asked by agencies to care for related children, often with little notice, may not have to undergo all the licensing requirements of foster parents but they will generally have to undergo a criminal background check. Kinship caregivers filing for adoption are given priority in many jurisdictions. Kinship care and adoption policies vary from state to state, so it is important to understand what rights you have as a kinship caregiver in your state.

Over the past decade, researchers and practitioners have discovered a number of benefits of kinship foster care and adoption. In the care of relatives, children may be able to maintain stronger connections with their parents, community and culture. They also are more likely to be placed in the care of relatives with their siblings or in family situations where they have more contact with siblings.[4]

PROSPECTIVE ADOPTIVE PARENTS WHO ARE SERVING IN THE MILITARY

Active members of the armed services, based in the United States or abroad, are eligible to adopt from the US foster care system and internationally. They may also adopt an infant through the US system of private adoptions. It is important that active service members learn about special benefits and services they are eligible for when they adopt and about some of the barriers they may face during the process. Generally, military families follow the same process of adopting a child from the US foster care system as other families, including an agency orientation, pre-adoptive training, paperwork, background check, home study and working with the agency to be matched with a child.

Military families interested in adopting an infant should find a private agency to work with. Likewise, military families interested in intercountry adoption should find a Hague-accredited agency to work with either in the United States or in the country where they are based. Several agencies specialize in working with service members based abroad who are interested in adopting domestically or internationally.

According to AdoptUSKids, active service members must follow the laws of adoption of the state where they are currently based. Military families move often, which can complicate the process. Two laws regulating interstate adoptions will be important to military adoptive families: the Interstate Compact on the Placement of Children (ICPC) and the Interstate Compact on Adoption and Medical Assistance (ICAMA). Both laws were enacted to facilitate the placement of foster and adoptive children across state lines and ensure that families receive vital services. It is important that older children legally free for adoption have as many opportunities as possible to be placed with adoptive families, even if the family lives in another state. Although interstate adoptions are common, families do report delays and challenges when they seek to adopt a child living in a different jurisdiction. The best approach for military and other families to take when adopting from another state is to ask their agency of choice a lot of questions and also do as much research as possible about adoption laws in the state where their prospective adoptive child currently resides.

As active service members, military families are eligible for the Department of Defense adoption reimbursement program, which covers $2,000 in eligible adoption expenses per adoptee in one calendar year.[5] Members of the armed forces are also eligible for up to twenty-one days of leave upon the adoption of a child. In addition to Medicaid if they qualify, pre-adoptive and adoptive children of active and retired service members are eligible for TRICARE benefits, the healthcare program of active and retired service members.[6] Military family service centers should be able to provide members of the military with additional information about benefits they can expect to receive when they adopt a child. Service members should complete as much research as possible on their own as well and find an attorney skilled in military family adoption.

PROSPECTIVE GAY AND LESBIAN ADOPTIVE PARENTS

Sometimes a waiting child does have preferences in terms of an adoptive parent's characteristics; this is often true when it comes to lesbian, gay, bisexual and transgender (LGBT) foster children. According to the Human Rights Campaign, LGBT youth are disproportionately represented in the foster care system.[7] Sadly, many of these LGBT children and teens in the foster system are rejected or even abused and neglected because of their sexual orientation or gender identity. The discrimination or rejection that each may have experienced in their adopted or fostered lives can create a strong bond of understanding between gay or lesbian adoptive parent and LGBT child or teen.

Because there is such a need for accepting parents of LGBT foster youth and because of the large number of waiting children in general, lesbian and gay prospective adoptive parents of older children and teens are critically needed. Gay and lesbian parents bring different perspectives and experiences to parenting. Because of discrimination they themselves may have suffered in their lifetimes, lesbian or gay parents can be particularly empathetic to the pain of children who have been removed from their biological families through no fault of their own. Lesbian or gay parents may know more than some about feeling isolated or marginalized—feelings that so many older children and teens in foster care unfortunately experience. When lesbian or gay people or couples parent an adoptive child, that child may experience a sense of love and acceptance he or she never knew before. Gays and lesbians may confront barriers to adopting an older child internationally. The United States and other Hague-accredited nations allow gays and lesbians to adopt, but several nations have laws prohibiting adoption of children by gay or lesbian individuals or couples. According to Beth Brindo, LISW, "There was a time when many agencies held a 'don't ask, don't tell' attitude toward adoptions by gays and lesbians. Today, reputable agencies are not willing to turn a blind eye to falsification of sexual preference. In fact, the applications required by some countries actually ask prospective parents if they are gay or lesbian."

Thus, older child adoption through an American public or private agency may be a lesbian or gay prospective parent's best option. Still, prospective lesbian or gay parents may need help navigating older child adoption due to their sexual orientation and marriage status. More agencies are developing specific resources and supports for lesbian or gay applicants. It is highly recommended that prospective lesbian or gay adoptive parents research which public and private agencies are open to working with gay and lesbian applicants and choose an agency with which they feel comfortable. Find out which agencies are accredited through The Human Rights Campaign (www.hrc.org). Lesbian or gay singles and couples considering adoption should also join adoptive parent discussion forums and local in-person support groups geared toward the lesbian and gay parenting community to get inside information and advice from those who have already gone through the process.

An increasing number of public and private agencies are becoming sensitized to lesbian and gay prospective parents' needs and many are even actively recruiting lesbian or gay foster or adoptive parents. The following statistics and information about the adoption of older children by gays and lesbians have been reported:

- Gays and lesbians are more likely to adopt children of a different race or culture, or special needs children, as compared to heterosexual adoptive parents. Fifty percent of adoptions by gay and lesbian parents are through the public child welfare system.[8]

- According to Gary J. Gates et al for The Williams Institute, same-sex couples raising adopted children are usually older, more educated and have more economic resources than other adoptive parents.[9]

- Legal victories allowing gays and lesbians to marry and changing social attitudes have contributed to the increase in adoptions by gay and lesbian couples since 2000.[10] According to the 2010 census, same-sex couples are raising over 22,000 unrelated adopted children.[11] Most recent estimates hold that gays and lesbians are raising approximately 4 percent of all adopted children.[12]

It is important that lesbian or gay prospective adoptive parents research and understand local laws and practices that will impact their effort to adopt, prior to starting the process. Only two states in the United States, Utah and Mississippi, legally prohibit single and coupled gays and lesbians from adopting. While some states expressly prohibit discrimination based on sexual orientation in adoption practice, most states do not, leaving much to the courts to decide. Even though a state may not expressly prohibit gays from adopting, unmarried persons may not be legally permitted to adopt jointly. As such, only one partner may be able to adopt a child. Laws governing same-sex second partner adoption are rapidly changing, so look into the laws in your state.

PROSPECTIVE ADOPTIVE PARENTS LIVING ABROAD AND NON-US CITIZENS

American citizens living abroad may adopt domestically or internationally. There are several agencies that specialize in working with US citizens living abroad who wish to adopt. It is critical that prospective adoptive parents living abroad research the adoption process and find an agency sensitive to their needs. These families should know that the US Department of State has advised US citizens living abroad who wish to adopt to follow the "adoption laws and procedures" of the country where they reside. This requirement pertains to families adopting US or foreign-born children, according to the National Council for Adoption.[13]

State laws govern the citizenship and residency requirements of adoptive parents. Most states allow lawful permanent residents to adopt an American child. Permanent residents of the United States must be very careful when adopting a foreign-born child, because there are legal restrictions on non-citizens adopting internationally. The US Department of State stipulates that either the non-citizen must be married to a citizen to adopt internationally or must meet certain criteria to be able to legally bring a non-US citizen child into the United States.[14] US citizens living abroad, non-US citizens wishing to adopt American-born children and foreigners wishing to adopt a US-born child should work with an agency that can meet their needs and consult an immigration attorney knowledgeable about adoption.

PROSPECTIVE ADOPTIVE PARENTS OF COLOR

There is a disproportionate number of African-American children in the US foster care system. In 2011, while representing only 14 percent of the total population, 27.5 percent of children in out-of-home care were African-American. There also is a slightly disproportionate rate of Native American children in foster care nationally and, according to Alicia Summers and associates for the National Council of Juvenile and Family Court Judges, in five states Latino/Hispanic children are overrepresented in the child welfare system.[15]

Researchers and child welfare professionals have a number of theories about why certain groups are disproportionately represented in the child welfare system. Some believe that racial discrimination influences the number of African-American children removed from the home. Others believe Caucasian-dominated agencies may not make adequate efforts to work with communities of color to address higher reported and substantiated rates of maltreatment. Additionally, staff may not be "culturally competent"—that is, they may not be educated about culturally specific parenting practices or problems in communities different from their own, leading to biases in how they handle cases and work with families. A Caucasian child protection services professional may have difficulty obtaining treatment and other services for a Latino family due to language barriers or being unfamiliar with the local community and services offered.

Others argue that disproportionality has more to do with corollary factors that increase the rates of child maltreatment in communities. They argue that higher rates of abuse and neglect do not occur in these communities *because* parents are of a certain race or ethnicity, but because of the prevalence of factors that have been linked to higher rates of child maltreatment such as poverty combined with substance abuse. Families living in poverty may have less access to preventive services that can help keep families together and quality therapeutic services to address addiction, domestic violence or mental illness.

The reasons for disproportionality are complex and continue to be studied. A number of organizations are working toward addressing the problem through staff training, advocating for preventive services and other measures.

Not only are there more African-American children in the system, but older children of color also are more difficult to place. Reasons include a smaller pool of prospective adoptive parents of color and greater hesitation among Caucasian prospective adoptive parents to adopt older children of color, possibly because they don't want the child to be a minority in a largely Caucasian community, prejudice, racism or concerns they hold about adopting transracially.

Increasing the number of prospective adoptive parents of color may improve permanency for children of color who statistically experience longer stays in foster care. In recognition of this fact, many states have developed adoptive parent recruitment and support programs geared specifically toward certain racial and ethnic groups. There also are a number of adoption agencies that specialize in recruiting and working with prospective adoptive parents of color.

CHAPTER 3

Adopting Within the United States

UNDERSTANDING THE AMERICAN PUBLIC CHILD WELFARE SYSTEM

"Over the last five years, opinions of foster care adoption improved to be as good, if not better, than those of private domestic infant adoption or international adoption," according to The Dave Thomas Foundation.[1]

The number of older children being adopted through the American child welfare system may be increasing in recent decades due in part to a greater awareness among prospective adoptive parents of the need for permanent homes for waiting children; a decrease in the number of infants being placed for adoption and a greater willingness by kinship and family caregivers to legally adopt children in their care. Should you decide to adopt an older child domestically, learn all you can about the American child welfare system, because you will interact with many parts of the system as you go through the adoption process. You will have many choices to make along the way, including what kind of agency to work with, what type of adoption you would like to pursue and the characteristics of the child you would like to adopt.

The American child welfare system emerged from concerns about the lack of protections afforded abused and neglected children. Interestingly, the first child welfare agencies in the United States served both abused children and animals. Over the centuries and in modern times the US child welfare system has grown in complexity.[2]

The three pillars of the American child welfare system are safety, permanency and well-being. Local and state child welfare organizations are responsible for investigating allegations of abuse and neglect, removing children from the home when they cannot safely stay there, developing case plans for families and finding permanent homes for children when parental rights are terminated. While most child protection work is carried out by public agencies, an increasing number of private agencies are becoming involved in child abuse and neglect prevention and treatment services. Private agencies licensed by the state also commonly deliver foster care and adoption services. Although child protective services largely fall under the jurisdiction of the states (states decide how to administer services and enact child welfare laws and policies), federal legislation has significantly impacted local agencies. States must comply with federal child welfare laws and regulations to receive federal funding for services and programs.[3]

Public child welfare agencies have come under intense scrutiny by the media. Underfunded in many counties and states, some agencies struggle to provide the best child protection and permanency services possible. Notorious for being overworked and underpaid, many public agency caseworkers and supervisors quickly become discouraged and burn out. The good news is that millions of federal dollars have been invested in child welfare system changes, capacity building and professional development for the child welfare workforce over the past two decades.[4] Public funds help support the development of programs by county and state agencies to enhance recruitment and retention of quality child welfare staff. Furthermore, schools of social work have partnered with public child welfare agencies to increase the number of MSWs entering the field and provide agency staff with comprehensive training. Publicly funded programs to help agencies become more "trauma informed" and implement "evidence based practices" have made great strides in improving service delivery in cities, counties and states throughout the country.

Foster parents provide temporary homes for children who cannot live safely with their parents or legal guardians. Many children are placed with relatives, while others are placed with foster parents. In 2012, there were about 400,000 children in foster care at any given time, according to the Adoption and Foster Care Analysis and Reporting System (AFCARS 2012).[5]

When allegations of abuse or neglect are substantiated, parents must follow a case plan if they want to remain with or be reunified with their children. Parents who satisfactorily meet the requirements of their case plan are reunited with their children. In other cases, courts terminate parental rights and children become "legally free" for adoption. In 2012, the case plan for about half of all children in foster care was reunification with parents or guardians while the plan for about a quarter of the children was adoption. Other permanency goals include long-term foster care or guardianship placement with relatives.

Children whose parents' parental rights have been terminated and are legally free to be adopted are often referred to as "waiting children." While waiting for a "forever family," children are most often placed in relative or non-relative foster homes while a small percentage, usually children with severe mental, medical or physical challenges, are placed in group homes or hospitals. Some foster children experience multiple foster placements before they are adopted. Approximately 100,000 children in the United States are waiting to be adopted, according to AFCARS 2012.[6]

TRUTHS ABOUT OLDER CHILD ADOPTION

Adoption of children from the US foster care system, sometimes referred to as public adoption, has been increasing over the past three decades and accounts for about 40 percent of all adoptions by Americans (the remaining adoptions are of American-born infants voluntarily relinquished by biological parents and international adoptions).[7] A majority of older children adopted in the United States are adopted by their foster parents. Not all foster parents adopt children in their care, however—they may be unwilling or unable to make a lifetime commitment to the child. A growing number of foster children are being adopted by family members, due in part to state programs and federal incentives encouraging kinship adoption. In most states, relative caregivers of children removed from their parents have first priority in adoption.[8] Some family members prefer legal guardianship to allow the child's parents a greater measure of involvement in the child's life. The remaining children adopted out of foster care—many considered "hard to place"—are adopted by persons unrelated to them.

COMMON MYTHS ABOUT OLDER CHILD ADOPTION	
MYTH	FACT
Most foster children are juvenile delinquents.	Most foster children are caught up in the child welfare system through no fault of their own.
Most older children and teens waiting to be adopted have significant mental health problems and need to live in institutions.	Very few foster children live in institutions and the vast majority function normally.
Domestic older child adoption is expensive.	Generally there is no cost to adopting from the public system, and you may receive monthly adoption subsidies.
Older teens in foster care don't need adoptive families; they will do just fine on their own.	Were you able to live independently at sixteen, eighteen or even twenty-one? Teens aging out of foster care without a permanent family face serious lifelong challenges.

ADOPTIONS FROM THE AMERICAN PUBLIC CHILD WELFARE SYSTEM

It is important that prospective adoptive parents of older American children become familiar with the foster care system, because their future child most likely will have spent time in foster care. Foster care is meant to be a safe place for children but sometimes it does more harm than good if children are moved from home to home or experience maltreatment in a foster home. Children in foster care already have experienced the trauma of being separated from their biological parents. Being moved in and out of foster care homes can aggravate this trauma and cause further emotional and behavioral problems. One adoptive mother told us, "...Regardless of what happened with her first family, I believe the five years bouncing around foster care is what caused [my daughter] the most trauma." Most children only have one or two foster placements but about 15 percent experience multiple placements. According to AFCARS in 2012, close to 30 percent of all foster children have been in care for more than two years.[9] Children who are in foster care for many years are more likely to experience multiple placements.

Children also suffer when they are not integrated in a meaningful way into a foster family. Some foster children describe feeling as if they are little more than house guests. Despite the problems some foster children experience, living with a foster care family can be positive for many children, especially if the foster family is loving and supportive and wants to have a permanent relationship with the child.

Prospective adoptive parents considering adopting a specific foster child should ask questions about how long the child has been in care and what his experience was like. This knowledge will help adoptive parents develop empathy for their child and understand why certain behaviors are manifesting. Pre-adoptive parents may even want to speak to the child's current and/or former foster parents to get a sense of what type of experience the child had and how well he adjusted to a positive family environment.

FOST-ADOPT

Achieving "permanency" for children is a guiding principle in contemporary child welfare practice. In order of priority, permanency for a child engaged in the system means either reunification with parents or relatives, adoption or long-term foster care. Generally, for older children and teens interested in being adopted, an agency pursues two concurrent tracks toward permanency: reunification with the biological parents or adoption by a foster or relative caregiver. Agencies prefer to license and place children with foster caregivers who are willing to adopt them should they become legally free to be adopted.

Foster adoption, or fost-adopt, programs allow foster parents to adopt a child in their care should that child become legally free for adoption. In many areas, participating in fost-adopt programs is the quickest and surest way to adopt a child. Fost-adopt parents undergo screening, preparation and have to fulfill foster parent licensing requirements. Each state sets its own guidelines about the amount of training and preparation foster parents must receive. Fost-adopt parents receive public subsidies for their service and may receive reimbursements and other benefits to assist in the care of their foster child(ren).

Some prospective adoptive parents decide the best route to adoptive parenthood is through a fost-adopt program; however, foster-adoption is not for everyone. Foster parents must accept the risk that their foster child, whom they may grow to love very much, could be reunified with his or her biological parent(s). Not being able to adopt a beloved foster child can be heart-wrenching, so prospective adoptive parents must understand this risk before entering a fost-adopt program. Some prospective adoptive parents may prefer the fost-adopt route to parenthood, because it can be easier and faster than adopting a legally free child, because they will have time to get to know the child prior to permanently adopting him or because there is a greater likelihood of adopting a baby or toddler. Contact your local or state child welfare agency to learn more about fost-adopt.

WAITING CHILDREN

Think about the background and characteristics of the child you would like to adopt. Educate yourself about the common problems and issues that waiting children may face and think about the types of behaviors or challenges you think you and your family could cope with. As you decide what type of child you would like to adopt, think about or discuss with your partner or spouse the following questions:

- Do I/we want to adopt an elementary-school-age child or a teenager?
- How important are the racial or cultural characteristics of the child?
- Am I/Are we open to transracial and/or transcultural adoption?
- Am I/Are we open to adopting a sibling group?
- Can I/we parent a child with special needs?

- Am I/Are we open to ongoing contact between the child and his/her biological family members?

You will encounter the term "special needs adoption" during your adoption journey. "Special needs adoption" is a designation ascribed to children who are "hard to place" by states. The definition of which children qualify for "special needs adoption" assistance varies by state but may include children over a certain age, children who are part of a sibling group, male children of color, children who are ill or disabled or children who have several mental health or behavioral challenges. States receive federal funding to increase the number of special needs adoptions in that state. Funds may be used to provide additional subsidies and services for adoptive parents. Many foster children and adoption professionals are uncomfortable with the term "special needs adoption" because it can stigmatize older children who truly do not have any special needs but simply have been in the system for a long time.

Since African-American children in foster care wait longest for permanent families, states often designate older African-American children in foster care as "special needs adoption" cases. Because African-American prospective adoptive parents are more likely than prospective parents of other races to adopt African-American children from foster care, there are special recruitment efforts in some states to increase the number of prospective African-American adoptive parents.

Transracial or transcultural adoption may not be the best choice for every family and thus should be carefully considered. Prospective adoptive parents must think about whether they will be able to help a child from a different culture or background connect with their cultural heritage. They also must think about the degree of openness and acceptance of their extended family, the people where they live and whether their child will face serious challenges fitting in or even experience negativity because of his or her race or culture. One couple who adopted a child from the foster system decided transracial adoption was not best for their family:

We were open to white or Hispanic children. I received some anger on an adoption forum when I revealed that we were open to Hispanic children but not African-American. Older child adoption is complicated and difficult. Each family needs to evaluate their strengths and challenges to determine the children they are best suited to parent. Due to prejudices in our small town and extended families, we didn't feel we would be the best choice for an African-American child. (We were worried) the child would face serious challenges fitting in or facing prejudice.

Families that do decide to adopt a child from a different racial or cultural background must be prepared to handle cultural issues in adoption. Although the prevalence of multicultural and multiracial families has increased over the past twenty years, some families still face prejudices. Children of transracial adoption or interracial unions may still deal with identity issues or wonder where they fit in. Most agencies, especially those that handle international adoption, require parent training on cultural issues in adoption. Parents can also prepare for cultural issues by reading books and articles, speaking to other adoptive families or joining transracial adoption discussion forums. (Read more about multiracial/multicultural adoptive families in chapter 8.)

According to data from the Federal Adoption and Foster Care Analysis and Reporting System (AFCARS 2012):

- Fifty percent of children in foster care were reunited with their families.
- The average age of children in foster care was nine years old.
- The average age of children waiting in foster care to be adopted was 7.8.
- There were slightly more boys in the system than girls.
- Twenty-two percent of children in foster care were adopted.
- The average amount of time children waited to be adopted from foster care was 34.4 months.[10]

Despite the increase in older child adoption, too many older children languish in the foster care system for a number of years or age out of the system by the age of eighteen or twenty-one with few or no family or kinship connections. In 2012, 23,000 young adults aged out of the system without being adopted.[11] Young adults who age out of the system without permanent family connections are less likely to graduate from high school, attend college, find a secure job or have stable relationships. They are more likely to become homeless, have children at a young age or become involved in criminal activity.

Some prospective adoptive parents may believe older teens are too old to be adopted. They fear older teens will not be able to adapt to a new family or will have ingrained and intractable behavior problems that cannot be addressed. While some older teens will have significant difficulties adapting to a permanent family after so many years "on their own," for most it is not too late to benefit from having a stable, loving family for a lifetime.

Some teens who have been in foster care for many years also believe they are too old for adoption or that adoption will not make their lives any better. For The Urban Institute, Kate Chambers and colleagues explored some concerns and beliefs teens in foster care have about adoption, including:

- Adoption is only for young children.
- I will lose contact with my friends and biological family.
- I will have to follow too many rules in an adoptive home.
- Independent living will be easier and I'll be free to do what I want.[12]

Many older teens in foster care miss out on the opportunity to be placed in a permanent adoptive home because they hold assumptions, many of which could be inaccurate, about what adoption will mean for them. Fortunately, agencies are doing more to convince older teens in foster care that adoption is still an option. Child-centered adoption practices, now being used by many agencies, prioritize the needs and concerns of older children in care. Older teens are asked what type of family would be best for them and the process of matching teens with prospective adoptive families is done with much careful thought and consideration.

CHOOSING AN AGENCY

After deciding to adopt a child from the US foster care system, you will need to choose an agency. First you must decide if you want to work with your public child welfare agency or with a private agency. Public child welfare agencies have the authority to investigate allegations of abuse and neglect, remove children from homes where they are at risk and place children in foster care. They also complete home studies and work with foster and non-foster parents interested in adopting children in care. Private adoption agencies generally are nonprofit (although there are some for-profit agencies out there—avoid them) and do not carry the same child protection responsibilities as public agencies; they do, however, conduct home studies and match prospective adoptive parents with waiting children.

Adoption agencies and organizations must be accredited by the state. To meet higher standards, some obtain voluntary accreditations such as those offered by the Council on Accreditation.

Virginia Volante-Appel, a Denver-based adoption professional with over thirty years of experience, advises prospective adoptive parents to choose an agency carefully. She writes, "Look at accredited agencies that have a good track record, find out what others' experiences have been with that agency, visit your county and find out about fost-adopt; just learn as much as you can."

Some of the benefits and disadvantages to working with public versus private agencies are:

PUBLIC CHILD WELFARE AGENCY	PRIVATE ADOPTION AGENCY
+ Adoption costs are negligible and may be more familiar with federal or state subsidies for special needs adoption	+ May have access to a more diverse population of prospective adoptive children, including younger or out of state children
+ Works directly and is familiar with children in care needing permanent homes	+ May have programs targeted to specific groups of prospective parents (e.g. gays and lesbians, singles or parents of color)
+ City or county agencies may have a better service referral system since they are rooted in the local community	+ May serve as a buffer between you and the county or state (i.e. communicate with them for you)

PUBLIC CHILD WELFARE AGENCY	PRIVATE ADOPTION AGENCY
– May be slower to return phone calls and process applications	+ May return phone calls faster
– May be slow to respond to requests about a child's photo listed by other organizations or states	– May charge more than public agencies
– May be slow or have difficulty with interstate or inter-county placements or in securing services for an adoptive family from another jurisdiction	– May only work with prospective parents from a specific religious background
*This chart was compiled based on information from the North American Council on Adoptable Children and interviews with adoptive parents and agency professionals.[13]	

In one study conducted by Ramona W. Denby et al, prospective adoptive parents who were comfortable with their agencies and trusted the information that they received from the agencies about waiting children experienced greater stability in their adoptive placements.[14] Visit, or communicate by phone, with staff members from several prospective agencies. Agency staff generally will be happy to meet with you and answer any questions you have (if they're not, don't work with them).

Ask prospective agencies:

- About parent requirements (e.g. Sexual orientation, marriage status, religious background)
- About their application and pre-adoptive training requirements
- What types of children they place (e.g. Age, race, special needs, sibling groups, etc.)
- What subsidies might be available to you
- How they facilitate the adoptive parent/child match
- What post-placement services they can provide or refer for you
- What their fees are
- For references from several families with whom they have worked

Other adoptive parents can provide you with a wealth of information about specific agencies. Join an online discussion forum for adoptive parents and ask parents which agency they used and how their experience was. Some of the larger forums already have areas for prospective parents looking for agency recommendations.

Co-author Stephanie will never forget a visit she and her husband had with the director of an adoption agency that specializes in older child adoption, at his home. The man took the time to explain the adoption process, was honest about the challenges older adoptees face and the therapeutic services they may need and shared his own inspiring story about adopting a number of older children. One point he made about the need for adoptive parents of teens has stayed with Stephanie. He asked her and her husband to compare the amount of time they spent as children with the amount of time they have been adult children to their parents. Pointing out that time spent as an adult child is equal to, if not longer than, time spent as a child, he then asked in so many words—don't you need your parents as much when you are an adult, albeit in different ways, as compared to when you were a child? His point was that teens, just as much as younger children, need the guidance of loving parents to see them through young adulthood and to love and support them all through life.

THE APPLICATION PROCESS

Some pre-adoptive parents feel they are being placed under a microscope. They wonder: "Why do I have to go through all this paperwork and preparation to become a parent, when people who are unprepared for parenthood can have children without any kind of evaluation?" Such feelings are understandable, especially when prospective adoptive parents have experienced the heartbreak of infertility or miscarriage. But there is another way of thinking about the situation: Adoptive parents receive guidance and preparation for parenthood that many biological parents never receive. They receive the support of adoption professionals and other adoptive parents. Engaging in the home study process affords adoptive parents time for introspection and time to think about their financial and emotional readiness for parenthood. This is support and preparation from which any parent would benefit.

A mother of four children adopted through her state's public child welfare system had this advice for pre-adoptive parents beginning the application process: "Take your time. Expect that you will answer the same question many times over. Understand that the bureaucracy that surrounds you during this time is necessary and often helpful in making you take the time you should before making this life-changing decision."

The next list illustrates major steps in the adoptive process, including common core elements of the application and pre-adoptive procedures. Paperwork and other requirements may vary by state, agency and your relationship to the child you want to adopt (i.e. relative caregivers or foster parents may already have completed some of the core requirements).

Steps to Expect

- Complete the agency's common application form
- Submit completed tax returns, your marriage license (if applicable) and other identifying documents to the agency
- Complete a household budget
- Submit letters of recommendation from friends, family and or/employers
- Complete a criminal background check
- Get a physical and submit vaccination records for existing children
- Complete a self-study, which is generally a set of questions you answer about your personality, relationship with your spouse or partner, family, childhood and how you would parent your adopted older child
- Engage in a home study conducted by the agency which involves agency and home visits
- Complete any required training or reading

PRE-ADOPTIVE TRAINING AND EDUCATION

No one can obtain a degree in parenting, but there are many ways you can prepare for the role. Pre-adoptive parents of older children and teenagers need to be as ready as possible for parenting children who have experienced early adversity. Being prepared for the challenges of older child adoption may decrease your chances of experiencing adoption disruption, wrote the adoption expert David Brodzinsky for the Evan B. Donaldson Adoption Institute.[15] Through agency training, independent learning and networking, pre-adoptive parents can ensure they know as much as possible about older child adoption.

It is important that you ask agencies you are interviewing what their training requirements are and how they approach adoptive parent preparation. Pre-adoptive training requirements vary by state. Your adoption agency may require you to attend a set number of training sessions at the agency and/or online as well as read several adoption-related books. Relative caregivers may be exempt from some training requirements or may be able to complete these requirements at a later time (almost all states require at least a criminal background check of relative caregivers, however) since they often have very short notice that the child is being placed in their care.

To be as prepared as possible for adoption, pre-adoptive parents should seek additional training and educational opportunities outside their agency, such as:

- Reading adoption-related websites and blogs
- Registering for online classes or webinars offered by nonprofit organizations
- Joining an adoptive parent support group
- Participating in one or more online discussion forums for adoptive parents (locate areas of the forum where people are discussing older child adoption)

We recommend the websites listed in the appendix for comprehensive and accurate information about domestic older child adoption. The list also includes organizations that offer training and education for prospective, pre-adoptive and adoptive parents.

THE MATCHING PROCESS

Before you find an agency, you can begin learning about waiting children through photo-listing sites. These sites feature children who are legally free for adoption and who are hard to place. On them you will find some information about the child's interests, background and whether he or she is part of a sibling group. Often you can search for children that belong to a specific age or ethnic/racial group. If you are interested in learning more about a particular child, you will be asked to complete a form that is submitted to the photo-listing agency.

Private adoption organizations or agencies that have a regional or national focus may photo-list waiting children, as do many city, county and state child welfare agencies. When you submit an inquiry about a specific child in whom you are interested, you should receive a phone call shortly from the sponsoring agency which will explain the next steps you need to take to learn more about or meet the child.

Although federal laws have been passed to facilitate interstate adoptions, you may still experience challenges adopting a child from another state. For this reason it may be best for you to begin searching online for a child who has been photo-listed by a public or private agency in your state or region. In working with an agency or organization from another state or region, you may experience delays in getting responses to inquiries about specific children. If you are working with a local agency to complete your home study and other pre-adoptive requirements, your agency may have difficulty obtaining complete and accurate information about a child from another state or region.

In addition to photo-listing waiting children, public agencies may host events where prospective adoptive parents and waiting children can meet and get to know each other in a group setting. These events may be held in conjunction with National Adoption Month (November) and National Foster Care Month (May) to increase the number of prospective adoptive parents of waiting children. If you are interested in attending such an event, call your local child welfare agency to find out if they are holding one.

You may choose to forego using photo-listing services altogether and instead allow your agency to guide the matching process. Your agency may direct you to their own public photo-listing site of waiting children, or ask you to view private listings available only to clients of that agency. Some children are never photo-listed and you simply learn about them from their adoption caseworker. Based on your application materials, your adoption caseworker may talk to you about specific children he or she believes would be a good match for your family. It is especially important that agencies engage teens during the matching process. A good match between adoptive child and parent can decrease the risk of adoption disruption. When choosing an agency, ask whomever you speak with how the agency matches waiting children with prospective parents.

You will only get a few details about the child from a photo-listing service; the in-depth information you need will come from the child's case files. In order to cope with your child's needs, issues and problems, you must make every effort to learn all you can about a child's history of maltreatment, foster care or group home placements and behavioral issues. Your adoption caseworker may review the child's history with you verbally but you should also examine the case file yourself. The file may include hand-written notes and should date back to his earliest involvement in the system. If you see content that is redacted (blacked out), ask why. After examining the file, ask your counselor additional questions about the child's behavior, history of maltreatment, relationships with biological family members and foster care placements. Having as much information as possible about your adoptive child can greatly help you be the best parent to that child.

You may also want to speak with the child's current and/or former foster family to get a more current picture of how he is functioning in a family setting. Beware; some foster families may not be completely forthcoming with information or even willing to speak to you at all, for any number of reasons including lack of interest, a desire to adopt the child themselves or a desire to paint a rosier picture of the child's behavior so he or she is adopted into a permanent home more quickly. Most foster families will be forthcoming and very helpful. In addition to the foster family, you may also want to try speaking with others close to the child such as teachers, mentors or extended family members.

Many prospective adoptive parents of older children are concerned their agency will withhold information about the child or that the agency will not have a complete case history. Unfortunately, some adoptive parents do report that they did not receive accurate or complete information about their child. There even have been instances of adoptive parents suing their agency for allegedly withholding information. While the majority of agencies and adoption professionals are honest and competent, as in any profession you have some people who cut corners, are unethical or do not place the child's best interests ahead of their own. If you are not happy with your adoption caseworker, ask to be assigned to someone different.

If you are interested in getting to know a specific child you have learned about from a photo listing or your agency, ask your caseworker to arrange a meeting with the child. They most likely will be willing and able to do this. During the meeting, ask the child what her interests are, what she enjoys learning in school or what she wants to be when she grows up. Your child's caseworker will have ideas about which questions to ask her. Engage her in a conversation to try to get a sense of what she is like but don't be discouraged if she seems shy or is short on words—it can be overwhelming for a child to be considered for adoption by a complete stranger. Don't make commitments but do try to get to know the child.

ADOPTION COSTS

Adopting an older child in the United States is much less expensive than adopting an infant. Specific costs you may incur as you move through the adoption process include agency and legal fees. Because the government has decided to invest in special needs adoption by providing subsidies to families who adopt children from the US foster care system, adopting an older child can cost little to nothing for many families. In 2012, AFCARS reported 92 percent of families adopting with public agency involvement qualified for an adoption subsidy.[16]

Prospective adoptive parents participating in fost-adopt programs receive monthly payments from the child welfare agency for providing foster care services, but once foster parents adopt a child in their care, financial support may change. Some foster parents are concerned about legally adopting children in their care because they fear losing subsidies that help them care for the child, but new federal programs are ensuring that adoptive parents of older children continue to receive support. A major source of support for foster parents adopting the children in their care comes from the federal Title IV-E program. States vary in determining eligibility for payments through this program so parents should ask their agency if they qualify. Title IV-E benefits may be negotiated or renegotiated.

See http://www.acf.hhs.gov/programs/cb/monitoring/title-ive-reviews for additional information.

Families that adopt children from foster care also are eligible to receive the federal adoption tax credit regardless of how much they incurred in adoption expenses. The credit, however, has been made non-refundable, meaning that because it is based on tax liability it does not benefit lower and moderate income families as much as higher income families. The adoption tax credit can be confusing, so you should ask your agency or a tax preparer how to go about claiming the credit. The North American Council on Adoptable Children has some of the most up-to-date information about the adoption tax credit on its website.[17]

Adoptive parents also may receive one-time or recurring payments from the county or state (again, rules vary by state and on a case by case basis). Pre-adoptive parents can negotiate with public child welfare agencies about how much support they will receive for the child's care. Some adoptive parents receive deferred subsidies, sometimes called "dormant subsidies," for the future care of an adoptive child. If a child has inherited a mental or physical illness that is known to manifest in adolescence, adoptive parents may ask for dormant subsidies to cover the costs of expected therapeutic or medical services that will be needed. Pre-adoptive parents should research what payments and benefits their adopted child is entitled to receive from the county or state for medical care, higher education and other services.

It may be more difficult to obtain financial support for needed services or adoption subsidies from a different state if you are adopting across state lines. There may be a lack of understanding about services you are eligible to be reimbursed for or receive for free (e.g. counseling services or medical expenses) on the part of the local child welfare agency or the private adoption agency with which you are working. Most children in care receive health benefits through Medicaid, which may continue after adoption, but state rules and regulations vary so you must become knowledgeable about what coverage the child's home state allows. A child may be eligible for other benefits, such as higher education tuition reduction from the state where he spent a number of years in foster care, but he may become ineligible for such benefits once he is adopted by a family in a different state. To ensure that you receive as many benefits, subsidies and other supports as possible, you need to ask your caseworker a lot of questions and do your own research.

Should you find that you need additional support in helping you pay for adoption-related costs, you may be eligible to apply for private grants or loans. Another source of financial support for adoption may come from your employer, so be sure to find out what your company's policies are.

HELP NAVIGATING THE ADOPTION PROCESS

Navigating the adoption process can be confusing at times and you may feel as if you need someone to walk you through each step. We do not suggest that you hire an adoption consultant when adopting an older child, because most, if not all, of the information you will need to successfully adopt an older child will be free to you. Be wary of for-profit adoption consultants or organizations that charge exorbitant fees or make unrealistic promises.

If you feel that you do need a paid advisor, select such services very carefully and make sure you will be receiving services, information or support that your agency, a parent support group or a nonprofit organization isn't already offering. Many public agencies and nonprofit organizations can match you with experienced adoptive parents or adoption professionals who will help you navigate the adoption process from beginning to end, at little or no cost.

CHAPTER 4

Intercountry Adoption

Before deciding whether domestic or intercountry adoption is best for you and your family, become familiar with the process, requirements, costs and post-placement services available in your state for both types of adoption. Also, learn about the different needs of children adopted domestically versus internationally. For example, older children adopted from non-English speaking countries face language, cultural and educational barriers. They may also have different health problems such as malnourishment, cleft palates or bone malformation, as well as significant developmental delays and attachment difficulties.

Intercountry adoptions to the United States increased after World War II and reached their peak in the 1990s. After World War II, a number of children, both orphans and children of parents in the military, were adopted from Europe to the United States. The next big wave was Korean adoptions after the Korean War. During and after the Vietnam War, a number of families adopted Vietnamese children. After the fall of communism, thousands of children were adopted from Russia and Eastern and Central Europe. At the same time, due to its one-child policy and the value of male children over female children, China became a major country for intercountry adoption of mostly females. Intercountry adoption started

43

as a humanitarian response from families or individuals in other countries (typically high-income or western industrialized countries) responding to the needs of children left orphaned or abandoned as a result of war.

Intercountry adoption now reflects a different scenario based on changes that started in the 1960s. Since then, there have been a number of sociological changes in high-resource countries including high infertility rates, later age of marriage with women's increased participation in the labor market, the social acceptance of single parenthood and the availability of legal abortions.[1] One result has been that the demand for available infants to adopt is more than the number of infants eligible for adoption within high-resource countries. This has contributed to increased intercountry adoption and the emergence of the role that money plays within the intercountry adoption process, according to Dr. Peter Selman.[2] In some instances, intercountry adoption has been viewed not from a child rights perspective but rather from a right-to-a-child perspective.[3] That is to say the demand for adoptive children has driven the availability of children, which can lead to unethical practices and illegal activities such as child trafficking, baby buying or the abduction and sale of children, according to David M. Smolin in his report for the *Valparaiso Law Review*.[4] In areas where disasters have recently taken place, both natural and human-made, this is a very specific concern.

The Convention on the Rights of the Child (CRC) in 1989, The Hague Convention of 29 May 1993 on the Protection of Children and Co-operation in Respect of Intercountry Adoption (The Hague Convention) and the UN Guidelines for the Alternative Care of Children (2009) provide a child rights-based framework for intercountry adoption. These legal instruments act as guides as to how intercountry adoption should be practiced. In particular, The Hague Convention established international standards of practice for intercountry adoptions including transparency, protections against child trafficking and agency accreditation.[5] In 2008, the United States began abiding by Hague Convention rules. According to the US Department of State, if only one country in adoption is a Hague Convention country, both countries must follow Hague Convention procedures, practices and rules. In practice, this is not happening. Americans adopting from non-Hague countries are advised to proceed with caution or reconsider their decision to adopt from these countries. The regulations that protect children and families do not exist in non-Hague countries and the process is less certain. As one adoptive parent we interviewed said, "Hague treaty countries are more predictable during the adoption process [i.e. China, Bulgaria] and might be a better fit for first-time adopters. You are officially matched with your child earlier in the process."

You may be familiar with recent media controversies concerning intercountry adoption. There was the story of the American adoptive mother who sent her son back to Russia alone on a plane. There are stories about abuse of intercountry adoptees as well as "rehoming," in which adoptive parents advertise for new homes for their adoptees in online discussion forums. While a rare occurrence, the children caught up in this unprofessional practice often are older intercountry adoptees and have significant special needs. Also, there are the concerns of child advocate groups, legislators and others about corruption and unsound adoption practices. Some of these concerns have been substantiated and adoption programs have been shut down.

Some argue that aid to foreign nations for the care of orphans and other impoverished children is not enough and that these children need permanent homes, even if that means they are removed from their native culture and adopted by foreign families. As Elizabeth Bartholet stated:

> We assert that children's most fundamental human rights are to live and to grow up in a nurturing family so they can fulfill their human potential. These rights have been largely ignored in the debate surrounding unparented children and related international adoption policies. We argue that unparented children have a right to be placed in families, either their original families, or if that is not feasible, then in the first available permanent nurturing families. This includes the right to be placed in international adoption if that is where families are available. We argue that children have a related right to be liberated from the conditions characterizing orphanages and most foster care.[6]

Others argue that US aid for international child welfare should be more focused on helping foreign nations strengthen their own families by reducing poverty and building up child welfare systems so orphans have better lives and more children are adopted by families living in their own countries.

Despite recent controversies surrounding intercountry adoption and the ongoing debate about how the United States should focus its foreign aid and other efforts when it comes to international child welfare, one fact remains: millions of children around the world do not have one of their most fundamental human rights met—the right to grow up in a loving, supportive and permanent family. UNICEF reports that there are millions of orphans throughout the world who have no permanent family or kin caregivers.[7] Reflecting on this very large number, one cannot help but conclude that intercountry adoption is a vital component of child welfare; however, it should not be the only intervention.

Scandinavian countries lead the world in the rate of intercountry adoptions. The United States also is a leader in intercountry adoption but over the past ten years the number of intercountry adoptions by Americans began to decline. There are a number of reasons for this decrease, including new restrictions placed on which children may be adopted by foreigners. For example, some countries are restricting the number of infants that can be adopted internationally and allowing only special needs or older child adoptions by foreigners. Some nations are building up their own domestic adoption programs in response to high domestic demand for infants or to reduce the number of infants and children being removed from their native cultures. Intercountry adoptions have also slowed down due to Americans' concerns about child trafficking in foreign countries and their mistrust of foreign adoption agencies and programs. The decrease is also because some countries' adoption programs simply have been shut down due to corruption or non-adherence to Hague treaty standards.

The Russian international adoption program was discontinued in 2013, ostensibly in response to stories about abuse and abandonment by American adoptive parents, but other political considerations may have been in play as well. Adoptions from Guatemala, another popular program in the United States, have ended due to the lack of safeguards for children, according to Kelley Bunkers McCreery et al.[8]

At the same time, intercountry adoptions from some established programs are increasing and new programs are opening. Each country sets its own processes and procedures for intercountry adoptions, so prospective parents should research international programs carefully before deciding which is best for them. Your agency can help you become familiar with different programs. You also should search online for the latest information on country programs.

WAITING CHILDREN

As noted, there is unfortunately an abundance of orphans throughout the world whose parents have died and have no other family members to care for them, who have been abandoned because their families cannot care for them or who have been abused and neglected and are being sheltered. Many of these children have a reduced quality of life. In countries where child welfare systems are better developed, children may have some of their basic needs met in orphanages, but life in an orphanage is far from ideal. Staff often do not provide babies and children with love, caring, responsiveness or a relationship through which they can grow and develop.

One adoptive parent we interviewed traveled to an Eastern European country to adopt her toddler from an orphanage. She described a sad, desolate place where the few toys available were out of reach of tiny hands, where staff chatted with each other but rarely talked to or played with the children, where youngsters were blocked off in a small area when not in cribs and clamored for any modicum of stimulation or attention and where special needs children not adopted by a certain age were sent to harsher institutions.

For many children living in foreign orphanages, intercountry adoption is their only hope for a better life. Infants and toddlers who have spent even a few months in an orphanage without proper care and attention often suffer developmental delays. Older children who have resided for years in orphanages may suffer even worse developmental delays, behavioral problems and health difficulties (read more about the health of adopted children in Part III). Prospective parents of older children available for intercountry adoption should learn all they can about children eligible to be adopted from different countries and how these children are cared for while waiting to be adopted.

CHOOSING AN AGENCY AND COUNTRY PROGRAM

Before choosing an agency, get a free subscription to Guidestar, which provides tax returns for all nonprofit agencies. Not only will you be able to review the top salaries at the agency but, if you are good with math, you can decipher the percentage of their budget that goes to help a country where they are working.

The best source of information about country programs and adoption agencies is other adoptive parents. Join blogs, networking sites and use search engines to locate information about programs you are considering. However, be aware that some agencies hire companies to expunge negative comments about their programs. If you are considering an agency, ask them to connect you with a parent who used their service and lives near you. It is worth the effort to meet adoptive parents face-to-face so you can learn about their experience.

Choose your adoption agency carefully. Public agencies typically do not offer intercountry adoption services, so you will probably have to work with a private agency. Some families prefer to work with an independent adoption facilitator, but we recommend you work with an agency. Facilitators may be unqualified, corrupt or charge exorbitant fees. Be wary of any too-good-to-be-true promises made by private consultants or facilitators that they will find you an infant, for example, in a country that has closed their infant program.

To find a reputable private agency that facilitates intercountry adoptions:

- Visit your state's adoption or child welfare information websites, which often include lists of licensed private agencies.
- Check the website of your state's attorney general or your state or county's Better Business Bureau to find out if any complaints have been made against an agency.

- Visit the Council on Accreditation website and look for agencies with a COA accreditation that is also a Hague accreditation (http://coanet .org/accreditation/who-is-accredited/who-is-accredited-search/).
- Get agency recommendations from other adoptive parents by joining an online adoptive parent discussion forum (see the list at the end of chapter 6).

Once you have narrowed your choices to several agencies, call or visit each agency and ask the following questions:

- With which country adoption programs do you work?
- How much interaction will I need to have with the foreign agency?
- What are your adoptive parent requirements or the requirements of each country's program?
- What ages are the children available for adoption from each country's program?
- What pre-adoptive training do you offer or require?
- What support do you offer pre-adoptive parents as they go through the process?
- What post-placement services do you offer, including visits to the home, support groups and education or training?
- What are your fees?
- How many visits do I have to make to the country for each program and what will I have to do while I'm there?
- How do you match waiting children with prospective parents?
- Typically, how long is the process from application to homecoming?

Don't hesitate to ask the agency as many questions as you need to, because intercountry adoption can involve a lot more steps than domestic adoption and you will need to learn about each country's program before deciding which is best for you. The agency you choose should be willing to answer all your questions, address your concerns and make you feel comfortable about the path you have chosen to adopt a child.

In choosing a country from which to adopt, think about travel requirements. You should ask your agency about required travel prior to selecting a country if you think travel will be an issue for you. It is in the best interest of your child for you to plan on going to the child's birth country and not have your child escorted. The number of required trips, and the required length of stay for each, varies by country. Pre-adoptive parents may have to make one trip to meet and choose a waiting child, then make a second to bring the child home. A parent may need to stay in the country for several weeks or even months to collect all the papers the child needs to exit the country.

Also research which countries you are eligible to adopt from (for example, gay and lesbian couples are prohibited from adopting by many countries), the characteristics of waiting children, the reputation of the program and the costs. Most importantly, think about which culture you are most drawn to or which you are unwilling to adopt from. All intercountry adoptions are transcultural and some are transracial. Think about how you might support a child from a different culture develop a strong sense of self and identity. For example, do you live in a diverse community where a child from a different race or culture would be welcome? Are you willing to travel to your child's country of origin to help him reconnect with his birth culture, should he be interested in doing so in the future? Do you have friends from specific ethnic or cultural backgrounds from whom your child might enjoy learning?

Popular foreign programs for American adopters over the past three decades have included China, Russia, Poland, Colombia, Guatemala, South Korea, Romania and Vietnam. Programs that have grown in recent years include Ethiopia, the Philippines and Ukraine (prior to the Russia-Ukraine conflict). Almost all adoption programs have special programs for older youth, sibling groups and children with special health needs.

A mother who adopted a nearly four-year-old child with blindness and other special needs from Ukraine has this advice for prospective parents in the process of choosing an intercountry adoption program:

> I recommend that parents look at all open countries. Assess needed travel (as length of time in countries varies in the number of trips needed and length of stay, etc.), time waiting before travel after submitting dossier, the country's qualifications and the type of children available for adoption. There is no best country for all. For us,

traveling to Ukraine and living there for sixty-one days was not an issue, but for families with other children it may be more challenging, although we did have the option to make multiple trips versus a longer stay. We did not qualify for some countries due to medical history. Country laws and restrictions are constantly changing.

With Ukraine, since you cannot pre-select a child, we did not get any information on a child before traveling, but other countries will give full profiles and match a family before traveling. For us, since we were adopting an older child, Ukraine worked well, as we could meet the child and see her personality before saying yes or no to adopting the child (it worked for us—before we met our girl, we met a girl who neither of us connected with so we declined the referral and got a referral to our child). Ukraine allows three referrals (allowing a family to meet up to three children) before sending a family home. Also, Ukraine was good for us as we were open to a child with special needs so we were able to adopt a younger child (under five). For families who are not open to special needs and want a younger child, Ukraine would not be best.

Note that this parent was interviewed prior to the Russia-Ukraine conflict that erupted in 2014. Such incidents adversely impact adoption programs, adding to the unpredictability of intercountry adoption.

BEING MATCHED WITH A CHILD

Prospective parents interested in intercountry older child adoption may be able to begin the process of searching for a child before they even choose an agency. There are numerous photo-listing sites featuring older foreign children and children with special needs waiting to be adopted. Some of these sites are affiliated with agencies while others are simply photo-listing services. Be careful when using sites run by consultants or independent adoption facilitators. Find out how they get access to the photo listings and whether you can work with an agency to adopt a child found on their site (more about intercountry adoption facilitators in the next sections). Like domestic photo listings, you should be able to search for children by location, age and other characteristics, including whether they are part of a sibling group.

Be aware that, according to Hague Convention rules, adoptive parents cannot choose the child they will adopt; they can indicate an interest in a specific child but the match usually will be made by professionals in the child's country of origin.

More commonly, families receive referrals to children eligible to be adopted. Your agency may direct you to their public or private photo listings or engage in their own matching process that involves looking at your profile and home study.

Prospective parents should learn as much as possible from the foreign agency about the child's life, including her family history, care and special needs. Many parents adopting internationally complain they did not receive adequate information about their child's background. Problems with getting accurate information include inadequate record-keeping, corruption, fraud or a straightforward lack of knowledge about how the child became an orphan on the part of the foreign government and/or agency. Some parents have even discovered that they did not receive an accurate birth certificate or correct information about their child's date and location of birth.

THE PRE-ADOPTIVE PROCESS

The pre-adoptive process for domestic and intercountry adoption involves many of the same elements including the application, home study, pre-adoptive training, a background check and physicals (see the domestic adoption chapter for more information about the application) but there are additional documents you will need for intercountry adoption:

- A passport for travel
- I-800A form: Application for Determination of Suitability to Adopt a Child from a Hague Country
- I-600 form: Petition to Classify Orphan as an Immediate Relative (required for adoption from non-Hague countries)

LEGAL ISSUES

Once you have been matched to the child you want to adopt, you must find out what type of visa she will need to enter the United States and obtain a passport for her. Most children adopted by Hague Convention countries automatically become legal citizens of the United States but there are some exceptions. For example, if you are a citizen of the country from which the child is being adopted, procedures may differ. Also, when adopting from a non-Hague country, you may need to obtain orphan status for the child, and the process for entering the United States and gaining citizenship status for the child may be different.

Accredited agencies will help you complete the paperwork necessary for legalization and obtain a visa. If you are not using an agency you will have to hire an attorney experienced in intercountry adoption to assist you with the adoption process and to achieve finalization. Paperwork that renders the adoption legal is processed in Hague Convention countries prior to the child's departure. Once the child is brought into the United States, he may not need to be re-adopted through the courts but sometimes parents do this. Please reference the Child Welfare Information Gateway factsheet on adoption from Hague versus non-Hague countries to gain a better understanding of the legal process governing intercountry adoption.[9] Laws can sometimes change, so please also reference the Department of State's website (http://adoption.state.gov/) for the most current information about the required paperwork and procedures for adopting a child from a foreign nation. You will also need to discuss with your attorney what the laws are in your state concerning re-adoption and citizenship for your child.

COSTS

Intercountry adoption is considerably more expensive than adopting a child through the US foster care system. Currently, you will pay between twenty and forty thousand dollars to adopt a child internationally. Costs vary according to the country's program and the agency. For example, certain countries may require more visits and longer lengths of stay than others. Furthermore, certain countries require post-adoption visits and reporting by the agency. You also will incur higher legal fees if the adoption process is more complicated. Be sure to ask agencies you are considering working with what their fees are and what the costs are for a different country's programs.

To help you pay for intercountry adoption you might apply for a loan or grant from a private organization that supports adoptive parents. You might also do your own fundraising through an organization or on your own through programs like Kickstarter (https://www.kickstarter.com/). One of the parents we interviewed said she raised money through Reece's Rainbow, a private organization that specializes in special needs intercountry adoption, to help defray the costs of adopting their child from Ukraine.

In some states, parents who have adopted a child from another country, especially those who have adopted special needs children, will qualify for a one-time payment from the state. Call your state's child welfare agency to find out if you qualify. Once the adoption is finalized, you may also apply for the federal adoption tax credit. The tax credit is more beneficial for families that fall in a higher tax bracket; be sure to ask your tax preparer how you may benefit.

CHAPTER 5

Post-Adoption Services

Prior to adopting an older child, families should evaluate their support systems, noting in which areas they are lacking formal or informal support. Adoptive families should feel no shame in seeking out formal support and services. It is a typical need and families should seek help early and often.

Virginia Volante-Appel has over thirty years of experience as an adoption professional, including running her own agency and finding foster and adoptive homes for hard-to-place children. She says, "I think there is a lot of support out there for adoptive families now." She tells new adoptive parents that love alone cannot solve every problem a child may have. "In the long run," she tells them, "most mental health and attachment issues can be dealt with. [Adoptive parents] must have unconditional commitment no matter what happens. Kids have their own timelines—give them a chance." She believes that, with adequate post-placement services and support, most older child adoptions can succeed.

It is evident that there are more post-adoption services available to families today than ever before. At one time, adoption agencies had little knowledge about the mental health problems and needs of older adoptees and therefore offered little support to families. Today, adoption professionals, policymakers, therapists, researchers and adoptive families themselves understand that families who adopt older children from foster care or from abroad need a range of specialized services and supports to help them succeed. A majority of the three hundred adoptive parents surveyed by the US Children's Bureau for a report to Congress on barriers and success factors in adoption from foster care said they found post-placement training, therapy and support groups very helpful.[1]

The availability and quality of post-adoption services may vary by geographic location. Families living in rural areas may have less access to services than those living in urban areas. Furthermore, just because services are available does not mean families are aware of them or that they will access them. According to the Children's Bureau report, 41 percent of the families surveyed said they had problems accessing post-placement services. A common barrier to accessing needed services noted by the families was a lack of insurance coverage.[2]

Post-adoption services may be available through the agency you choose, the state or a private organization. They may be free, covered by the child's insurance or your insurance or you may have to pay out of pocket for some services. Families who are waiting for an adoption to be finalized should qualify for most if not all post-adoption services. Post-adoption services and benefits available to families who have adopted domestically or internationally may include:

- Follow-up home visits by the agency (requirements vary by state and adoption type)
- Mental health assessment and treatment
- Respite care
- Medical, dental and vision care
- Physical or occupational therapy
- Educational services
- Tuition reduction
- Crisis intervention

- Residential treatment
- Walk-in centers

Parents of children who are adopted from other countries may receive fewer post-placement services than parents of children adopted from the US foster care system. Public agencies can connect parents more easily with public services as compared to private agencies. Recurring public adoption subsidies are only available to families adopting domestically and other free services, such as mental health care, may only be available to these families as well. Parents of children who are adopted internationally should call their county or state child welfare agency to learn about services available to their child.

Those who adopt domestically will receive post-placement home visits by their adoption caseworker as required by state law, while parents who adopt internationally may not receive any face-to-face post-placement visits.

Parents who have adopted internationally may be required to submit regular post-placement reports to the country from which they adopted. Certain countries also require the agency to file post-placement reports. Ask your agency what post-placement reporting your country program requires. A mother who adopted her daughter from Ukraine described that country's post-placement requirements:

For Ukraine we do not need any follow-up visits from a social worker but have to send yearly reports to the Ukrainian embassy for the first three years, then every three years after. Other countries have different requirements. Russia required visits and reports by a social worker at six months home, twelve months home and then every year after for the first three years home.

We received no financial support [for the adoption] from our government or from the Ukrainian government. We did some fundraising with Reece's Rainbow [www.reecesrainbow.com] where people could donate to our adoption and many friends and family did this since we did not have a baby shower or anything. We also got money from my husband's company when the adoption was finalized.

Additional post-placement support and services that may be available to families through their agencies include:

- Adoptive parent support groups
- Support groups for adopted children
- Culture camps
- Online discussion forums
- Mentors
- Parent training and education
- Special events

PART II

adoptive families

CHAPTER 6

Welcoming Your Child Home

For a child adopted from the US foster care system by someone who is not a relative or foster parent, the process of coming home is gradual. First you meet with your prospective child at the agency, then the agency arranges for the child to visit with you. The initial outings or visits will be short, while later visits will be longer. As the relationship grows, the child may come to visit you for a few days and then gradually increase to a week or two. The child's school schedule may affect the timing of these visits and you may need to discuss the timing of the visits with the child's foster parents.

During this visitation period, the child's caseworker as well as your caseworker will check in with you and the child about how you are getting along. If all parties are feeling positive about the visits and the placement, the agency will make a pre-adoptive placement of the child in your home. At this point he leaves his foster or group home to come to live with you until the adoption is legally finalized. During this time the agency will continue to make home visits and you may be asked to complete additional paperwork or training.

Children adopted by their foster parents or relative caregivers or guardians are already home, so the process of being legally adopted may not be as pronounced a transition as it is for other foster children. Nonetheless, they too have to adjust to the idea of having permanent parents. This could be scary for these children as well, because they will not want to do anything to disrupt the adoption. Some children may be confused about what being adopted means and how this will change their relationships with their caregivers. According to research by Tiffany Conway and Rutledge Q. Hutson, children adopted by relative caregivers may have fewer adjustment problems, because they can maintain closer contact with biological parents and other family members.[1]

For children adopted from another country, the coming home process is more abrupt but more countries are implementing protocols to make the transition easier for older children and teens. At first you may be permitted to visit with the child at the orphanage and take walks with her around the grounds. After that, you may be permitted to make longer visits and eventually have the child stay with you overnight.

Children adopted internationally may have more difficulty than children adopted domestically when adjusting to their new homes. Not only are they adjusting to living in a family, which they may never have done before, but they must adjust to a new culture, language and country too!

PREVENTING ADOPTION DISRUPTION

Adoption disruption occurs when an adoption never reaches legal finalization. Ten to fifteen percent of American domestic adoptions are disrupted while intercountry adoptions are rarely disrupted, because they are generally finalized before the child leaves the country.[2] An adoption can be disrupted because either the child or parent decides the placement is not working. The age at which children can consent to an adoptive placement varies from state to state.[3]

Adoptions are less likely to disrupt when:

- Parents are well prepared for older child adoption through training and education
- Adoptive parents have complete and accurate information about the child they are adopting
- The adoptive child and parents are well-matched

• Quality post-placement support is available

Adoption disruption can be very painful for pre-adoptive parents and traumatic for the child. If you feel the adoption is at risk, contact your adoption caseworker immediately. The agency may have specialized adoption preservation services or be able to refer you to such services. Remember that the pre-adoptive period is a very sensitive time; behavior that manifests may not be indicative of long-term behavior problems. Often, parents wait too long to contact their agency for help and the adoption cannot be saved.

FINALIZATION

Domestic adoptions must be finalized in court. During the pre-adoptive period you will need to hire an attorney and/or work with your agency to finalize the adoption. When an adoption is finalized, you become the child's legal parent. Your child usually lives with you for six months or more before this. Your attorney and/or agency will let you know what additional paperwork you need to complete, what legal fees you are responsible for and arrange a finalization date with the court. Reasons a finalization may be delayed include:

• Biological parents appeal termination of their parental rights
• Relatives or foster parents object (this is rare because agencies are required to give them first priority in adopting a child in their care if they are considered suitable permanent parents)
• The court has a backlog of cases
• The child is unsure he wants to be adopted

INTRODUCING YOUR CHILD TO RELATIVES AND FRIENDS

During the visitation and pre-adoptive period, your child should be getting to know you and his siblings, not the entire extended family. Do not overwhelm him with visits to your sister's house, outings with your best friend and her kids or a holiday at your mother's. Also be mindful of who is coming in and out of your home while your child is adjusting. Remember that your child may not be able to trust or feel comfortable with a lot of adults.

In the past he may have experienced abuse by biological parents or other relatives, or in an orphanage abroad. Just getting to know you and your partner or spouse and any new siblings may be difficult.

Allow your child to get to know his extended family including aunts, uncles, grandparents, cousins and friends of the family over time. Perhaps have your parents meet the child first (if you are emotionally close to them), then invite others to meet your child over the course of a year. Prior to meeting his new extended family, show the child photos of family gatherings and holidays. Tell him funny stories about people he sees in the pictures and let him know how excited they are to meet him. You may even ask other children in the family to write him letters or draw him pictures expressing how happy they are that he's joined the family.

ACCLIMATING YOUR CHILD TO HER NEW COMMUNITY

Your child may have left a community she knows well to become part of your family. It is very difficult for any child, especially a traumatized one, to make such a big change. Slowly acclimate your child to her new community by visiting parks, restaurants, shops, historical sites, museums and other locations you think she will like. Tell her stories about the times you and your family have spent at these spots. Then take her to her new school and introduce her to the principal and her new teacher(s).

Children adopted from foster care who have grown up in areas that are very different from yours may be excited about your community or may be intimidated or confused. Imagine growing up in an inner city, then suddenly finding yourself living next to a farm. Expose your child to all the wonderful things about your town and city and hopefully he will come to love it as much as you do.

A child raised in a foreign country should be expected to have more difficulty adjusting to his new community. He is a foreigner in a new land, as well as a new town! Develop a plan for helping your internationally-adopted child slowly adjust to his new surroundings using some of the recommendations we've made. Also, perhaps learn his native language before you bring him home and find out about culture camps or support groups for internationally-adopted older children.

SETTING ROUTINES AND EXPECTATIONS

Offer children many opportunities for building trust, including the seemingly mundane interactions of the day. Following through with the most trivial of promises is crucial to a parent's integrity. If you say you will read a book with your child before bed and you do, this is a form of building trust. There will be times when parents are unable to follow through, either for reasons beyond their control or due to unrealistic planning, and in those cases it is important to offer a simple rationale and let your child know that you did not forget. When your child sees that you are consistent in doing what you say and saying what you do, he or she will learn to trust you. Adoption professional Judy Schwartz recommends:

> When adopting from an orphanage, get as much info as you can regarding routine, foods, methods of discipline, sleeping arrangements, etc. There are behaviors that are referred to as "orphanage behaviors" that are generally institutionalized rocking or self-stimulating actions, self abuse, etc. Also, there is something about how children might position themselves in bed (they tend to turn around during sleep to maintain boundaries especially when beds are side by side). Also, sometimes children were disciplined by using water such as turning a hose on them and that might make them fearful of showers, etc. If a child never ate meat or had to chew food they may not be able or comfortable doing so and there might be a heightened risk of choking. They might be resistant to trying new foods while transitioning. Remember, your adopted child has gone through many losses; the loss of their biological family, the loss of caretakers and friends, the loss of culture, foods, familiar smells, sights, etc. They are sometimes overwhelmed when they come to their new family and home; generally their new bedrooms are full of interesting things to look at and bright colors and sunshine. This is sometimes over-stimulating and it might add to difficulties in transitioning. Introduce new things slowly. Do not make a party to welcome the child; give your child a chance to get used to their new family first. People will want to come and meet the child

and bring gifts; you need to put the needs of your transitioning child ahead of the wants of well-meaning loved ones.

Getting families on a regular routine as much as possible will make the days as predictable as possible. This will help establish clear expectations and combat feelings of disorder and chaos that a child might have become accustomed to in foster care or displaced adoptions. Using charts, calendars or graphics to depict the daily routine will add to a semblance of order and calm. There are times in the day where a sequence of actions is expected. For instance, establishing a bedtime routine might include the following: brush teeth, bath time (or basic washing), read books, bed. Using images in the desired order, posted at the child's level in plain sight, will serve as a reminder and enforce the routine. Turning routines into chunks or clusters of behaviors does a few things:

- Sets clear expectations
- Serves as a prompt or visual cue
- Forms a habit
- Empowers children by giving them a sense of control

AFTER THE HONEYMOON PHASE IS OVER

You know the saying, "The honeymoon is over." It is used to describe the reality that may set in for married couples after a year or two of marriage. The first years may be a time of romance and excitement, but then you start focusing on each other's faults and have to figure out how to really live with each other. This is when people say that the honeymoon is over. The same concept can be applied to the relationship between older adoptees and their new parents.

When an adopted child first comes home he may be on his best behavior. He may be quite pleased about the adoption and want to make his new caregivers happy. He doesn't want to do anything to disrupt the adoption or cause conflict. But after a period of time, the child will want to test boundaries. He wants to find out how much he can get away with, what his parents' steadfast rules are and how much they will tolerate.

In acting out, the child is trying to find out, "Are they truly committed to me?" Or he may be showing a part of himself that is hurt or confused. He may wonder, "Do they understand me? Do they know what I've been through? Can they put up with the part of me that is ashamed, frightened or angry?" Seek to understand what these different behaviors mean.

Your child may have early issues in the parent/child relationship when the honeymoon period is over, but many of these issues can be dealt with early on with the right professional help. As a new adoptive parent you should take time off from work after your child comes home. You will need time to get to know your child and your constant presence in the early days of her placement may help her adjust better. The Family Medical Leave Act (FMLA) allows foster and adoptive parents to take up to twelve weeks of unpaid leave from their jobs after their child comes home. Smaller companies may be exempt from the law, so ask your company what leave time you are eligible to receive.

Remember that the child acting out in these early weeks and months is normal within certain parameters—if the child is violent or ill you must seek immediate assistance from your agency and/or mental health professionals. Try to understand how his past influences his behavior. He may have experienced years in foster care going from placement to placement and now is being told that somebody wants to take care of him permanently. Wouldn't you be afraid of rejection or of doing something to disrupt the adoption? Wouldn't you be wary of your new parents? Years in an orphanage may have instilled survivor behavior that is no longer useful in a family environment.

Some adopted children will transition into their new families more easily than others. In all cases, building trust is a process that cannot be rushed. Your child's uncertainty about her new home and her trauma history may manifest in the following behaviors during the first weeks or months of the placement:

- Repeatedly asking adoptive parents to buy her things
- Being overly protective of toys and other possessions
- Lying
- Having difficulty sleeping or resting

- Acting out sexually
- Stealing
- Damaging or destroying items in the home
- Refusing to complete chores
- Hoarding or gorging on food
- Making false accusations of abuse
- Becoming easily startled or anxiety-ridden
- Demonstrating extreme bouts of anger or throwing tantrums
- Becoming easily overstimulated
- Disregarding rules or acting defiant
- Being manipulative, overly argumentative or defiant
- Hurting herself, family members, pets or others

Not every behavioral problem will need to be addressed early on, but some behaviors such as sexual acting out, violence and making false accusations of abuse will need to be addressed immediately. Your agency should be able to refer you to a mental health professional who is experienced in working with adopted children and their families.

CHAPTER 7

Adoptive Families are "Real" Families—Educating Friends and Family about Older Child Adoption

Think about your circle of friends and family. Do you know someone who has adopted or is adopted? The answer, most likely, is yes. Many children and teenagers also can identify at least one friend or classmate who is adopted. Adoption has become more common in recent decades and adoption in general is viewed favorably by the public; nevertheless, some myths about adoption persist and some even continue to question whether adoptive families are real families. To the extent there is a lack of understanding about adoption, older child adoption may be the least understood type of adoption.

The last thing you want to do as an adoptive parent of an older child is to have to educate others about adoption, when you yourself may feel that you still lack some of the necessary knowledge. But you may need to do so, because as the adoptive parent of an older child you have enough knowledge and experience to dispel myths and educate others about the importance of adoption.

Some people who are close to you may not have an accurate understanding of older child adoption and just need information about certain aspects of adoption that they don't understand. At the worst, some people close to you may not consider adoptive families, especially families that have brought an older child into their lives, "real" families. They may have tried to dissuade you from adopting an older child or told you you were crazy to actually go through with it. Before you adopt, build a network of people around you who understand your decision to adopt, who understand older child adoption and who believe in the healing power of families.

One couple who adopted an eight-year-old boy from the US foster care system was disheartened by people's negativity about their decision to adopt. The wife explained:

> *I wish I had known how many people in both our community and extended family would not be supportive of our decision or would continually question why we would want to do this. It would not have changed our decision, but we went into it feeling like this was a way to help a kid who was already here and needed us...and most people who we told about it seemed to think we were stupid and making a huge mistake. I think in general people just could not understand why we would possibly want to adopt an older child as opposed to an infant. I didn't feel that most people were prejudiced [about older child adoption], just surprised or shocked...and a little standoffish.*

It is disheartening to have to deal with such attitudes, especially after you've gone through so much to prepare for adoption or after you have actually brought your child home and are trying your best to adjust. You may feel the child is as much a part of your heart as if you had given birth to him, but having to explain this to others, you feel yourself growing resentful. Despite the stress that such ignorance can cause you, perhaps look at the situation another way. Who better to dispel myths and educate those closest to you about the realities of older child adoption? You are in a unique position to be able to change people's attitudes and maybe even turn them into advocates for adoption. What better gift can you give your child than to change perceptions about adoption among close friends and family and even in the larger community? Your child will benefit from your role as an adoption ambassador and so will you.

When you find yourself needing to educate those closest to you about older child adoption, try some of the following:

- Show your friends and family some videos of adoptive children and families speaking about what adoption has meant to them.
- Share this guide with them and suggest certain sections they may want to peruse.
- Bring friends or family to an adoption class offered by a local adoptive parent group or register them for a webinar.
- Prior to adopting, introduce them to friends who have already adopted older children and feel positive about the experience.

If friends or family remain reluctant to support you in your choice to adopt, gently explain that you have made your decision and hope they will support you, but if they can't, you will need some time to adjust to adoptive parenthood without their interference or negativity. Hopefully in time these reluctant family members and friends will come around to love your child, but if they don't, reconsider your relationship with them. This may be extremely difficult if the family member is a parent or sibling, but think about your child and yourself. In adopting an older child, you deserve the utmost respect from those closest to you. If there are people in your life who are making an already difficult journey even more so, you need to put some space between yourself and them.

As for educating people not in your closest circle of friends and family, take a slightly different approach. There may be people in the community with whom you are not personally close but who play an important role in your child's life—teachers, tutors, school social workers, other parents, babysitters, coaches or employers. Visit with each and talk to them about your child's adoption, as well as her history, if you feel that level of detail is necessary to help them understand particular behaviors your child may exhibit. For example, explain to a coach that your child may need extra help with aspects of teamwork because she had to be so independent in previous situations just to survive. Explain to her teacher how certain behaviors she may exhibit at school are attributable to past trauma, not a learning disability or unwillingness to learn. You may share some resources about older child adoption or trauma with individuals in your child's life, but don't be too aggressive about it because ultimately it is their responsibility to interact in an appropriate way with your child.

Help the people in your child's life *help you* raise a happy, healthy child. If you feel someone close to your child is not exhibiting the level of understanding they should, replace them if you can. If it is beyond your ability to do so, in the case of a teacher, school social worker or even employer, help your child navigate these difficult relationships. Help him develop resilience by telling him not everyone in his life is going to love him, but you and your partner or spouse always will.

You may feel that you don't want to simply educate people in your immediate circle about adoption, but want to educate others in a more formal way. If so, think about forming or leading a support group for adoptive parents or volunteer to help prospective or new adoptive parents navigate the system. Your willingness to become an adoption advocate shows your child, friends and family how important your child is to you. As an advocate, you will help others understand how older child adoption changes lives.

CHAPTER 8

Multicultural and Multiracial Adoptive Families

Transracial adoption is a term used to describe the adoption of a child who is a different race from his adoptive parents. For example, when white parents adopt a black infant or child, that is considered transracial adoption. Transcultural adoption is a term used to describe an adoption where the child and parents have different cultural backgrounds or nationalities. Children adopted from another country generally have a different cultural background from their parents (unless, for example, the parent is an immigrant and has the same cultural background as her adopted child). A transcultural adoption may also characterize an adoption in which the child is a different ethnicity or culture from his parents even though they are from the same country.

Often families that have adopted transracially or transculturally are referred to as multiracial or multicultural. According to the 2007 American National Survey of Adoptive Parents, children adopted internationally are most likely to be of a different race, culture or ethnicity from their adoptive parents (84 percent) compared to 28 percent of children adopted from the US foster care system.[1] Forty percent of all adopted children (including privately adopted infants) in the United States are a different race, culture or ethnicity from their parents.[2]

GROWING AWARENESS OF THE IMPORTANCE OF CULTURE IN ADOPTION

In the United States, agencies receiving federal funding cannot consider race as a factor in the placement of a child. Many families adopting domestically in the United States are now required to receive training about transracial adoption. Agencies recognize that children adopted transracially and transculturally may still experience important identity and other issues related to race and culture; therefore, the greater emphasis on training and awareness is a welcome development in US adoption practice.

Awareness about the importance of addressing cultural issues in intercountry adoption has grown as well. The Hague Convention established that member country agencies must consider a prospective family's ability to meet the cultural needs of a child when placing that child.[3] Individual countries set their own cultural training requirements, but all Hague Convention countries are encouraged to educate prospective parents about the importance of valuing and celebrating their child's cultural heritage. Intercountry adoption agencies in the United States, for example, do require that prospective parents adopting internationally receive training in cultural issues.

ADOPTING MATURE NATIVE AMERICAN CHILDREN

If you are interested in fostering or adopting a child who belongs to a federally recognized tribe, you must educate yourself about the Indian Child Welfare Act (ICWA) and the tribal child welfare system. ICWA is a federal statute passed in 1978 that set specific requirements governing the removal and placement of Native American children who are members of federally-recognized tribes. Concerned about the high rate of removal of Native children from their parental homes by the domestic child welfare system, ICWA was passed to protect tribes' greatest resource—their children—and ultimately protect tribal sovereignty. ICWA requires county and state child welfare agencies to notify tribes when a child who is a member of a federally-recognized tribe is removed from the home and requires them to work with the tribal child welfare system to find placements with Native American families or tribal members, among other requirements.

There is a troubling history of Native American children being removed from their families and tribal communities. By 1880, Native children were required by federal statute to attend boarding schools to be assimilated into white culture; incredibly, it was illegal for Native parents to have their own children in their homes. Being sent away to military-style boarding schools was traumatic for Native children separated for long periods of time from their families, tribes and cultures. Prior to ICWA's passing in 1978, 20 to 30 percent of Native American children were living outside their parental homes due to removal by domestic child welfare authorities. Often Native children were removed for reasons such as the home not having running water or electricity; a high percentage of those removed were placed with non-Native families.[4]

ICWA REQUIREMENTS

In addition to requiring that tribes be notified when Native children come to the attention of child welfare authorities and are removed from the home, ICWA now requires that:

- Culturally appropriate services be provided for Native children and families engaged in the child welfare system
- Tribes be contacted by domestic child welfare agencies when a child is being removed or placed in foster care
- Agencies prioritize placements with family, tribal members or members of another tribe
- "Active efforts" be made by agencies to prevent removal of children from their parental homes and to reunite families

Tribal child welfare agencies commonly serve multiple tribes in a region and oversee foster care placements, adoption and foster and adoptive parent training and recruitment. The tribal child welfare system works with county and state child welfare agencies and receives funding from the

US government. Should a tribal child welfare agency not have adequate resources to provide families with comprehensive child welfare services, it will refer cases back to the county or state. ICWA specialists are available in many state and county agencies to ensure ICWA compliance. Preserving tribal culture is central to ICWA, which requires county and state child welfare workers to make culturally informed services available to Native families.

Child protection practices vary from tribe to tribe. For example, one tribal child welfare system may allow for the termination of parental rights and adoptive placements, while others may not process terminations, which means children remain in the care of foster parents or relative guardians until the age of eighteen. ICWA requires a higher standard of proof than the Adoption and Safe Family Act (ASFA) for termination of parental rights and expert witnesses are often brought into proceedings.

Many tribal child welfare systems are confronted with resource limitations. Tribes must refer cases back to the state if they are under-resourced. Furthermore, many tribes struggle to recruit and retain foster and adoptive parents. Clarissa LaPlante, ICWA Specialist/Child Protective Worker Supervisor at Dakota Tiwahe Service Unit in Santee, Nebraska, says many tribes are using federal funding to improve their child welfare systems, including increasing the availability of parenting classes and rehabilitation and therapeutic services for children and families. LaPlante adds that many agencies are taking steps to improve foster and adoptive parent recruitment and retention. Her agency is allowing prospective parents leave time from their jobs to become licensed.

ICWA is subject to interpretation by the courts. One recent high-profile ICWA case that went all the way to the Supreme Court involved a girl whose Native American father sued for custody after she was placed in a non-Native adoptive home. The father refused to support the little girl's mother when the mother was pregnant and did not make any claim to custody until after she was born, leading the adoptive family to argue he no longer had a valid claim. Ultimately the father dropped his custody battle and pledged to work with the adoptive parents to develop a plan for being involved in his daughter's life. Some believe the court's decision threatens tribal sovereignty while others feel the decision correctly subsumes some provisions of ICWA to the best interests of a specific child.

A LEGACY OF KINSHIP CAREGIVING IN TRIBAL COMMUNITIES

Under ICWA, priority out-of-home placements are with the child's extended family or other members of the tribe. Related guardians, foster parents and adoptive parents may be eligible for special funding to help cover the child's expenses. Family and kinship foster and adoptive parenting in tribal communities today reflects the notion of kinship care in Native culture.

Elders especially have always played an important role safeguarding the youngest generation and passing the culture and traditions of the tribe on to them. Today, many Native grandparents are raising grandchildren and great grandchildren their family members can no longer care for and often ensure that siblings stay together. Mothers and grandmothers who take in foster and adoptive children are modern-day clan mothers responsible for the protection and safe keeping of the tribe's children.

FOSTERING OR ADOPTING A CHILD COVERED BY ICWA

ICWA gives first priority for fostering or adopting a Native American child to the child's extended family. Secondary priority is given to members of the child's tribe, with tertiary priority going to members of other federally recognized tribes. Non-native persons may be eligible to foster or adopt children under ICWA should a family or tribal placement not be available. If you are interested in fostering or adopting through the tribal child welfare system you should begin by taking the following steps:

- Educate yourself about ICWA and tribal child welfare.
- Contact your regional tribal child welfare service unit about becoming a licensed foster parent (Note: it is important to get licensed early in the process of becoming a foster parent because only licensed foster parents are eligible to receive Title IV-E funds for reimbursement of medical and other expenses related to the child. Payments are not retroactive; you are not reimbursed for expenses incurred prior to becoming licensed).

- Find out if your tribe terminates parental rights, allowing adoptive placements to be made.
- Attend foster or adoptive parent training classes in the community, online or by video. At-home training may be available as well.

MIDWEST NATIVE AMERICAN COUPLE RAISES TWO GENERATIONS OF ADOPTED CHILDREN

This particular Native couple's parenting responsibilities did not end with their six biological children. They raised an adopted grandson and, in their sixties, they are raising nine and twelve-year-old adopted children related by blood. They also are considering adopting two of their great-grandchildren, ages seven and eight, and the children's two siblings who are three and four.

They fostered their youngest two adopted children for over a year prior to adopting them. The adoption did not go through the tribal child welfare system because the children have significant mental and physical illnesses including Attention Deficit Hyperactivity Disorder, Oppositional Defiant Disorder and spina bifida. The two children were devastated by having lived in a dozen different foster homes prior to being adopted. Unaware initially that they were in foster care, the couple tried to stay in touch with them during their most recent placements. They say the children simply wanted to belong to one family and repeatedly asked the couple if they would adopt them. When the older of the two children came to live with them, his behavior was challenging, but since his medication was adjusted his behavior has improved. "It's been a 50 percent turnaround for him and he keeps heading in the right direction," the adoptive mother said.

POTENTIAL CHALLENGES FOR CHILDREN OF TRANSCULTURAL OR TRANSRACIAL ADOPTION

In the past, multiracial families, including adoptive families, were stigmatized. Today, with the growing number of transracial and transcultural relationships and marriages, multiracial and multicultural families are becoming more common. Multiracial and multicultural families through adoptions also are more numerous. Nonetheless, race and culture are important factors in adoption and thus understanding the impact of transcultural and transracial adoption on children is essential.

According to the Donaldson Institute for Adoption, "Transracial adoption in itself does not produce psychological or social maladjustment problems in children." However, children adopted transracially or transculturally may face additional challenges related to fitting into their families and communities and in developing a healthy racial or ethnic identity.[5]

Children adopted domestically into communities that are very different from where they previously lived with biological or foster families may feel disconnected or even alienated from both communities. Children, especially teens, may be confused about where they fit in. Friends from where they once lived may tease them about having parents of a different race or culture or tell them they no longer fit in with friends from their old neighborhood. Children of a different race may feel their adoptive parents don't understand where they come from or how they experience the world differently. They may feel their parents don't understand what it means to be a member of their racial or cultural group. They also may feel their parents do not understand the prejudice or racism they encounter or will encounter as adults.

Children often don't disclose incidents of racism, prejudice and discrimination to their parents. One reason is that the family does not have a regularly structured opportunity to allow for such discussions. Parents often think children will tell them when something happens because of their race or ethnicity but the children don't share it with them. Building identity is not the same as having a strategy to deal with being different.

Families should have meetings on a set schedule to discuss race, ethnicity or culture. The meetings could include watching a movie where someone was discriminated against or taking a story from the news for discussion. It means setting aside time for communicating openly related to this topic. It is about building a safe family space where children can participate in a discussion about their differences with their adoptive family. Remember, if you don't ask, they won't tell.

Older children adopted internationally will probably experience issues related to their cultural identity. Older children brought to a new country by their adoptive parents after living in their home countries for five, ten or fifteen years will almost certainly experience culture shock. All at once they must adjust to a new family, new culture, new language and new diet. This is a dramatic adjustment for an adult, let alone a child! These children must contend with learning not only about their new nation's culture in general, but also about how people of different racial and ethnic backgrounds fit in. Help your child adjust by teaching him English or learn some words in his native language before he comes home. Ask your agency if your child will receive any English language classes to prepare him for adoption.

Children with a different cultural background from their parents and siblings may not understand holiday traditions or the meaning of the holidays that their new family celebrates. Take time to explain these traditions and the meaning of various holidays to your adopted child. If your child was brought up in a different religion, celebrate the holidays of his faith as well. Show him that you value his religious upbringing by learning about his earlier religious faith, holidays and traditions. Make all the holidays (his and yours) fun for your transculturally adopted child by baking together, doing arts and crafts projects and listening to holiday music. Involve your biological or same-culture adopted children in participating in their adopted siblings' holiday traditions.

BECOMING EDUCATED ABOUT RACE AND CULTURE

You know in your heart your child's skin color or culture does not make you love him any less. You want everyone in the world to reflect the color-blindness of your love, but unfortunately the world simply isn't always color-blind. You must be realistic about the community and world you live in and prepare your child for racism, prejudices, discrimination, uncomfortable questions or even curiosity he may encounter.

The 2010 Donaldson Institute report concludes that parents who are better prepared for transracial and transcultural adoption will be better able to help their children with issues related to their cultural/racial identity. Furthermore, a study conducted in 2009 by Charlotte Paulsen and Joseph R. Merighi of 326 parents who adopted children internationally found that parents who were better prepared for issues related to their child's cultural heritage or racial identity felt more prepared for intercountry adoption in general and, in effect, more satisfied with the adoption.[6]

You will serve your child well by learning all you can about his cultural/ethnic/racial background and making an effort to understand how he may experience the world differently from you. Agency training on transracial adoption may focus on how people of different races and ethnicities experience the world, how to prepare your children for prejudice or racism they may encounter and how to celebrate your child's birth culture. In addition to agency training and taking other adoption classes or seminars, read books, review online resources and talk to other adoptive parents about transracial/transcultural adoption. Part of building your own cultural competence that you can pass on to your child is to become aware of the history, social institutions and everyday customs of the culture of your child's birth.

A second strategy is to promote bicultural socialization. Bicultural socialization is a process via activities, events and relationships where children are socialized into the values, attitudes, beliefs, norms and behaviors of the dominant culture in which they live as well as their birth culture. It allows children to attain bicultural competence and negotiate, navigate and relate between the two cultures. Bicultural socialization can result in positive psychological outcomes for adoptees such as better parent-child relationships (i.e., attachment), higher self-esteem, more positive racial or ethnic identities, higher educational achievement and adult adjustment.[7] These effects are most pronounced if the activities begin when children are younger. Your children will let you know when they no longer wish to participate in them.

Parents who adopt transracially or transculturally should also think about where they are raising their child and sending him to school. Is your community culturally and racially diverse? Are the schools culturally or racially diverse? Are people in the community accepting of people from different racial, ethnic and cultural backgrounds? Studies have shown that living in a diverse and accepting community can help children adopted transculturally or transracially adjust and develop a more healthy sense of racial/cultural identity.

CELEBRATING YOUR CHILD'S CULTURAL HERITAGE

Here are some ideas for cultural activities you can do with your child and ways in which your entire family can celebrate your child's cultural heritage:

- Send your child to a culture camp where he can meet other children adopted from his birth country.

- Participate in a homeland tour (arranged by some adoption agencies) or visit your child's home country.

- Spend time in a part of your city where there is a large population of people who share your child's cultural background.

- Connect your child with a friend or mentor who shares his cultural heritage.

- Reserve one night of the week for cooking or ordering ethnic food your child enjoys (i.e. Korean food night, Mexican food night).

- Learn your child's language while he learns yours.

- Decorate your child's room with items, designs and pictures from his native country.

- Do cultural arts and crafts projects.

- Go to museums that feature art or artifacts from your child's native country or that focus on your child's ethnic or cultural history.

- Attend cultural parades or events.

- Listen to culturally-relevant music.

- Celebrate holidays native to your child's culture or that focus on a historical event important to his community of origin.

- Buy him culturally-relevant toys, story books, music, cookbooks, clothes, literature and other age-appropriate items.

- Attend salons or barber shops that cater to your child's race or culture of origin.

- Expose your child to different faiths or attend religious services at a house of worship with which your child is comfortable.

- Speak frankly about historical and present discrimination and prejudice.

- Create a cultural life book with your child that explores his cultural and family history.

CHAPTER 9

Sibling Relationships

It is important to understand the importance of sibling relationships in adoption. Whether the relationship is between siblings who have been adopted together, an adopted child and his non-adopted sibling or an adopted child and sibling-like friends or relatives, sibling relationships, like peer relationships, can significantly impact a child's well-being, identity, sense of belonging and overall happiness.

Sibling relationships contribute to the development and growth of individuals in numerous ways. They influence individual formation of identity, establish norms of interaction, serve as a cultural reference and help children with their emotional development such as coping skills and perspective-taking. Siblings may comprise a child's first peer group, where they learn how to negotiate, cooperate, share and engage in a reciprocal relationship.

Any child, adopted children included, may consider children who are not their biological brothers or sisters to be like siblings.[1] Your child might have a sibling-like relationship with a family member such as a cousin, a non-relative he lived with at one time, a step-sister or brother, the son or daughter of a parent's partner or a child he lived with in a group or foster home. Prospective parents preparing to adopt a specific child should learn who the child has a sibling-like relationship with so they can ensure their child's relationships with his "sibling" is not disrupted.

SIBLING PLACEMENTS IN ADOPTION

In the United States, about two-thirds of children in foster care have a sibling.[2] The Fostering Connections to Success and Increasing Adoptions Act of 2008 is a federal law that encourages states to make their best efforts to keep siblings together in foster and adoptive placements.

Sibling relationships can be a tremendous support for children placed in foster and adoptive homes. Having a sibling can increase a child's sense of security and belonging at a time when he has experienced so much change and loss. For foster and adopted children who have limited familial ties and smaller networks of support, siblings can be a source of comfort and attachment. A healthy sibling connection may promote resilience in foster and adopted children and give them the sense that "we're in this together."

Placing siblings together in an adoptive home can reduce the risk of adoption disruption due to the protective aspects of sibling relationships, such as emotional support and kinship.

WHEN SIBLINGS ARE PLACED IN SEPARATE ADOPTIVE HOMES

Typically it is recommended that siblings be placed in foster and adoptive homes together, but this is not always possible. Various factors can contribute to sibling separation such as the number of siblings, aggression or abuse between siblings or a lack of foster or adoptive parents for sibling groups. Children may be placed in separate orphanages because of their ages.

When there has been sibling abuse, some believe it is best to first explore therapeutic interventions before the children are placed in separate homes. If treatment options have been exhausted to rehabilitate the abuser, separation may be deemed necessary to protect one sibling.

According to Cherilyn Dance and associates, when an older child is separated from siblings and placed without them, he could be at risk of poorer outcomes in the first year.[3] There is ample grief and loss in adoption but when sibling separation also occurs a child's grief and loss is compounded. Children in the foster care system have described separation from siblings as another form of "punishment."[4] Even if the siblings haven't always had a healthy relationship, they may grieve. There can be a higher risk of disruption when siblings are placed separately, because of the emotional or behavioral issues that follow separation.

The Fostering Connections to Success and Increasing Adoptions Act of 2008 encourages states to allow for visitation between siblings placed in separate foster or adoptive homes. Siblings may be included in formal or informal contact agreements between biological and adoptive families but legal enforcement of such agreements varies by state. In addition to playdates or visits, your child might also stay in contact with his sibling through video calls, e-mail and letters.

Grief and loss may occur not only when a child is separated from his biological sibling, but also when he is isolated from a child with whom he has a sibling-like relationship. If your child is being separated from another child with whom he has a sibling-like relationship, it's important that you think about how to foster the continuation of this relationship. You might include the other child in a visitation plan, but be aware states vary in their definition of sibling relationships when it comes to legal visitation rights. (This is, of course, impossible with intercountry adoption.) You should validate the relationships and let your child know you understand the sadness he feels about seeing less of such a special family member or friend.

A SIBLING IN THE ROLE OF CAREGIVER

In cases of abuse or neglect, siblings can provide protection and comfort to each other, with older siblings often taking on the role of caregiver for younger siblings. This dynamic sometimes leads to strong connections in sibling relationships, in some cases stronger than the biological parent-child connection, that can last a lifetime, and it can be incredibly traumatic if separation occurs.

Despite the love she has for a sibling, a child forced into the role of caregiver may become resentful. "Parentification" of children is commonly seen in families where parents are substance abusers; however, it can occur in any home environment where the primary caregivers are not responsive to the children's needs. In lower-resource countries, children may be forced to take on the role of breadwinner and parent.

Older sibling caregivers may grow to resent their roles and lash out at the younger child in anger or frustration. This type of situation is typically resolved when the older child is relieved of his or her role as caregiver, thus it usually does not warrant sibling separation. However, the child should be monitored and therapy is generally warranted to help reestablish a sibling dynamic that is parallel rather than hierarchical.

Conflict may also arise when the "parentified" child is expected to relinquish her caregiving role to the new adoptive parent. It is important that adoptive parents try to understand the dynamics of sibling relationships and roles in the biological family home. Take the time to gradually introduce family roles and expectations. Recognize that an older child's anger may be rooted in a history that is known only to the children.

In some cultures or families, older siblings are expected to care for younger siblings. If an older sibling is unwilling to pass along the caregiver role to the adoptive parents, try to maintain some of the older sibling's responsibilities for the younger one, or create new roles such as reading to younger siblings or helping them with their homework.

SIBLINGS THROUGH ADOPTION

In some cases, agencies recommend children be adopted into homes where there are no other children present, because they need one-on-one attention or have significant behavioral problems and could harm another child in the family. Most normally functioning children will do just fine in a home with other children. For some adoptive children, gaining a sibling increases their sense of belonging, helps them adjust better to a new family environment and increases their overall happiness.

Some adoption professionals recommend that birth order be preserved when adopting a child. In effect, the adopted child should not become the oldest sibling in the family—they should become the youngest so as not to disturb the other child or children's feeling of entitlement to being the first children in the family. An exception might be made when an existing child really wants an older brother or sister and the adoptive child is mature enough to step into that role.

Bringing an adopted child home can be stressful and exciting. Being aware of what to expect and planning ahead can make all the difference in how everyone responds to and experiences the change. Arleta James asserts, in *Brothers and Sisters in Adoption: Helping Children Navigate Relationships When New Kids Join the Family*, that the adjustment process requires that parents maintain existing relationships with current children while building a strong parent-child relationship with the adoptee.[5] Biological children will have varying responses to an adopted child joining the family, but the one thing they share is how the changes will impact their lives in the long term, according to Amanda Baden and John Raible.[6]

Empathize with your child or children's apprehension about how their lives will be affected by the adoption. Uncertainty is a common feeling for any child who will be become a big brother or sister, but the adoption of an older child can bring added complications. There may be opportunities for your children to participate in pre-adoptive training which can help prepare them for behaviors their new siblings may exhibit. Ask your agency if they offer training for siblings. If they don't, look into training or even a webinar offered by a nonprofit.

After their adopted brother or sister arrives, children already in the home may become jealous of all the attention he or she is getting. Special needs adoptees certainly will take up a lot of parents' time, so make sure you set aside some special time to spend with your other children.

Older children who are living in the home may express an interest in assisting with the care or needs of the adopted child. While adoptive parents may appreciate and welcome the assistance, it may help the older child to know it is okay to set boundaries and limits, particularly with regard to an adoptee who has developmental issues or behavioral problems. Give the older child permission to express his or her concerns or frustrations. Be supportive of him or her and offer assurance that you are listening and you care.

Your children may also have difficulty understanding why their adopted sibling seems so much younger than his age. Explain to them that because he was deprived of many things in his past including attention, schooling or even love, he may not behave his age. Make sure other children don't make fun of an adopted child who has emotional, cognitive or social delays. When an adopted child is acting in a way that is surprising or even funny to them, make sure your other children simply ignore his antics or comments and walk away if the adopted child is doing or saying something that is upsetting them. This may be difficult advice for some children to follow, but enforce your instructions and praise them when they handle a situation well.

Caroline is the mother of nine children—three biological children and six children adopted at various ages (including older children over the age of four) from Eastern European orphanages. She describes the willingness of her biological children to help with the younger adopted children and how sometimes the adopted children are more willing to listen to their siblings than mom:

My nine-year-old biological daughter was the biggest help with my eleven-year-old adopted daughter who was brought home from Ukraine, raised in an orphanage her whole life (with no special needs). Things that would cause a "power struggle" between the eleven-year-old and myself (like trying to get her to shower, change clothes after three days, etc.) were accepted much better from her sister (who would be very blunt and say "you smell—the other kids at school won't sit by you"). My four-year-old biological daughter got mad at the adopted eleven-year-old for something yesterday and yelled at her. The eleven-year-old burst into tears and said "Family no love me." My biological children don't take anything a younger child says seriously but my eleven-year-old adopted daughter has no idea how to differentiate—if it comes from a four-year-old it is just as if it was coming from me or "the family." My fourteen-year-old biological daughter is very mature compared to my almost-twelve-year-old adopted child who looks up to the fourteen-year-old more like a parent than a peer. I was not expecting that level of separation [in maturity]. My nine-year-old biological daughter is more emotionally mature than my eleven-year-old adopted daughter as well. I truly see my eleven-year-old adopted daughter and four-year-old biological daughter as having the same "emotional IQ" due to my adopted eleven-year-old child's history.

BLENDING ADOPTED AND NON-ADOPTED CHILDREN

Younger children in the home may be more accepting of a new family member and may adapt more easily than older children; however, they may also demand more of their parents' attention or show signs of distress if their routines change or their needs are not consistently met as they have come to expect.

Children of different ages will have different concerns about how their adopted sibling will affect their lives. Young children may adapt more easily but have more difficulty sharing their toys, while teenage children may be more concerned about privacy and boundaries.

Your other children may not understand why their adopted brother or sister is crying so much, throwing tantrums, stealing, lying or being hyperactive. Do your best to explain to your child that her new sibling experienced some difficult things when he lived with his other family and needs help to heal. You might share reading material or videos with a teen to help him understand a specific condition his new sibling may have. Younger children may actually become fearful of their new sibling's behavior or actions. Explain to them in an age-appropriate manner that their new sibling is upset or angry about something that happened in the past but that he will get better with the love and support of his new family and doctors.

Bringing home an adopted child is difficult enough but when an adopted child is brought home to a family where there are already biological, foster or adopted children, extra care will need to be taken to help all the children adapt to each other and cope with any negative feelings (resentment, guilt, anger, sadness, etc.). If you've adopted a child who requires more time and attention, because of medical, behavioral, developmental or other reasons, even more preparation will be needed.

The following are some additional areas of concern to think about when considering adopting an older child if you already have a child or children at home:

- The adoptee will need time to adjust to his or her new family. Keep expectations realistic and reserve celebrating the adoption until the child has had a chance to adjust to his new family.

- It may take time for children to start referring to each other as brother or sister. Refrain from using labels and be careful not to force anyone to behave or think like siblings before they are ready. First comes the rapport and relationship, then the title of brother or sister.

- Introduce the adopted child's future siblings to her before she moves in. Perhaps your child can write the child you will be adopting a letter or draw her a picture before she comes home.

- To make the transition easier, establish family rules, rituals, patterns of interaction and roles. Be flexible while initiating routines of eating, interacting, self-care, etc.

- Adoptive parents should try to spend more time at home after bringing home their child to provide a stable presence for all. If possible, reduce outside influences while everyone adjusts. Ease the children into their new life slowly.

- Encourage children to be patient and to share feelings constructively. Praise positive efforts.

If your children are having a lot of difficulty adjusting to the changes older child adoption can bring or in navigating new sibling relationships, consider going to family counseling. Choose a therapist who has experience working with adoptive families. He or she should understand the dynamics of adoptive families and utilize the most effective evidence-based approaches. The therapist will work with family members to adjust to the changes the adoption has brought and how to prevent or manage conflicts.

SIBLINGS IN MULTIRACIAL AND MULTICULTURAL ADOPTIVE FAMILIES

Children adopted into families that are already multicultural or multiracial may not be used to diversity of that kind and may need help adjusting to and being proud of belonging to such a family. Biological children of the same race and culture as their parents should be prepared to have a sibling of a different race or culture. Adoptive parents can help with the transition by educating them through age-appropriate books, by looking at maps, attending cultural events, singing or playing songs from different cultures, eating foods from other regions or teaching them the language of their new sibling.

Once your family has officially become multiracial or multicultural, celebrate the cultural heritage of every child in the family as well as the fact that you all belong and you are now a multicultural family.

There are many factors that can negatively or positively affect how a biological child feels about having an adopted sibling from a different culture and being part of a multicultural family, including:

- Whether the adopted child was adopted domestically or internationally
- Travel experience
- Their family's existing attitudes toward people of different races and cultural backgrounds
- Their family's interests in foreign cultures
- Family education and preparedness
- Community acceptance of the adoptee's racial or cultural background
- Their mental health, behaviors, perspectives and coping skills
- Sensitivity toward differences in physical appearance
- Prejudices they have grown up with in their home or community

The more differences there are among family members, the greater the potential challenges. According to Harold Grotevant and Ruth McRoy, adoption status, shared or diverse heritages, special needs, ages, languages, siblings placed together versus singly and connections with biological families can factor in.[7] It will take time for your family to adjust to all of the changes and differences, which may seem significant at first, but in time your children will cease to view their new sibling as "my adopted brother [or sister];" rather, they will simply view him or her as "my brother [or sister]."

CHAPTER 10

Navigating Biological Family Relationships and Understanding Adoption

A difficult area for some adoptive families is their child's ongoing contact and relationships with previous foster and/or biological family members. One strength of many adoptive families is their capacity for flexibility and one way in which they are flexible is how they define family. For many adoptive families, including an *adoptive kinship network* is beneficial for the adopted child and the entire family. Adoptive kinship networks include extended family members of the adoptive family, former foster family members and biological family members. Adoptive families are typically quite adept at maintaining kinship networks that enhance the child's sense of well-being, connection and personal identity.

Adoptive families are not unique in being able to blend multiple family relationships into kinship networks that benefit all. How many people do you know who have adopted their spouse's biological child? Parents with children from previous marriages or unions also are adept at creating blended families that may include former spouses or partners and extended family members of the child's step-parents and biological parents. In the U.S., new family structures have emerged. Involving kinship networks in the raising of children is increasingly seen as important, even critical, in societies where both parents work and need as much help as possible to raise happy, healthy children. In some cultures, involving extended family and kin in the raising of children is a practice that has never faded. For example, in many tribal cultures, members of the "clan," which may include grandparents, aunts, uncles and members of the tribe, have important roles in the raising of children and are expected to step into the caregiving role if a parent is temporarily or permanently unable to care for their child.

POST-ADOPTION CONTACT WITH BIRTH FAMILY MEMBERS IN OLDER CHILD ADOPTION

Open adoption in infant adoption refers to the adoptive family having an open relationship with the child's biological parent(s). This relationship may involve regular meetings, phone calls, an exchange of gifts or photos or attendance by the birth parents at milestone events in the child's life such as graduation ceremonies. Semi-open adoption in infant adoption generally refers to agency-mediated contact. For example, meetings may take place at the agency or the agency mediates the exchange of letters, photos or gifts. A closed adoption is one in which there is no contact between biological and adoptive parents.

Contact with the birth family in older child adoption may also be described as open, semi-open or closed. Whereas it is likely that adoptive parents will formally meet the birth parents in private infant adoption, adoptive parents rarely meet formally with the biological parents when they adopt from foster care. With public adoption, the child has been removed from the biological parents' care due to neglect or abuse and parental rights have been terminated by the courts; therefore the birth parents play no role in selecting adoptive parents. Once rights are terminated, a public agency is legally responsible for the child until he or she is legally adopted and is responsible for finding an adoptive placement for the child.

Today, open or semi-open adoption is recommended in infant adoption. At one time, closed adoption was the only choice biological parents and adoptive parents had, but more recently adoption experts have realized that openness in adoption is healthier for the child, the biological parents and the adoptive parents. Openness can help adoptees learn about inherited medical conditions, strengthen their sense of identity and alleviate feelings of abandonment.

For biological parents, having ongoing contact with their child can provide peace of mind that their child is being brought up well. Openness may also benefit adoptive parents who will feel there are no secrets. Most adoptive parents want to answer their children's questions as forthrightly and completely as possible and, with greater openness, the children may even get answers directly from their biological parents.

In public domestic adoption, the fact that the biological parents' rights may have been terminated does not mean that they are legally prevented from seeing their child, although in some cases they could be. Likewise, the foster parents are not automatically legally prevented from seeing their former foster children in most cases (unless there was substantiated abuse).

Because older children adopted from the public system usually remember life with their biological families, the nature of ongoing contact is different from contact in infant adoption. Children adopted from foster care are likely to have been abused or neglected or lived in a family where neglect or abuse occurred; therefore, contact with biological family members must be carefully considered. With public adoption, adoptive parents will receive at least some information about the child's biological family and history, enabling them to make an informed decision about contact.

Openness in intercountry adoption often is not an option because the biological parents may be deceased, difficult to locate or, in some cases, unscrupulous practices have left them out of the process altogether. Some biological parents have not fully consented to the adoption (i.e. cases of child abduction or coercion to relinquish an infant). Children become lost to biological family once they are placed in an orphanage.

Contact with biological parents can be healing or harmful depending on each child's unique situation. In some cases, children may not harbor anger towards biological parents or feel unsafe with them, so having a continuous relationship with them may be healing. Older children may be more interested in maintaining contact with biological parents, just because they have a longer history with them than younger children do.

Contact with biological parents for children who were too young to clearly remember their time with them may help eliminate any fantasies they have about their biological family or their lives before adoption. Take cues from your child on contact with biological or foster family members. If your child seems anxious or depressed after a visit, perhaps contact is not in her best interests, at least for the time being. It may be difficult to figure out if post-visit behavior is about loss or fear. Seek the assistance of a counseling professional if necessary.

Adoptive parents usually have a lot of control and authority about the frequency of contact and type of relationship their child has with biological or former foster family members. Adoptive parents may decide that foster parents were a positive force in their child's early development and want to keep them involved in their child's life. Likewise, they may feel positively about their child's relationship with a biological grandparent, sibling, aunt or uncle and want to maintain that relationship.

In their analysis of data from the US National Survey of Adoptive Parents, Monica Faulkner and Elissa E. Madden found that children adopted from foster care had less contact with biological parents and other biological family members than those adopted privately as infants.[1] Children adopted from foster care were more likely to have contact with biological family members, including siblings, if they had lived with their biological family prior to being adopted. The authors also found a lower incidence of written post-adoption contact agreements in foster care adoption. Finally, they reported that children who experienced abuse prior to being adopted were less likely to have contact with biological family members.[2]

Adoption agencies can assist in the development of post-adoption contact agreements and help mediate contact. In domestic older child adoption, post-adoption contact can be negotiated and placed in writing. A court may mandate a pre-finalization contract regarding contact between biological and adoptive family members. In some jurisdictions contact agreements are legally enforceable but when they are not, adoptive parents have the final authority about those people with whom their children have contact.

Even when contact agreements are not legally enforceable, it is important for adoptive parents to make an agreement in good faith and carry out the terms to the best of their abilities. Breaking an informal contact agreement can create unnecessary friction between people who truly care about a child. However, there are some situations in which an informal contact agreement should be broken, because it is not serving the child well.

A mother of four siblings adopted from the American foster care system described the nature of her children's contact with their birth mother:

Our children do not have any relationship with birth family members on a personal level. We have photos of the birth family (parents, other half-siblings, grandparents, aunts, etc.) and we permit gifts from their birth mom on birthdays and Christmas. We talk about their birth family openly and honestly in an age-appropriate fashion. Feelings change over time. Sometimes they are angry and sometimes they miss their birth mom. Contact is through the foster mom of our youngest. They are still in contact and as long as birth mom remains sober and appropriate we will continue to permit this contact. I am comfortable with the arrangement. We live in close proximity and the children are at times nervous that we may see her in public without warning, but we continue to talk about what that would mean and how we can all be emotionally safe in that case. It is my belief that the birth mother is currently concerned with the well-being of her children and understands that if she entered their lives without permission it would jeopardize any future contact or relationship she may have with them.

Here are some ideas for how your child can maintain healthy contact with his or her biological or former foster family members (some ideas are more appropriate for open contact):

- Chat online.
- Make video calls.

- Share photos electronically via a private photo-sharing page.
- Write letters.
- Exchange gifts, artwork or photos.
- Share videos of events.

WHEN CONTACT IS HARMFUL

While extended family and friends generally enhance a child's sense of security and stability, there are some instances when contact with specific members of the kinship network is not healthy for or in the best interests of the child. Adoptive parents should be cognizant of their child's emotions regarding contact and look for cues that the relationship is helpful or harmful. It might be helpful to establish rules for contact if biological family members are acting inappropriately.

In some cases an ongoing relationship with a family member may be clearly harmful to the child, such as when a family member abused the child or did nothing to stop the abuse. In the case of a child who was abused, contact may lead to a worsening of trauma symptoms or mental health conditions such as anxiety or depression and should be carefully considered. Sometimes the court will recommend whether post-adoption contact with specific biological family members is healthy for the child. If you believe contact with a family member is harmful, ask your attorney to petition the court to prohibit such contact. If your child is being harassed or stalked, obtain a restraining order from the court.

TALKING TO YOUR CHILD ABOUT ADOPTION
AND HER BIOLOGICAL FAMILY

Your child will understand the meaning of adoption more concretely as she matures. Children younger than five may simply understand adoption as meaning they did not come out of their mommy's "belly." Your child may need your help in learning how to answer her friends' or others' questions about her past and her adoption. It is important that you talk to young children about adoption in a way that is developmentally appropriate.

Expect children who were very young when they were removed from their parents' home to ask you for details about their time in foster care, their adoption, their past and their biological family. Children adopted at a younger age may not retain memories of their time with their biological family but will express curiosity as they mature. Children may ask difficult questions about why they were removed from their biological family. As their parent, you must try to provide an explanation that is age appropriate, empathetic to problems that biological family members may have had and that does not vilify them (as much as you may resent specific family members for the harm they have done to your child).

When they are older, children adopted internationally may want to search for biological family members. There are individuals and organizations that can aid the search but make sure they are professional and ethical.

Also speak honestly about adoption and the differences between adoptive and non-adoptive families. Some children will be more curious about adoption, their past and their biological family than others. One adoptive mom we spoke to said it best: "I know hundreds of adopted kids and adults—your personality and disposition [have a lot to do with how you process adoption]. Some crave knowing all the info they can, some don't care at all, and they were raised by the same parents in the same house. Everyone thinks differently."

"Last Mom" blogs about raising a daughter adopted from foster care at age nine. "Princess," as she refers to her in the blog, experienced multiple foster placements and a psychiatric hospitalization prior to being adopted. Princess suffers from the effects of early trauma and struggles some days to function normally. In one post, "Last Mom" described a difficult conversation she had with her daughter about her birth father:

> Sometimes the questions come when you least expect them—like explaining child abuse at breakfast.
>
> "Momma, why did my biological father keep us for so long if he hit us?"
>
> I'm always torn with these questions—half grateful that she feels comfortable asking me and half devastated that she has them to ask.

Her first mother walked away when she was eighteen months old. Her little brother was four months old. Her four older sisters were all under seven. This mother of six was only twenty-one when the last baby was born. She got pregnant at thirteen and was fourteen when she became a mother. The children's father was thirty when he began a relationship with a twelve-and-a-half-year-old child.

The father tried to care for all six babies on his own for a while. They were severely neglected. Princess's foster care file describes the home as filthy, the children dirty and infested with lice and no food in the kitchen—or even running water. There were also reports of abuse. There were notes of the father having alcohol issues. Then there was no home at all. They lived in a van.

He tried to work the plan [that the Department of Children and Families] set for him for a while. He went to some parenting classes. And then he threw in the towel when Princess was four. He dropped the six kids off at a children's shelter and never returned.

Princess knows her story. I've told it to her in bits and pieces over the years. It's hers to know. She's trying to reconcile how her father could hit them if he loved them enough to try to keep them on his own for over two years. In her mind, hitting children is the opposite of love.

So I acknowledged how messed up and confusing it is.

"Well, Sweet Pea, I think he did love you. How could he not? You're awesome. But I think he had problems that had nothing to do with you. We know he drank a lot and he might have had other mental health things going on with his brain. He wasn't able to be the father you needed and deserved. He couldn't keep you safe—even from himself—and I think he wanted to give you a chance to have a different life. I'm so sorry all of that happened to you. I wish it didn't."

And ya know what my sweet girl said? "It's okay, Momma. It brought me to you and for that I'm glad." Heart melted. Again.

The manner in which "Last Mom" answered her daughter's question is exemplary in its empathetic tone toward the birth father and how she assures her daughter that her birth dad's problems were not her fault. "Last Mom" also is effective in providing an age-appropriate response that doesn't overcomplicate the story. If you are unsure how to talk to your child about his family history or biological family ask other adoptive parents and/or mental health professionals for advice. Especially when there's a history of abuse, you must be careful how you talk to your child about his past, as these discussions can trigger a traumatic response.

Older children usually remember being removed from their biological family and being adopted into a new family. They can explain that they are adopted to friends and others who may ask and understand what that means. Teens remember fully and have the most sophisticated understanding of their past, including why they were removed from their biological family, what foster care was like and what it means to be adopted into a permanent family.

Some adoptive parents fear their child will never love them as much as their biological parents and it is true that for some children, especially those who were removed at a later age, their primary loyalties will remain with the biological parents. The majority of adopted children, however, know that their adopted family has given them the sense of belonging and normalcy they need, according to Michele Hanna et al.[3] It is important that adoptive parents validate the grief and loss that adopted children feel for their biological families. Jessica Nonnemacher, a therapist who specializes in child attachment and an adoptive and foster mom herself, told us:

> *Most adopted children, at some point, wish that things were different and they could be with their family of origin...Many seem to forget the negative things that brought them into care, and instead idealize their bio families. I usually just try to affirm their feelings...that it's okay to love both families and to want to be with both. I have found that it's usually harder to convince the adoptive parents of this (that their child will always love/miss their family of origin) and that it's okay, but once parents are understanding of this the child is able to reconcile it too.*

CONNECTING WITH AND UNDERSTANDING THE PAST: LIFE BOOKS, MEMORY BOXES AND TIMELINES

There are several useful tools for helping your child learn about and stay connected with his personal and family history. These tools may also help your child process loss and grief. Life books provide a medium for your adopted child to:

- Record memories
- Celebrate milestone events
- Enter information about biological family members
- Explore the child's talents and interests
- Process difficult memories and feelings

You may order a life book or create your own using a photobook service or scrapbooking materials. There are many resources online for parents interested in creating a life book with their child (see the appendix). Contents of a life book could include:

- Documents related to your child's birth, foster placement or adoption
- Medical information
- Photos of biological family members and the adoptive family
- Scrapbook materials including fun cutouts and stickers
- Your child's artwork
- Cards and letters from biological family members
- Report cards and other items from school
- Souvenirs from school trips and vacations
- Invitations and other items from birthday parties with friends
- Poetry and creative writing
- Items related to your child's birth culture such as artwork, songs, poems or recipes
- Awards and certificates
- First day of school photos

In addition to creating a life book to help your adopted child understand his history, the entire family might create a family life book together. This book can celebrate your time as a family after the adoption of one or more children. Each family member might contribute to the book in his or her own unique way. Dad might share ticket stubs from the first sporting event he attended with his kids, while mom might share a favorite family recipe. Biological children might include written memories about when their sibling was first adopted while adopted children might share their favorite family photos. Additional items for your adoptive family life book might include:

- A family tree that includes birth and adoptive relatives
- Adoption day photos
- Memorabilia from events and trips
- Copies of the family's favorite recipes
- Family photo holiday cards
- Items related to each family member's cultural heritage
- Photos and information about extended adoptive family members
- Items related to family holiday traditions
- Handprint collages
- Children's artwork that depicts the entire family
- Collages made from magazine cutouts that depicts family members' interests and/or the types of things the family enjoys doing together

Other ideas for celebrating your child's history and preserving memories include creating a memory box filled with some of the items listed above as well as larger souvenirs and memorabilia that do not fit into a book. One adoptive parent recommends that adoptive parents, especially those who have children struggling with behavioral problems, create a timeline for their child. The timeline, which can be taped to a wall or table, can be used to record information about the child's time with his biological and adoptive family, note significant milestone events or measure progress with behavioral or health issues. Use stars to represent your child's improvement at school or with negative behavior, or use before and after photos that show improvements in a health condition that required corrective surgery or therapy. These visual representations can instill in your child pride and confidence that he or she can overcome any challenges that life may present.

PART III

understanding your child

CHAPTER 11

The Traumatized Child

Understanding the impact traumatic events have on the lives of children is a field that has grown tremendously over the past thirty years. Very little was known about the impact of traumatic stress on children's development, psychological well-being, cognition and physical health. Today there is a growing group of child trauma clinicians and researchers who are making it their life's work to understand and treat psychological trauma in children.

According to the National Child Traumatic Stress Network (NCTSN), a psychological trauma "occurs when a child experiences an intense event that threatens or causes harm to his or her emotional and physical well-being."[1] It is important to distinguish a potentially traumatizing event from its impacts. A potentially traumatizing event will not cause traumatic stress in every person.

TRAUMATIC EXPERIENCES

According to William W. Harris et al, most children who come into the foster system have experienced one or more traumatic events such as:

- Sudden bodily injury
- Abuse

- Neglect
- Parental substance abuse
- Witnessing household or community violence
- Experiencing man-made or natural disasters
- The sudden death of a primary caregiver
- Witnessing the violent or sudden death of a parent[2]

Children adopted from other countries may also have experienced some of these events in addition to spending time in an institution or orphanage. Simply growing up in an orphanage is traumatizing for many children.

Just because a child has experienced what most would consider a traumatic event does not mean that he is traumatized or, as clinicians might say, is suffering from traumatic stress. It's important to first be aware of various traumatic events that may have occurred in your pre-adoptive or adopted child's life before you can begin to assess how these events may be affecting him psychologically, cognitively or socially.

CHILD ABUSE AND NEGLECT

Child maltreatment is another term for parental neglect or abuse. According to the child maltreatment report released by the National Institute of Justice there were 686,000 substantiated (proven) cases of child maltreatment in the United States in 2012 and there may have been many more incidents that went unreported. In four-fifths of the cases, one or both parents were the perpetrators. Laws regarding what constitutes child maltreatment vary across states/provinces and countries.[3]

Parental neglect is the leading form of child maltreatment in the United States. Due to drug or alcohol abuse or mental health problems, neglectful parents or caregivers are unable to responsibly care for their children. A neglected child may not have adequate food, furniture or hygiene. Parents may allow excessive truancy from school, provide inadequate supervision, place the child in dangerous situations, allow the child to be supervised by another child or someone else who is incapable of caring for the child or may fail to stop acts of abuse by another adult or child. A neglectful parent may also fail to secure needed medical or psychological help for a child.

In the United States in 2012, substantiated cases of physical abuse were about equal to the substantiated number of cases of sexual and psychological abuse combined. According to the National Child Traumatic Stress Network: "Legal definitions vary from state to state, but, broadly, child physical abuse is any physical act by a caregiver that results in a child being hurt or injured."[4] Adopted children may suffer from a history of physical abuse at the hands of a parent, other caregiver or sibling. Physical abuse can leave both physical and psychological scars, can damage a child's cognitive, physical or social development or even kill the child.

It is estimated that, in the United States, one in four girls and one in six boys will experience some form of sexual abuse before adulthood. Parents will be the perpetrators in many cases of childhood sexual abuse. Child sexual abuse is forcible or coercive sexual touching or intercourse with a child under the age of eighteen by an adult over the age of eighteen. Child sexual abuse also includes exploitation of a child such as being sold into prostitution, allowed by a parent or other caregiver to be used sexually in exchange for money or drugs or for child pornography. Children can also be sexually abused by an older child or peer. Sexual abuse harms children physically and emotionally and may impede normal social, emotional and cognitive development.

Psychological or emotional abuse may be perpetrated by a parent, a sibling or other relatives. According to the American Humane Association, the emotional abuse of a child includes acts of ignoring, rejecting, isolating, exploiting, corrupting, verbally assaulting or terrorizing a child.[5] Psychological abuse can be just as harmful as other types of abuse in terms of the long-term damage it can cause to a child's social, emotional and cognitive development and sense of self-worth.

In some cases of child removal due to parental neglect or abuse, families can be rehabilitated and children can be returned to their parents, guardians or caregivers. Parents or other caregivers must follow a case plan developed by the court to correct behavior that has led to a child being removed from the home. About 50 percent of children removed from parents or guardians and placed in foster care in the United States are eventually reunited with their parents, according to AFCARS.[6] In cases of abuse or neglect where children are deemed to be in immediate danger of being severely harmed or even dying due to parental abuse or neglect, the child will not return to the home and parental rights will be terminated by the court.

MALTREATMENT IN THE UNITED STATES IN 2012

In 2012, 1,640 US children died as a result of parental abuse or neglect. According to the data, victims of abuse were more likely to be exposed to domestic violence and to have a caregiver who abused drugs or alcohol. Furthermore, very young children were more likely to be maltreated than older children. For example, infants less than one year of age experienced twice the rate of maltreatment compared to five-year-olds.

Child maltreatment is a global problem. According to the World Health Organization (WHO), "international studies reveal that approximately 20 percent of women and 5 to 10 percent of men report being sexually abused as children, while 23 percent of people report being physically abused as children."[7] It is difficult to track psychological abuse and neglect in countries with less developed child welfare systems but the problem is most likely widespread around the globe. Culturally sanctioned child abuse such as child selling, child trafficking, female genital mutilation and child marriage still takes place in some societies.

The WHO estimates that, globally, 34,000 children under the age of fifteen die from abuse each year. WHO reports, "This number underestimates the true extent of the problem, as a significant proportion of deaths due to child maltreatment are incorrectly attributed to drowning, falls, burns and other causes."[8] The number of infant girls killed by their parents in patriarchal societies around the world is unknown as well.

An adoptive mother described the parental abuse and neglect her son experienced prior to being placed in her home as a foster child at the age of nine:

He had been physically and sexually abused by his older brothers. His older brothers had beaten him to force him to sexually abuse his younger sisters. He had witnessed his [biological] dad beating his [biological] mom on multiple occasions. [Child Protective Services] was actively involved in his life since before he was born. There were multiple reports of the kids coming to school with suspicious bruises and multiple times the police were called because the kids were left home alone for hours on end. He spent most of his time wandering around the city with his older brothers—ten and thirteen-year-old boys left in charge of their four-year-old brother. They taught him all of the worst habits you can think of, roaming an inner city unsupervised. He remembers watching them set a kitten on fire and stealing from the library. In school he missed more days than he attended of both kindergarten and first grade.

TRAUMATIC BEREAVEMENT

Traumatic bereavement occurs when a child is overwhelmed by the death of a parent or other family member. The child may be traumatized by the death but by also the manner in which the person dies. For example, some children who end up in foster care have witnessed a domestic homicide. They might also have witnessed or heard about a parent or other family member being killed violently. Children of war may witness multiple violent deaths but when it's the death of a loved one the trauma can be severe. According to the National Child Traumatic Stress Network traumatic bereavement is characterized by "a combination of trauma and grief symptoms so severe that any thoughts or reminders—even happy ones—about the person who died can lead to frightening thoughts, images and/or memories of how the person died."[9]

NATURAL OR MANMADE DISASTERS

Millions of children throughout the world have experienced multiple traumas due to war, including the loss of family members, having to flee their homes and countries, having to live in squalid refugee camps or being injured themselves by bullets, bombs or machetes. Some of these children will end up in orphanages and some will be adopted. If you adopt from a country that has or recently had civil conflict, try to find out what violence your child has experienced or witnessed.

Prospective adoptive parents also should research the adoption policies and practices of the nation from which they are interested in adopting a child. Some children placed for adoption have living parents and family members. Parents who are victims of war or poverty may be coerced or forced to give up or sell their children to adoption officials. You don't want to have to learn from your child that a caregiver is somewhere out there looking for her or missing her. Do your research and make sure the agencies and countries you are dealing with are Hague accredited and have sound adoption policies and practices. Great trauma is inflicted on a child who is trafficked and then adopted into a foreign country.

Children may also end up in orphanages when there has been a natural disaster in their community and there is no one left to care for them. These children may have experienced multiple traumas including losing their home, having to stay in a relief camp, becoming separated from family members, being injured and witnessing suffering and chaos. UNICEF has issued a very strong policy statement about these situations. In essence, the only children who should be adopted after a natural disaster are those already in the adoption process.[10] If you are adopting a child from a region that has experienced an extreme natural disaster, learn all you can about what happened to him or her from the foreign adoption agency.

WITNESSING HOUSEHOLD OR COMMUNITY VIOLENCE

Family violence is a common occurrence in families where there is drug or alcohol abuse. Although your child may not have been physically or sexually abused, his siblings or a parent may have been. Try to find out if your child witnessed the physical, sexual or psychological abuse of another family member. Witnessing the abuse of a family member can be just as traumatic as experiencing abuse for a child. He may feel helpless to stop the abuse or feel in some way responsible for it. A child may even experience guilt for having felt relieved that the perpetrator chose a sibling to abuse instead of him.

Many children witness violence in their communities as well. Try to learn more about the community where your child lived with his biological or foster family. Was there a lot of crime, problems with gangs or drug dealing? Did your child witness someone on the street or in school being shot, stabbed or assaulted? Your child needs space and time to process witnessing or experiencing violence in the community or at school, as well as at home.

OBTAINING INFORMATION ABOUT YOUR CHILD'S TRAUMA HISTORY

Do your best to find out about potentially traumatizing events your adopted child has experienced. During the pre-adoptive phase, ask your adoption caseworker for all the information she has about prior abuse or other traumas the child may have suffered. Ask your caseworker if your child witnessed domestic violence, lewd activity or adults abusing drugs or alcohol. If the child was neglected, find out what type of supervision he was lacking and any dangerous situations he experienced as a result of parental neglect. Ask the caseworker and former foster parents how the child has responded to traumatic events and if he has received treatment. You may not always get the best information about your child's trauma history, but find out as much as you can.

Also be aware that the caseworker or former foster parent may not know about these experiences. Children, once they are safe, will divulge information never recorded in their case files.

For intercountry adoption it is even more complicated. The records are often poor overall. Added to this problem are different views of what constitutes abuse and neglect across cultures. Finally, many low-resource countries are sensitive to how the world views them and their child welfare systems. They are less likely to report information that would make them look bad.

SYMPTOMS OF TRAUMATIC STRESS IN CHILDREN AND TEENS

According to the National Child Traumatic Stress Network, child traumatic stress occurs "when children and adolescents are exposed to traumatic events or situations that overwhelm their ability to cope."[11] Traumatic stress in children may result in chronic disturbances to cognitive, social and emotional functioning, report Alicia F. Lieberman and Kathleen Knorr.[12] A child who has survived multiple traumatic events is said to have a complex trauma history.

Research on the brains of children who have experienced early trauma illustrates that a child's brain literally changes after she experiences a traumatic event. It can become rewired for hypervigilance and anger;

parts of the brain responsible for empathy may be compromised. Hormones released as a result of chronic stress may also cause damage to parts of the brain responsible for social or emotional functioning.

However, there is not always a cause-and-effect relationship between such events and mental health problems. It may be that the child would have developed or had the potential to develop these disorders and the traumatic event simply triggered their manifestation. According to Lieberman and Knorr, these behavioral symptoms may indicate traumatic stress in children:

- Moodiness
- Heightened anger or aggression
- Frustration
- Inability to cope with stress or minor challenges
- Intense fear
- Uncontrollable crying
- Temper tantrums
- Sleep problems
- Reenactment of the traumatic event through play
- Avoidance of people, places and things that remind the child of the traumatic event
- Hyperarousal and hypervigilance
- Regression (i.e. Acting like a baby, toileting problems)
- Clinginess and separation anxiety
- Inability to follow rules
- Defiance
- Lying
- Controlling behavior
- Sexual acting out[13]

Additionally, children who have experienced natural disasters may ask a lot of questions about storms, be easily startled by weather events and ask how strong the house in which you live with them is, if it can float away, be blown away, etc.

The daughter of "Last Mom," who experienced abuse and neglect prior to being adopted, suffers from severe traumatic stress. "Last Mom" blogs about her daughter's day-to-day struggles with stress, mental health issues, grief and loss. She writes: "Our poor little girl. The information in her file is only what the case worker knew. She is holding all the trauma of her day-to-day life for her first nine years deep inside her. I wish I could just vacuum it all up for her."

Teenagers who have experienced traumatic stress may demonstrate the same behavioral symptoms listed earlier, but in accordance with their developmental age. For teens, reenactment behaviors will be more extreme and destructive. Teens who have been victims of sexual abuse may become sexually promiscuous or abusers themselves. Some teens may take unnecessary risks that could harm themselves or others or turn to drugs or alcohol to dampen their pain. Others will become aloof, avoid social activities and/or miss school or work. Teens who have been traumatized may also demonstrate a lack of moral judgment and/or refuse to take responsibility for their actions.

Children and teens might also develop these mental health disorders as a result of traumatic stress:

- Depression
- Anxiety
- Obsessive-compulsive disorder (OCD)
- Oppositional defiance disorder (ODD)
- Post-traumatic stress disorder (PTSD)
- Reactive attachment disorder (RAD)
- Borderline personality disorder (BPD)
- Eating disorders

Traumatic stress may also lead to cognitive problems such as an inability to focus and learn, impaired thinking and learning disabilities in children and teens. Physical injuries to the brain as a result of abuse may cause or contribute to cognitive problems in some children. Traumatized children and teens may also develop physical issues such as weight loss, rashes, stunted growth, obesity, loss of bladder control and sleep disorders. Finally, children and teenagers may develop the following social and relational problems after experiencing a traumatic event:

- Difficulty attaching to caregivers and other family members
- Difficulty with peer and family relationships
- Lack of respect for authority figures such as teachers, coaches or work supervisors

Each child's developmental age, temperament, family support, community support and trauma history will contribute to his or her unique trauma response. While one child may be completely incapacitated by a traumatic event, another may be more resilient and come through the event without major problems. Family functioning is an important factor in a child's ability to cope with traumatic events.[14] Traumatized children whose parents are highly functional, loving, supportive and have the economic means to get their child help will do better than children who live with parents coping with their own traumatic stress and other problems.

LONG-TERM EFFECTS OF TRAUMATIC STRESS

Adopted children and teens who have suffered past abuse and other traumas can improve significantly with the right treatment and therapeutic parenting techniques. (See chapter 18 for suggestions.) Children and teens who do not receive proper treatment for traumatic stress will continue to suffer from serious symptoms and disruption in their day-to-day functioning and will struggle with these problems into adulthood.

Robert Anda reports that early trauma can have long-term effects on neurobiological systems that control "emotional regulation, somatic signal processing (body sensations), substance abuse, sexuality, memory, arousal, and aggression."[15] It is important that children and teens who suffer from traumatic stress receive treatment as early as possible, because as they mature into adulthood it may be more difficult to correct resulting cognitive, emotional and behavioral problems, according to psychiatrist Julian D. Ford.[16]

A landmark study, the Adverse Childhood Experiences Study (ACES), examined the long-term consequences for adults of childhood trauma and adverse experiences including abuse and/or neglect, witnessing family violence, growing up with substance abusing, severely mentally ill and/or criminally involved parents and even experiencing the divorce or separation of parents.[17] The study found that early adverse experiences increase the likelihood an adult will:

- Experience problems in their relationships with peers and family members
- Become re-victimized through partner or spousal abuse
- Abuse drugs or alcohol and develop related diseases
- Smoke and develop related diseases
- Suffer from depression and attempt suicide
- Become obese[18]

Sadly, adult survivors of childhood abuse also may die at a younger-than-average age due to health problems and/or high-risk behaviors.

GETTING PROFESSIONAL HELP FOR YOUR TRAUMATIZED CHILD

Traumatized children may need several different types of professional intervention. A child may need medical intervention to address physical illnesses brought on by traumatic stress or to treat physical injuries due to abuse. The child may need psychological services including individual and/or family counseling or psychiatric attention if medication is needed. He might also need residential behavioral treatment, psychiatric treatment, occupational therapy or educational services.

Getting your traumatized child the appropriate mental health services is critical to his recovery. Many children with traumatic stress are misdiagnosed or go undiagnosed for many years, even into adulthood. William W. Harris, Alicia F. Lieberman and Steven Marans report that there are dire consequences for many children when not correctly diagnosed with traumatic stress and related mental health disorders:

The majority of severely and chronically traumatized children and youth are not found in mental health clinics but in the child protective, law enforcement, substance abuse treatment, and criminal justice systems, where the root of their problems in exposure to violence and abuse is typically not identified or addressed. Before reaching these systems, traumatized children are often identified and/or mislabeled as "behavior and discipline problems" in childcare and school settings, where their maltreatment is also routinely unrecognized.[19]

Adoptive parents who are educated about trauma can save the life of a child who has been in one of these situations, whose symptoms are misunderstood or undiagnosed and/or has not received the right help. Adoptive parents of traumatized children should learn all they can about child trauma. They may begin the learning process by visiting the website of the NCTSN or by searching for child trauma information on the Internet. Trauma-informed parents are more effective in getting their traumatized child the professional help he or she needs.

Here are some tips from the NCTSN on finding a qualified, trauma-informed therapist for your child:

- Ask a pediatrician, family physician, school counselor or clergy member for a referral to a professional with expertise in traumatic stress.

- Talk to close family members and friends for their recommendations, especially if their child or adolescent had a good experience with psychotherapy.

- Contact a community hospital, medical society, psychological association or the division of child and adolescent psychiatry, or the department of psychology in any medical school or university.

- Contact agencies in the community that specialize in trauma and/or victimization. These might include sexual assault or rape programs, victims' advocacy agencies, the local crime victims' compensation program, the children's advocacy center or local domestic violence programs.

- Contact local community mental health centers, mental health associations and support groups.[20]

EVIDENCE-BASED TRAUMA TREATMENTS (EBTT) FOR TRAUMATIZED CHILDREN AND TEENS

Quality psychological services for traumatized childen can significantly improve a traumatized child's quality of life, cognitive functioning, relationships with parents and other family members, mental health and physical health. Thankfully, today there is an entire discipline of research and practice dedicated to helping children and teens who have experienced psychological trauma.

Psychological trauma treatment approaches have become more effective over the past decade. A number of evidence-based trauma treatment (EBTT) approaches have now been studied, evaluated and demonstrated to be effective. Most EBTTs involve the parent or caregiver in therapy, consider the child's developmental stage and employ the use of a trauma narrative to help the child process what has happened.[21]

When choosing a therapist for your child, ask the person what type of treatment approach he or she uses. Therapies not devised specifically for traumatized children could end up doing more harm than good for a traumatized child.

Other types of therapy that may help your traumatized child include play, music and art therapy.

It is important to take cultural factors into consideration when you are seeking professional help for your adopted child. Children adopted from foreign cultures may not respond well to certain types of therapy.

If you are unhappy with a provider, do your own research to find a trauma-informed therapist who is experienced working with traumatized children and adopted children in particular. If you feel your child needs to be assessed by a mental health professional prior to finalization of the adoption, don't hesitate to ask your agency for a referral to a trauma-informed therapist.

In some locales, rural areas in particular, it may be difficult to get help for your child. You may have to rely on Internet-sourced medicine to be in contact with qualified providers.

THERAPEUTIC PARENTING

Traumatized children need safety, support, love and understanding to heal. The home and family can be a healing, therapeutic environment for the traumatized child. Parents can help their traumatized child simply with the way they parent. Parents adopting and raising children who have experienced trauma need to adjust their expectations, because their traumatized child will not behave, respond or relate like the typically-developing child. These parents need a different set of strategies.

Arleta James, an attachment expert, explained that removing toys or other possessions from a traumatized child most likely will have no effect on behavior. She explained that the traumatized child has experienced so much deprivation in his life that having a possession taken away is like—so what—for the child.[22] James notes that time-outs and grounding most likely will not be effective either. Isolating a child through time-outs or groundings, she explains, may actually come as a relief to a child who already experiences difficulty with family relationships. Allowing the child to spend more time alone may be just what he wants. Finally, James and others recommend that parents do not spank or use other physical punishment on children who have suffered past abuse. Physical punishment could trigger a trauma response or make them afraid of you. They may also try to provoke such punishment because they believe they deserve it.

James and Brenda McCreight recommend greater emphasis on rewards than punishment when seeking to modify a traumatized child's behavior. James urges parents to correct a traumatized child's behavior in a way that teaches cause and effect, repercussions for mistreating others, taking responsibility for one's actions and moral thinking.[23] Remember that your traumatized child's cognitive and social development may have been seriously compromised, so you may need to think about how you taught your typically-developing child these concepts when he was younger. Although he may have developed moral thinking around the age of seven or eight, your traumatized child may still be grappling to understand the effects of his actions on others at the age of fifteen or sixteen.

Here are some additional parenting tips for parents raising adopted children who have been abused, neglected or have experienced other traumatic events:

- Reassure the child that she is safe in your home. Emphasize your commitment to the child, express empathy for all she's been through and communicate that you understand that some of her difficult behaviors are related to past trauma.

- Explain in the most basic way what kind of touch, including hugs, kisses on the cheek, snuggling or hair brushing, is used in the family to express affection.[24]

- Describe how each family member has a right to his or her own personal space and privacy, as recommended by therapist and international speaker Brenda McCreight.[25] Discuss the rules regarding entering siblings' rooms, borrowing toys and other possessions, closing bathroom and bedroom doors and other physical boundary issues between family members.

- Give a child who has experienced past sexual abuse his own room if necessary.[26] Until you know the existence or extent of any sexualized or sexual acting out behavior your child may exhibit as a result of past abuse, protect other children (especially younger) in the home from this behavior.

- Explain family routines to help the child understand how the family functions as a unit. Create personal routines for the child that help her feel in control of her life and so that she knows what to expect on a daily basis. Examples of family routines that may be helpful to explain or establish include family meetings, take-out night, movie night, Saturday chores, Sunday worship or bowling night. Establishing personal routines for the child might include scheduling study/homework hours after school, TV or computer time, outdoor activity time, time for athletics or music lessons and a regular bedtime. You might also allow a set schedule for when your child can spend time with friends. To establish the right kind of routines for your traumatized child, take into consideration developmental and chronological age, temperament, sense of responsibility, interests, behavior, etc.

- Monitor internet use. Traumatized children may have boundary issues related to dealing with strangers, making "friends," sharing personal or intimate information, sharing photos, etc. These boundary issues can spell disaster online where there is an abundance of adult predators, bullies and other unsavory characters eager to exploit vulnerable children and teens.

- Allow your child to discuss past trauma when he feels comfortable doing so. For the younger child, you might explore traumatic events and feelings through play. For the older child or teen you may do so while playing sports, reading a book or watching a movie that triggers a memory or emotion or while putting together a life book or memory box.

- Explain that the place where he is now living is relatively safe to the child who has experienced war, terrorism or community violence and, although bad things can happen anywhere, it is very unlikely to happen in his neighborhood. However, don't be unrealistic if you live in a neighborhood that does experience significant crime or violence, but do teach your child coping skills. You may need assistance from a trained professional to learn how to help your child cope with the realities of life in a community where crime and violence are unfortunately the norm.

Parents may need the assistance of a skilled therapist, other parents of traumatized children or teachers to develop an approach to parenting their traumatized child that takes into account her unique strengths, weaknesses, history, mental health problems and cognitive and social functioning. It is no small task for parents to discard much of what they thought were sound parenting techniques for a whole new set of approaches, but it can be done. They must do this to ensure their child has a chance to heal and perhaps even move forward in an area where they thought their child was doomed to failure forever.

RESILIENCE AND POST-TRAUMATIC GROWTH IN TRAUMATIZED CHILDREN AND TEENS

Some victims of trauma, whether children or adults, are more resilient than others. Each individual's unique temperament, personality, mental and physical health, social support, spiritual beliefs and past experiences contribute to different reactions to traumatic events. There is evidence that girls and young women are more resilient in the wake of traumatic events, perhaps because of their sometimes greater ability than boys to seek comfort in friends and seek out other relationships that are healing. Children who are more resilient regarding traumatic, stressful events in their lives may experience fewer social, emotional and physical effects.

Some individuals, whether they are children or adults, also experience what is known in psychological literature as "post-traumatic growth."[27] This is a phenomenon wherein people who undergo extremely stressful or traumatic life experiences grow emotionally and spiritually in the wake of the event. These individuals may become more empathetic toward others suffering similar or even different types of traumatic experiences. Individuals experiencing post-traumatic growth may become more spiritual and seek out greater meaning in their lives. They may question whether their current vocations or interests provide them optimal opportunities to serve others. If not, they become activists, counselors, social workers, teachers or nurses.

Although it may seem difficult to believe that children could experience post-traumatic growth, some studies have shown this is possible. Older adolescents and young adults can also experience post-traumatic growth. Young people who have experienced trauma or great stress may become more resilient in the face of other life stressors. The attitude is, "I've survived the worst so nothing else can defeat me." Resilience in young people should not be mistaken for taking dangerous risks or living in an excessively carefree manner, free of goals or positive relationships. Rather, for young people, resilience is an ability to accept what they cannot change, get the help they need and be able to move on with their lives with hope.

Young people who have experienced past trauma may find themselves drawn toward service to others, helping other children or teens with their struggles or toward studying for a career in one of the above-mentioned fields. They might also start seeking answers in religion or spirituality. They may begin asking why such terrible things happen to some people.

Young people's ability to be resilient or even grow from their experiences should be praised by the adults in their lives, including therapists. Simply surviving a traumatic event should be praised. Tell your child that he is still standing and that's an incredible thing. In praising the resilient child, don't take anything away from people who need a lot more help than your child to heal from such an event. Explain to your child that everyone is different and some people need more assistance to recover from a bad experience, but you are so proud that she has found a way to heal.

For the child or teen who is not healing quickly and does need a lot of assistance, point out and discuss all the areas of her life where she is functioning. Tell her that her ability to function is a testament to her own strength, determination and resilience. Let your adopted older children know that they have overcome tremendous hardships and should feel proud and empowered by their ability to move forward in even the smallest ways.

CHAPTER 12

Grief and Loss in Adopted Children

For older adopted children, feelings of loss and grief may stem from temporary or permanent separation from their biological parents. It may be difficult to understand why a child would mourn the loss of an abusive or neglectful parent, but grief associated with any caregiver is rooted in our biology and emotions. Abusive or not, the parent-child relationship is a primal bond. A deep fear of losing or being separated from a parent is etched into the psyche of every child. Primal attachment to a caregiver is rooted in the survival instinct. The relationship with the caregiver does not have to function well for this attachment to occur. In fact, unhealthy co-dependency created by emotionally unbalanced parents (in cases where parents lean on their child for emotional support) may only deepen the child's attachment and increase the fear of loss.

The sibling bond is primal as well. Removal from the only parents and family he has ever known, whether abusive or not, is traumatic, but when a child is also separated from siblings, his whole world may seem to fall apart. Other relational losses may include separation from extended family members such as grandparents, aunts and uncles, cousins or close friends of the family and their children, friends, teachers, coaches, caseworkers or pets. Children may also grieve the loss of a familiar community, school, culture, state or country. Finally, adopted children may grieve the loss of more abstract things such as routines, living in a neighborhood that is culturally familiar, cherished possessions, a house or even dreams.

Many adopted children also grieve the loss of one or multiple foster families. A child may have grown close to children he lived with at these homes and feel a sibling-like relationship with them; therefore, being separated from them is like losing a sibling. A minority of foster children experience multiple foster placements before being adopted or aging out of the system. Some children have even experienced five, eight or more placements. Multiple foster placements can exacerbate the already present feelings of grief and loss a child may have from being removed from his family of origin. A child who is moved so many times may come to believe he is unworthy of having a loving, permanent family.

Adopted children may also grieve the loss of an adoptive family they had to leave due to adoption disruption or dissolution. A disruption may occur when the family realizes that they cannot meet the child's needs and the adoption never reaches finalization. Dissolution occurs when an adoption is dissolved after finalization and is rarer than disruption. Disruption or dissolution can be a devastating loss for a child even if it seemed that he did not love his adopted family or care that he was no longer part of the family.

AMBIGUOUS LOSS

Children in foster care or adoptive homes may experience *ambiguous loss*, which occurs when a person close to them is present physically but not psychologically. Psychologically-absent parents may include those who are abusive, neglectful, ill or addicted to drugs or alcohol. Ambiguous loss can also happen when a caregiver is in their lives psychologically but not physically. This occurs when a parent is present in the child's life and shows him affection and love but cannot be around physically. This type of scenario could involve a child separated from a parent due to the parent's incarceration. The child may not harbor fear or anger toward the parent and still loves him very much but suffers from his physical absence.

Many children removed from their birth families are uncertain whether they will be reunited with their parents. Some adopted children hold onto the hope that one day they may rejoin their biological families. Long after being removed from their biological parents and even years after being placed into a loving and caring home, it is not unusual for a child to fantasize about being reunited with her abusive parent and dreaming about how things could be different for her if she was still with her birth parent(s).

Living in a state of emotional limbo makes it harder for adopted children to resolve feelings of grief. When children have even the slightest hope that they will be able to go back to their family of origin, they are more reluctant to accept living with a new family and less likely to get over their feelings associated with separation from their birth parents.

FEELINGS AND SYMPTOMS RELATED TO GRIEF AND LOSS

Feelings of grief and loss are typical among adopted children and are often accompanied by a host of other emotions. Grief is an expected and normal reaction to loss and typically involves a myriad of emotions such as sadness, anger, anxiety, guilt, shame, betrayal, yearning, despair and numbness. Each adopted child will experience a unique journey of emotions that may begin with shock and branch out to a variety of other feelings. Expressions of grief and mourning may surface unexpectedly and heighten at the very time a child is receiving love, support and help. One adoptive mother described her son's expressions of grief over the loss of his birth mother:

> My son is nine, and we adopted him over a year ago—but when we have foster kids leave our house, he still gets sad that he "never got to go home." If you ask him, he will say he doesn't want to be with (his first) "Mommy Kelly." He remembers what life was like there and he does not want to leave us. But there is still and always will be a part of him that wishes things were different.

Feelings, behavior and other symptoms related to grief and loss may be immediate or delayed. As a child's cognition develops into more formalized or abstract thinking in adolescence, questions about her adoption may become more complex and, at the same time, she will understand reasons behind adoption in more sophisticated ways. In adolescence, a child's feeling of grief and loss may multiply simply because she understands more.

Symptoms of grief come in many forms and often are not clearly linked to the experience of loss. A child may throw a tantrum when least expected, because of a specific trigger (that may have gone unnoticed by the parent), such as something she saw or heard earlier in the day. Some children do not exhibit any symptoms of grief and loss. Sometimes a child is in denial, copes by avoiding the problem or masks it by being an overachiever or perfectionist. While there is a wide variety of symptoms that *may* point to issues related to grief, certain symptoms could indicate other problems.

Not all children suffering the effects of grief and loss require professional or therapeutic intervention. Whether help is warranted depends on the age of the child, the severity of the symptoms and the circumstances surrounding the behavior (was there a recent relocation, did she attend a new school, etc.).

The following are potentially serious manifestations of grief and loss. Typically, parents become more aware of a problem when it is severe or there is a constellation of symptoms present. If you observe any of the symptoms on this list, consult with a doctor or family therapist for further exploration.

Serious Grief and Loss Symptoms

- Difficulty coping with frustrations
- Bedwetting
- Food issues (hoarding or refusing to eat)
- Internalizing behaviors (e.g., social withdrawal, depression)
- Sleep disturbances
- Difficulty adapting to change
- Problems in school
- Lack of peer relations

- Externalizing behaviors (e.g., aggression, vandalism)
- Avoidance or denial about a specific topic related to loss

DEMOGRAPHIC DIFFERENCES IN GRIEF AND LOSS REACTIONS

Culture, ethnicity, age, gender, family dynamics and other factors may effect behavioral manifestations and coping related to grief and loss. Children raised in cultures that encourage open expression of emotions may fare better than those raised in cultures that are more inhibitive of individual expressions of feelings. Assistance that a child adopted from another country may have received to help him process grief and loss may vary in quality as well. Learn how your child's cultural heritage may affect his expressions of grief and ability to cope with loss.

Girls often are better at expressing their feelings than boys. Boys are more likely to express grief by lashing out at others or through anger or violence, whereas girls are more likely to blame themselves and become depressed. There are potential differences in the ways girls and boys respond to and cope with loss. Talk to other parents and mental health professionals about how to help your child based on these differences.

UNDERSTANDING THE BEREAVEMENT PROCESS

Bereavement is one type of reaction to grief and it occurs over time after a loss. Traumatic bereavement may occur when a loved one has died violently or suddenly. The traumatically-bereaved child may be affected daily by intrusive images or thoughts about the event that ended their loved one's life.

The late Elizabeth Kubler-Ross was a renowned expert in the field of grief, loss and bereavement. She identified stages of grief that occur when individuals experience the loss of a loved one. She found that the process of grieving or bereavement tends to occur in non-linear stages. The "stages" are emotional states that can be experienced in any order and cycled back and forth. The grieving process depends on many factors as the individual works through his or her pain. Kubler-Ross initially focused on the loss of a loved one as a result of death or dying, but later expanded her model to reflect a variety of other losses, including the loss a child experiences upon being separated from a parent.[1]

Learning about the stages of grief can help you identify your child's emotional states as they relate to grief and loss. These emotional states will most likely include:

- Denial
- Anger
- Bargaining
- Depression
- Acceptance

At the onset of being displaced from their home, children may be in denial and imagine being reunited with their family. This may overlap with anger, depression and bargaining as the child attempts to make sense of his or her separation and whether it will be temporary or permanent. During the bargaining stage, children may try to behave "better" to be returned home or to influence other desired outcomes.

Numerous factors dictate the onset, severity and duration of emotions during your child's process of grieving. A mix of emotions and behaviors can be evident in any stage; however, anger and depression are dominant emotions throughout the cycle. In acute stages of grief, the child may experience more extreme levels of emotions which could surface as being hypersensitive, emotionally explosive, overanxious, self-blaming, easily overwhelmed, neglectful of self-care, disorganized in thinking or behavior, giving up easily and developing new fears or disorders. Acceptance of loss often does not come quickly for children and teenagers and acceptance tends to be anticlimactic. Some young people may never reach the acceptance stage at all.

HELPING YOUR CHILD COPE WITH GRIEF AND LOSS

Early experiences of loss form the basis of a child's identity and beliefs about others. However, with the proper guidance, parenting style and necessary interventions, children can reframe loss in a way that enables them to be open emotionally, to be receptive to unconditional love, to cope with their difficult emotions, to experience feelings of hopefulness and to find fulfillment in their lives.

There are ways to help children process their grief, improve their outlook, cope or, at the very least, improve daily functioning. Parents can provide an emotionally safe environment where children are permitted and encouraged to express their emotions in a constructive way. This is demonstrated through actions and modeling more than through talk. The way parents express their emotions and respond to each other sets the stage for children. Also, messages sent verbally or nonverbally have an impact on how the adoptee frames the loss. Conveying to the adoptee that absence does not necessarily signify abandonment can help the child cope in a more constructive, less destructive manner.

Adopted children who are grieving multiple losses, when raised in a climate of cooperation and collaboration where the family is emotionally open and supportive, will heal more quickly than in families where emotions are not processed and there is no open discussion of feelings. Allowing children to express their thoughts and feelings freely in a nonjudgmental setting helps them feel accepted and more comfortable. This also builds empathy, which is an antidote to aggression. David M. Brodzinsky et al recommend creating a climate that encourages your child to ask questions about his past and biological family.[2] As children develop, the complexity of their questions may evolve. At all times, it is important to let children know that being removed from their original home and the abuse or neglect they may have suffered was not their fault.

Grief can wreak havoc on a child's social and emotional development. Parents need to be attuned to children who have missed out on certain stages of development, due to absent or emotionally unavailable parents or heightened turmoil in their family life. Children showing signs of regression will need to be given those opportunities for growth and development. A child is "stuck" at a stage of development, for instance, when an eight-year-old throws tantrums like a three-year-old. He or she will benefit from specific parenting techniques that are suitable for a toddler or preschooler.

Older children and adolescents are more verbal and expected to be able to articulate their feelings with greater competency, though this may not be the case with children locked in an unresolved stage of grief. Identity development can be a crisis during this time when teens are most concerned with fitting in, peer rejection, dating and being judged. Extra care needs to be taken to help the older child work through fears and concerns. Encourage dialogue in the way that most suits the child. Be accessible for times they may want to talk.

When someone dies, there are rituals that help people gain closure and work toward healing. Wakes, funerals, religious ceremonies, spiritual events, cultural rituals, bereavement journals, memorials, photo memory books and even medical settings, home services and hospice offer ways of coping for patients and their families. A ritual or ceremony offers a person a place to begin the journey of grief and move toward mourning and eventually accepting a loss, but in adoption, there is not a standard ritual that clearly marks the grief that results from loss or separation. Find out what your adopted child is interested in, perhaps a hobby or topic. There may be ways to incorporate his interests into healing activities.

Suggestions to Help Children Mourn Their Losses

- Creating a memory box
- Planting a tree
- Reading special books on grief and relevant topics
- Journaling or drawing
- Attending church services, praying or other religious activities
- Making a time capsule
- Creating family trees
- Devoting a small space to commemorate the child's past
- Drawing a timeline
- Creating photo albums
- Taking pictures
- Sculpting clay to depict family members
- Beginning new traditions

Some children may want to carry out certain activities in solitude (writing in a journal), while other rituals could be observed together as a family (planting a tree). Involving the adoptive family in the healing process allows for additional opportunities for bonding and spending quality time together.

In addition to grieving the usual losses inherent to older child adoption, one mother we spoke to said her three adopted children also have been forced to grieve the recent death of their adopted father. She wrote:

> *Since we adopted the kids, a lot has changed—the most recent is my husband Paul's death. It has been a rough eight months, but we are taking advantage of our counseling sessions to help us talk things through. The kids have been in counseling most of their lives— starting with their birth home issues and then adoption. We were told that they would be in counseling forever. I hope that is not the case, as I'd like to think that all three will be able to be happy and lead successful lives without the issues/stress of their past haunting them. John is the most successful at this point. Cassie took a turn for the worse after Paul died. She has regressed to her younger years— I'd say about seven, when she came to live with us—which has hindered her ability to move forward. She favored Paul over me and let me know it whenever she could. Paul protected Cassie, too, so I am guessing she feels very vulnerable without him. We are working our way through this tough time. It's awkward: for the past seven years, she only relied on me when she "needed" me—and now she really needs me. I am the one who is having the tough time accepting the fact that she needs me now. But again, we are slowly working through this in therapy.*

GETTING PROFESSIONAL HELP
FOR YOUR GRIEVING CHILD

It is important that adoptive parents seek professional help for their child if feelings of grief or bereavement interfere with the child's daily functioning or are resulting in depression or anxiety. Post-traumatic stress disorder (PTSD) is a common reaction to the trauma of loss in adoption. Locate a therapist who specializes in grief and loss in adopted children to help your child cope more effectively and assist you in providing the most effective measures at home. The quality of care a child receives may determine the extent to which she is progressing in healing, coping and managing emotions and behavior.

The therapeutic approach the therapist chooses to employ with your child and family will vary depending on the child's age, culture, presenting issues, contextual circumstances and family dynamics. A qualified clinician will use clinical expertise plus appropriate forms of assessment and knowledge to determine which treatment approach is best suited for the child and family's unique situation. There is no one-size-fits-all approach and any treatment depends heavily on expertise and judgment.

LONG-TERM CONSEQUENCES OF UNTREATED FEELINGS OF GRIEF AND LOSS IN CHILDREN

When feelings of intense grief are not adequately addressed in children, lifelong problems can result. Managing emotions and helping children cope with their loss is fundamental to their functioning. Without proper guidance, the long-term consequences of unresolved grief and loss or feelings of abandonment may result in issues related to trust, relationship difficulties, problems with emotional regulation and behavioral concerns. Adults who have never processed childhood losses may have difficulty developing and sustaining intimate relationships, managing family life, engaging in a successful career and maintaining social relationships. They may also have developmental or physical health problems.

There is also an intergenerational component to resolving grief and coping with issues surrounding loss. Children's abilities to resolve their grief and loss will ultimately affect their own relationships, including those with their own children if they decide to become parents. Children who learn to manage their emotions in healthy ways will be more equipped to work through life's challenges and be better able to express and receive love. Adoptive parents are directly and indirectly teaching children through their own emotional and behavioral modeling how to handle challenges. Ultimately, it's their actions more than their words that will provide their children with templates for coping.

CHAPTER 13

Attachment and Adoption

Attachment is a physical, social, emotional and psychological bond between a child and a parent. According to John Bowlby, the eminent scholar on the subject of attachment, it is biologically based. Attachment emerges after the first six months of life and becomes selective and focused in the latter part of the first year of life.[1] One way to classify certain behaviors of children is as an attachment behavior system. These behaviors function to maintain or increase the proximity of a child to a mother or mother figure or cause the mother figure to move toward the child, Robert A. Hinde wrote.[2] The behavior system promotes and is affected by relationship experiences; as a child interacts with the primary caregiver and other people, he or she develops a sensitivity to and expectation about others or, as Bowlby suggests, a working or cognitive model of self, caregivers and others. While initially there is little coherence in behavior patterns, by the middle of the first year of life these patterns become organized.[3]

Patterns of attachment have been classified into types by researchers. Initially there were three classifications: secure, anxious-resistant (ambivalent) or anxious-avoidant, also known as avoidant, according to Mary

D. S. Ainsworth.[4] Anxious-avoidant attachment patterns include displaying minimal affect or distress, and avoiding attachment figures under circumstances that would elicit interaction from those who are securely attached. Anxious-ambivalent attachment patterns include eliciting ongoing interaction with attachment figures while simultaneously lacking the ability to be comforted or calmed when distressed. Mary Main and Donna Weston added another classification of attachment patterns that result from being abused or neglected as a child, a disorganized/disoriented pattern of attachment.[5] This pattern blends contradictory strategies; there is no coherent behavioral strategy for children to obtain security needs from their caregivers, according to Neil W. Boris and associates.[6] Disorganized attachment is highly problematic.

Early experiences shape attachment patterns. For many children placed when they are older, life experiences are often not conducive to developing a secure attachment. Trauma has a major impact on attachment. Some children may have attachment problems so severe that they have a diagnosis, although the incidence and prevalence is quite low. In the most recent *Diagnostic and Statistical Manual of Mental Disorders* of the American Psychiatric Association (DSM-V), attachment problems can be classified as Reactive Attachment Disorder (RAD) or Disinhibited Social Engagement Disorder. Reactive Attachment Disorder is defined in DSM-V as a lack of, or incomplete formation of, preferred attachments to familiar people, the primary caregiver or parent. Disinhibited Social Engagement Disorder involves inappropriate, overly familiar behavior with strangers.[7] These diagnoses are only loosely related to the research typologies.

Most adoptees with attachment difficulties do not have a diagnosis. Older adopted children often show an array of attachment difficulties. One of the functions of having a strong, positive attachment is that children behave in ways that parents want and expect. Even when the parent is not physically present, children continue to act in ways that meet parental approval. That means when there is not this strong, positive attachment, children behave in ways they learned from previous families, use behaviors that helped them survive previous situations or engage in behavior as their temperament directs them.

A child may have an attachment problem if you tell him clearly not to do something and he does it anyway. This could also be an indication of other issues like an attention or hearing problem. Any list of behaviors indicative of attachment problems is tricky; the same behavior can be due to multiple reasons. The best indicator is whether you, as a parent, are happy and fulfilled in your relationship with your child. Another indicator is whether the child is happy and fulfilled with you as a parent. It is best to talk about attachment problems.

A strong, positive attachment means that you both feel emotionally close to each other. You can give and receive affection. You enjoy the time you spend together and, just as important, you want to spend time together. You respect each other. Most importantly, you trust each other. Not all these feelings are required to have a strong attachment. We have spoken to many families who feel many of these indicators of attachment except trust. Also, these attachments change over time as your child gets older. The way that you and your child interact when he or she just enters school at age five or six is not the same way you and your child interact at fifteen or sixteen. Attachment changes over time.

Parents are urged to use caution when using terms like RAD or attachment disorder unless qualified professionals who have been trained in adoption-sensitive mental health practice have made a diagnosis. There is a lot of misinformation about attachment. You don't want to label children or identify a problem incorrectly.

THE ADOPTIVE FAMILY AND ATTACHMENT

Post-adoption attachment is affected by not only pre-adoption child experiences, but also adoptive family characteristics. While an adoptive family can do nothing about the child's prior experience, they can pay attention to developing a family that promotes attachment. One particular component affecting attachment is maternal responsiveness, the ability to observe and respond to a child's signals for attention adequately and promptly.[8] Studies are accumulating about the association between maternal responsiveness/sensitivity and children's attachment.[9]

To this we would add paternal responsiveness or dad's responsiveness if your family has a dad, is a single-father adoptive family or a two-dad family. The best scenario is that both parents learn signals that the child uses to demonstrate he or she wants or needs attention. It should not only be when he or she is behaving poorly. A mismatch between parent responsiveness and child reaction may exacerbate or perpetuate attachment difficulties.[10]

Parents respond according to their own attachment style, based on their experiences growing up and through adult life. They respond to their child according to their model of attachment and with the expectation of a similar response. It is difficult to remember that the child has a different model of adult-child relationships than you do. It can be akin to a poor dancing partner—sometimes you both want to lead, sometimes one wants to dance to a fast song but the other one wants to dance to a slow song and sometimes neither of you knows how to dance very well. Understanding each other's attachment style is the foundation for developing an attachment that works well both for you and for your child.

It may take a long time for parents to be able to understand the child's model of attachment and the nuances of your children—the cues they give that something is wrong, they are anxious or they want to be loved/get affection/get attention. As the oldest of five children with a ten-year span between the oldest and youngest, co-author Victor was always amazed that his mother could tell when his little brother was going to be sick. She knew how to read his nuanced behavior. Getting to know an older child means getting to know their subtle cues and then responding quickly and consistently to those cues.

What are cues? Cues are emotions—crying, laughing, whining. Cues are cognitive—*I need something* or *I want something*, although many children have a difficult time finding and using the right words. Cues are behavioral—making noise, doing something you told them not to do, watching you to see if you notice what they are doing, being irritating. Remember, these are signals from the child that he or she wants or needs something. Your job as a parent is to be responsive and know how to interpret these cues. Responsiveness builds attachment.

Another issue to consider is family stress. High parental stress has been associated with problematic attachment in adopted children.[11] The manner in which parents respond to stress affects the child's adjustment, according to Brodzinsky et al.[12] Parents who are less stressed are more able to respond consistently and appropriately to the child's cues to facilitate positive or secure attachment. Parenting in and of itself is stressful but parents can reduce the stress in their lives. They can avoid or limit the situations that are stressful.

Some ways families can build attachment just by being a family are:

- Provide positive caregiving and consistency over time. As children change their cognitive models of caregivers and themselves, attachment difficulties become less pronounced.

- Facilitate attachment cognitively by assisting children in examining and understanding their past, giving children a vision for the future and using appropriate and positive physical contact. Life books are wonderful tools for talking about a child's life and should be read and reviewed often.

- Model and express feelings; modeling and expressing feelings are essential components to facilitating attachment between parent and child. They give children the language they need to talk about their feelings.

- Provide discipline without resorting to emotionally-laden words and with natural and logical consequences for transgressions. Don't call your children names!

- Look for opportunities to promote attachment (anxiety, fear, illness and fatigue).

  o When children are anxious, move closer to them and let them know you are there to help them feel less nervous.

  o When children are fearful, comfort them in a way they want to be comforted. Ask them how you can make them feel better and less afraid.

  o When children are ill, make every effort to stay by their sides and care for them. If you work, take time off. Every child wants his or her mom or dad nearby when he or she feels badly.

o Use bedtime as a way to build a connection. Develop a bedtime ritual. Reading a soothing story or developing a routine
at bedtime when children are vulnerable can be a positive way
to build an attachment, unless bedtime was a time of violence
or trauma. In these situations, you may have to work with a
professional to help figure out the best bedtime routine.

Any activity that builds a child's social competence—enhances social
skills, practices pro-social behavior of helping others or activities that aid
moral development—builds attachment. But be careful that you don't
over-program children. Children need activities but also need downtime.
The danger of too much programming is that children are not with you
and then you don't get to build attachment—they are building it with
the people with whom they do the activities.

You also need to provide structure and set limits. Children with
attachment difficulties do better with predictability—they know meal
times, bedtimes, bath times, homework times, etc. The schedule must
be consistent. Consistent is not unchangeable, but should be more rigid
than flexible. It is not unreasonable to have children adhere to a schedule. As children get into and understand the routine, they begin to relax
and the hard and rewarding work of becoming a family really begins.

Creating family meetings where values are discussed can be very helpful.[13] Value clarification can help both the parents and the adopted child; it
is a forum for educating the parent and child about each other's values to
clarify and modify value stances. Also, rituals can be used to mark significant events in the adoption, according to Lois Ruskai Melina.[14] It is important to remember that adoption is a process and not an event. Rituals help
the process of parents adopting the child but also the child adopting the
parents. There are a number of good books about adoption rituals that
could be helpful to parents (see Randolph Severson's *Adoption: Rituals for
Charm and Healing*, or Mary Mason's *Designing Rituals of Adoption: For the
Religious and Secular Community*).

Sometimes, when either everything you have tried has not worked or
the relationship is going badly, you have to obtain professional assistance.
Here is some guidance on finding competent help for attachment issues.

GETTING PROFESSIONAL HELP
FOR ATTACHMENT PROBLEMS

First, talk to other adoptive parents who have had similar problems. They will recommend who to go to and who to avoid. Second, find out the techniques the therapist uses. Parents are encouraged to look at the interventions rated by the California Evidence-Based Clearinghouse for Child Welfare that provides guidance on interventions to make sure you go to a reputable professional who is using the most scientific approach to treating your child and family.[15]

Children suspected of having attachment problems are better served if they are: (1) assessed for learning disabilities, regulatory disorders, sensory disorders and PTSD; (2) assessed by a multidisciplinary team of a physician, psychologist, occupational therapist and social worker; (3) observed in school or preschool and at home and (4) the family is evaluated and treatment is family-based as well as child-centered. Anything short of this comprehensive approach gives an incomplete assessment of the child.

Some of the best approaches for dealing with attachment problems are these interventions:

- Cognitive-Behavioral Therapy (CBT) with Trauma Focus

- Alternatives for Families: A Cognitive-Behavioral Therapy (AF-CBT) a.k.a. Abuse-Focused Therapy

- Trauma Affect Regulation: Guidelines for Education & Therapy (TARGET)

- Child-Parent Psychotherapy (CPP)

- Parent-Child Interaction Therapy (PCIT)

Families should avoid untested therapies or those widely viewed as harmful or dangerous to children. This includes rage reduction therapy, holding therapy, rebirthing therapy or the more generic attachment therapy. A number of professional associations such as the American Psychological Association, the American Professional Society on the Abuse of Children and the National Association of Social Workers have issued statements against the use of coercive therapies. Before you engage a professional person to work with you and your family if your child has an attachment difficulty, you should ask these questions:

- Is this person licensed at the highest level possible? If they are not licensed, be very careful.
- What disciplines are part of the assessment process and who provides the intervention (professional background and licensure)? If the individual is a student or trainee, you have the right to refuse treatment by that person.
- Does this person use evidence-based practices? Refer to the previous list and ask if they use these therapies.
- What professional training have they had in adoption? In working with attachment problems? You want to know about their adoption-specific and attachment-specific training.
- Has a child ever been harmed from the techniques they used? Have they been sued by a family or a child for using the technique they plan to use?
- Is their technique considered controversial?
- What evidence do they have that their treatment is effective?

Some practitioners may be nervous when you ask these questions. Some may be offended. Yet, you are putting the health and psychosocial welfare of your child and your family under the guidance of this professional. You have every right and every obligation to ask questions about the person providing the intervention. Sometimes desperate parents make desperate decisions. Unprofessional or unsanctioned treatment is never better than waiting or looking for a well-trained, competent professional with experience in the field.

CHAPTER 14

Emerging Sense of Self

Throughout childhood, adolescence and early adulthood we develop a sense of ourselves as unique human beings. Think back on your own sense of self during your teen and early adult years. How did you come to understand *who you were*? Perhaps family, friends and your community had the most impact on your sense of identity as you matured. As young children, our families are our world. They have enormous influence on our early development, sense of self and understanding of the world because we cannot yet fend for ourselves. Well into adulthood, we continue to develop an understanding of all the ways our families (for better or worse) have shaped our lives.

As we grow and mature, we are able to break away from family norms and expectations to find our own identities. In adolescence, our peer relationships become paramount and our emerging sense of self is greatly influenced by non-familial social relationships. The communities we grow up in also influence our sense of how we fit in and who we are. How many young people say "I have to get out of here...I don't belong here"? Some young people can't imagine living anywhere else and never leave the place where they grew up. They closely identify with what it means to be members of their community.

Identity formation in children and teens who are adopted can be more complicated. In addition to the often difficult issues any child faces as he matures, adoptees must integrate different life events into their sense of who they are and where they belong. Divided loyalties to biological and adoptive parents, past abuse, trauma, cultural differences with adopted families, feelings of rejection or lack of self-worth—all these can complicate an adopted child's search for a coherent identity and sense of self. An Evan B. Donaldson Adoption Institute report explores how children integrate adoption into their lives as they mature:

> Preschool children learn their own adoption/birth stories; elementary-age children may struggle with feelings of rejection, because they are recognizing the loss aspects of adoption and experiencing peer reactions to adoption; adolescents usually seek a deeper understanding of who they are in relation to both adoptive and birth families and may struggle with independence; and young adult adoptees come to terms with genealogy in making choices about marriage and parenthood and in deciding whether or not to search for birth parents (if they are not known).[1]

Growing up in situations that are volatile, insecure or downright cruel can be devastating for a young person's developing sense of self. Children who have been removed from their biological families may blame themselves and suffer from low self-esteem throughout their lives. They may feel they are not good enough, that no one can love them or that their lives have very little meaning.

Foster children who have lived in numerous homes may be especially confused about where they belong. Despite the abuse or neglect they may have suffered, adopted children often yearn for the familiarity of their biological families, home community and friends. They may even long for the stability of instability.

As adopted teenagers mature, in addition to contending with the usual stresses of adolescence—figuring out where they fit in, who their true friends are and dealing with changing family relationships—adoptees may also have to navigate biological family relationships, come to terms

with past abuse, try to fit into their new family and community and sometimes deal with issues related to their cultural or racial identities. During
adolescence, the adopted child may become more interested in his biological family and ask more questions.

For the adopted child, understanding his past may be an important part of understanding who he is, according to Leslie H. Wind and
associates.[2] Do your best to answer his questions in an honest and age-
appropriate manner.

It is developmentally normal for teenagers to distance themselves
from their parents and other family members in search of their own
personal identities. It can be very confusing for adoptees entering their
families during adolescence; they have the paradox of trying to build
attachments with a new adoptive family while trying to emerge as more
independent beings. Because they are still in the bonding phase or fear
separation from or the loss of their adoptive families, some teenage adoptees may even delay going away to college or taking a job in another state,
according to Cynthia Flynn, Wendy Welch and Kathleen Paget.[3] Adoption
at an older age changes the life cycle of the family. It can be quite confusing
to manage a typically-developing child while parenting an older adoptee
whose life cycle may be atypical.

According to child welfare specialists Gina Miranda Samuels and
Julia M. Pryce, although being removed from their biological family is
traumatic, many adoptees develop positive personal traits, such as resilience and the ability to cope, as a result of their negative experiences.[4]
Furthermore, adoption can improve adopted children's feelings of self-
worth and belonging.[5] Every adopted child is unique; factors that influence one child's sense of self-worth and personal identity may not impact
another child.

Younger children may face fewer challenges developing positive
senses of self and personal identity because they are too young to process many of the events that have occurred in their lives. However, being
removed from parents and siblings can certainly take its toll on a child's
sense of security and safety and some children may worry that their parents' problems are their fault. Trauma and loss experienced at a young

age, if left unresolved, can complicate a child's developing sense of self as she moves into adolescence.

RACE, CULTURE AND CLASS

Being a transracial or transcultural adoptee does not automatically confer behavioral problems, lower self-esteem or a lack of racial or ethnic identity for an older adoptee. Race, culture and class contribute to your child's emerging sense of self and belonging. It is important that adoptive parents acknowledge racial and cultural family differences, celebrate being a multicultural or multiracial family and honor the cultural heritage of their children. Your child may have spent many years immersed in the norms of her culture and community; thus, her cultural heritage may be an important part of who she is.

It is imperative that adoptive parents understand the meaning of being a particular race or culture in the context of the community where they live. For example, being black in the United Kingdom is not the same as being black in the United States. Being Latino or Hispanic may be a distinctly different cultural experience in one country as compared to another. Being Asian often comes with societal expectations of having talents in math and science. Parents need to learn how race and culture may contribute to their child's emerging sense of self in the context of their adopted regional or national community. They must seek to understand cultural norms the child has grown up with prior to entering the family, how she may be treated differently because of her cultural or racial background in her new community and the pressures she may feel to fit in with friends who share her culture or race. Parents must demonstrate empathy for a child's feelings of isolation, alienation or even embarrassment about being different.[6] If your child believes you are making an effort to understand how she experiences the world, she may feel more comfortable discussing racial and cultural issues with you.

Steps you can take to build your child's pride in his unique cultural heritage and cultural sense of self include:

- Connect your teenager with a friend or colleague from the same cultural background as he is. Ask the person to talk to your child about discrimination that he may face and how to navigate professional life as an African-American, Latino, Asian, etc.

- Take advantage of the many ways you can celebrate your child's cultural heritage such as visiting museums, attending cultural parades, learning your child's native language, cooking ethnic dishes together, doing cultural arts and crafts projects or celebrating cultural holidays.

- Talk to your child frankly about how people from his culture or race may have been treated unfairly in the past and how discrimination and prejudice can affect people even today. Read books with young children about how groups of people overcame discrimination or persecution.

- Bring your teenager to visit colleges that have a large body of students who share his religious, cultural or racial background. Encourage him to join cultural organizations at school or college. Share information about job fairs geared toward students of a specific racial or cultural background.

- Enroll your child in cultural extracurricular activities or summer camps where he will meet other adoptees and/or children who share his cultural or racial background.

Another strategy is to promote *bicultural socialization*. Bicultural socialization is a process via activities, events and relationships whereby children are socialized into the values, attitudes, beliefs, norms and behaviors of the dominant culture in which they live as well as their birth culture. Bicultural socialization allows children to attain bicultural competency and negotiate, navigate and relate between two cultures.[7]

If your child does not remember living in a different country, he may not relate as well to children who were adopted from his country of origin at an older age and who retain the language and customs of their native lands. Children who lose their first language often lose the memories associated with that language. Talk openly with your child about the kinds of activities and people with whom he feels most comfortable spending time. Talk to your child about any stress he is experiencing, because he does not know who he fits in with at school. Do not be critical or overly concerned if your child is simply not that interested in learning about his cultural heritage. Every child has different needs and interests; cultural identity may not be important to your child.

We spoke to Kim, a parent who adopted her daughter from Korea as an infant. Here is what she had to say about her daughter growing up as an Asian-American adoptee:

I don't have a lot of issues with the kids being Asian and feeling weird because they are. I have always been very proactive about it. She has attended Korea camp with two hundred and fifty Korean adopted kids every summer since she was four, has attended social functions with Asian adopted kids about three to four times a year and our church has about fourteen Asian adopted kids, which is a high ratio for a small church. I have always introduced her to families that look like ours and kept her friendships going with those kids. At Korea camp they always have adopted adults talk and some have been well socialized with other adopted kids growing up and some have not. I always thought the ones who have been socialized seem better adjusted. I found the kids that get a lot of trouble at school for being Asian tend to need this more than the homeschooled kids do. [My daughter] has never been teased for being Asian, not ever, but other kids at camp seem to go through it. My daughter has had so much exposure and socialization with other Asian adopted kids that I don't think she craves it, because she hasn't lacked that type of cameraderie. I prefer that she feels this way rather than to have her be the only Asian adopted kid she knows.

ROLE OF ECONOMIC POVERTY OR DEPRIVATION IN YOUR CHILD'S SEARCH FOR IDENTITY

You should also think about how economic class has contributed to your child's developing sense of where he fits in, what norms to follow, his understanding of achievement and his personal identity. A child or teenager who has grown up in an economically disadvantaged family and community will have had very different life experiences and expectations compared to a child who has grown up in an upper-middle-class home. A child who grows up in poverty may not expect to be able to afford college; therefore, he may develop a negative attitude toward school or college. A child who has been deprived of material things may become overly possessive of toys and other belongings.

When a child moves from an economically disadvantaged family to a family with greater financial means, he may feel confused or even angry. For a child who has grown up in abject poverty or in an orphanage, being adopted into a middle-class or wealthy family may be a complete shock.

A child from deprived circumstances may have unrealistic expectations about receiving gifts from parents or may even demand gifts in a manner that you find troubling. If your child expects you to constantly shower her with gifts, explain that although you have the means to buy her nice things, gifts are for special occasions like birthdays or when she has earned good grades. When your child first comes home (and later on), don't overindulge your child with trips to the mall, fancy restaurants or lavish parties, because this could be overwhelming if she is not used to these types of outings. Show her that time spent with family is more important than receiving gifts or money by spoiling her with your love and attention.

SEXUAL ORIENTATION AND GENDER IDENTITY

There is a disproportionately large number of LGBT youth in foster care, because some are rejected or abused by family members due to their sexual orientation. During their early teen years (and even younger), children become aware of their emerging sexual orientation and gender identity. When children or teens realize they are different in this way, they may experience considerable stress, confusion or feelings of isolation. The journey through foster care can be especially painful for LGBT and questioning children if foster parents don't understand or accept them.

Adoptive parents must demonstrate sensitivity toward their LGBT child. Hopefully a former foster parent or caseworker will inform you if the child has experienced rejection or other issues because of his sexual orientation, but they may not be aware of this history. All adoptive parents should be open to the fact that their child could be LGBT even if it is not evident during the matching process. LGBT adoptive parents may be the best fit for some LGBT children, because they are more likely to understand the hurt these children have experienced.

Adoptive parents may discover their child is LGBT a week, a month or a year after their child comes home. In this event, assure your child that you love and support him and want nothing more than for him to be himself at home and in the world. Tell him you are glad he felt comfortable enough with you to discuss his sexual orientation.

If you feel you cannot accept your child for who he is, seek counseling for yourself. It is your responsibility to love your child unconditionally. Parents can learn about parenting LGBT children and about LGBT issues by reading articles, reading books (try Anne Dohrenwend's *Coming Around: Parenting Lesbian, Gay, Bisexual and Transgender Kids*), taking classes or talking to LGBT friends who can share how it feels to grow up gay, lesbian, bisexual or transgendered. You might also want to join a discussion board or support group for parents raising LGBT children.

If your LGBT or questioning child has mental health issues such as anxiety or depression, get her professional help right away. Make sure the mental health professional you choose has worked with LGBT youth and understands the impact discrimination and bullying can have on their self-esteem. Work with a family therapist if you feel other immediate family members need help accepting your child for who she is.

THE TRANSITION TO EARLY ADULTHOOD

Emerging adulthood is a new concept of development proposed by development expert Jeffrey Jensen Arnett for the period from the late teens through the mid to late twenties.[8] This is a period of profound changes and independent explorations. Identity development begins in adolescence but doesn't become solidified until early adulthood.[9] Work experiences become more focused, setting the foundation for adult work. It is a time of great potential for positive changes but also a time of a high incidence of problems, according to Meredith O'Connor et al.[10]

Peter Martin and Michael A. Stayer suggest that when adults later consider the most important events in their lives, they most often name events that took place during later adolescence and early adulthood.[11] Jeffrey Arnett argues that emerging adulthood is neither adolescence nor early adulthood but is theoretically and empirically distinct from them both.[12] Erik Erikson, Kenneth Keniston and Daniel Levinson all contributed to the theoretical groundwork for the concept of emerging adulthood.[13] Emerging adults do not see themselves as adolescents but also do not see themselves entirely as adults.[14]

One of the central features of emerging adulthood is the exploration of various possibilities in love, education, work and personal values. If work on identity issues starts in adolescence, emerging adulthood offers new opportunities for clarification and learning more about what one likes and dislikes.[15] With regard to love, adolescents' explorations are more transient and superficial, while "emerging adults" are able to experience a deeper level of intimacy. In education and work, too, emerging adults are most focused on laying the foundation for an adult occupation versus adolescents' concerns with obtaining money to support leisure activities. Emerging adults can pursue novel and intense experiences more freely than adolescents.[16]

A largely unexplored area is the role of the adoptive family and the effects of adoptive parenting on adopted children's development in early adulthood. Meta-analytic evidence has shown that adoption is a remarkably "effective intervention," at least through adolescence, according to famed psychologist Marinus van IJzendoorn and Femmie Juffer.[17]

In contrast to youth leaving the foster system and transitioning to adulthood, adoptees have the benefit of family and community resources since they are adopted mostly by middle and upper-income families. However, the negative impact from pre-adoptive experiences continues to exert some influence even after joining higher-resource families and communities.

For children who joined their families when they were older, the transition to adulthood may be longer. There is nothing magical about age eighteen and adulthood. Also, parents should expect children to move in and out of the house and to be more financially dependent than independent. For more information, read Dr. Varda Konstam's book, *Parenting Your Emerging Adult: Launching Kids from 18 to 29.*

The path to adulthood is not linear. College is a difficult transition for adoptees, particularly ones going far away. If your adopted child goes to college, he will likely choose a campus closer to you than further away. If he chooses one further away to start, he may experience crisis and probably he will eventually choose one closer to you. During the college years, as your child matures into adulthood, the uneven development you witnessed early in your adoption experience will become more pronounced.

CHAPTER 15

Mental Health

There are inconsistent findings on the relationship between adoption and mental health. Some studies of adoptees suggest greater self-reported drug use, antisocial behavior, negative emotions and other behavioral problems compared to non-adoptees.[1] Other researchers such as Anu Sharma and colleagues report that adoptees engage in more pro-social behavior than non-adopted adolescents, such as helping disadvantaged populations.[2] In a meta-analysis of sixty-six studies, Michael Wierzbicki reported that adopted children scored higher than non-adopted children on measures of maladjustment, externalizing disorders and academic problems.[3] Ann E. Brand and Paul M. Brinich found mixed results regarding whether adopted children have more behavior problems than non-adopted children.[4] In their meta-analysis of over twenty-five thousand adoption cases and eighty thousand controls (non-adopted children), Linda van den Dries, Femmie Juffer, Marinus van IJzendoorn and Marian Bakermans-Kranenburg found small differences in behavior problems between adoptees and non-adopted persons (although they did find differences between domestic and intercountry adoptions, with domestic adoptees having more difficulties).[5] However, several studies have found adoptees are more likely to be in counseling than non-adopted individuals.[6]

Several studies suggest that adoptees are more likely to attempt or complete suicide but the number of cases, while statistically significant, is actually quite small.[7] Still, this finding has been a cause of concern.

It is clear that adoptees are more likely to be in counseling than general child populations but there could be multiple reasons for this. One, adoption is unique and brings unique issues to development across the lifespan. Adoptees encounter different issues from children born and raised by their biological families. As such, adoptees may need counseling more often than non-adopted children. Two, most adoptive families have had contact with social service agencies in order to adopt, so there is less stigma about going to counseling and getting social service assistance. We encourage adoptive families to seek professional help if they need it.

Most adoptees don't need or want counseling about their adoption and they should never be forced into counseling to address adoption issues. Sometimes that is at sixteen, sometimes it is at thirty-six and sometimes it is never. However, if you have a child with a mental health diagnosis, you will need to obtain professional help.

Nevertheless, we offer a caveat. Adoption is not a diagnosis. Many older children who have spent time in foster care obtained a diagnosis; it may or may not be accurate (but you want to know this information before adoption). Many intercountry adoptees have been in socially or globally depriving institutional care before adoption. These pre-adoptive experiences put children at more risk for mental health problems, Brodzinsky suggests.[8] Yet a diagnosis is not a child. It is based on the medical model that assesses/diagnoses/treats problems. The diagnosis is a way to communicate with other professionals about the problems the child may have. It is not unusual for children to have multiple diagnoses or different diagnoses—it is very difficult to adequately diagnose children and, as the child's context changes (for example, she moves from a foster to adoptive family), her diagnosis may change. There is great concern that children in foster care are over-diagnosed and over-medicated. In some low-resource countries from which children are adopted, medical training and access to the newest thinking about physical and mental health are hard to find. Sometimes diagnoses are used that are made up in that country without universal recognition of the diagnosis. If your child has a mental health problem, it may take some time after the adoption to determine the diagnosis and treatment plan. The history of the child in other settings may or may not be helpful in understanding his or her mental health in your family. It is complicated.

An additional caution is that in some periods certain diagnoses become popular and many children get that trending diagnosis. Both Reactive Attachment Disorder and Bi-Polar Disorder are popular at this time. This creates a problem when a diagnosis becomes almost a fad; you don't know if your child has a disorder or if the prism used by the mental health professional is swayed by the popularity of a diagnosis. This is the same with prescription medications for mental health problems; some prescriptions become heavily marketed and consequently are used too frequently, including being used for problems for which they were never intended.

That is not to say that some adopted children do not have serious or persistent mental health problems. Rather, we want parents to be careful about accepting historical or even current diagnoses if their experience with the child does not match the diagnosis. Treat children as individuals, not as their diagnoses.

MOST-DIAGNOSED PROBLEMS

Research literature is organized around behavioral problems and not diagnoses. As such, it is very difficult to know which diagnoses are most frequent. Also, the problems reported depend on the genetic and pre-adoptive backgrounds of the adoptee. These factors create a probability of behavioral problems/mental health diagnoses but cannot predict problems. We wish we could give you a list, but the list would have to be broken down by genetic propensity and pre-adoptive experiences—something that would be very difficult to construct. Even if we did construct such a chart, it would not say anything about your child. You cannot take data based on a group and apply it to the individual—to do so would be to create an ecological fallacy.

Clinicians report seeing patterns in adoptees, but you have to remember they do not see the majority of adoptees—they see a very small group of adoptees who come for services. Even clinicians must be careful because two children of the same age who lived, for instance, in a Russian orphanage for the first three years of their lives can have different issues. One could have a problem and one could be resilient, not demonstrating any problems.

According to the Centers for Disease Control and Prevention (CDC), 13 to 20 percent of children living in the United States experience a mental disorder in a given year.[9] According to the 2013 supplement, using parent reports, the most-diagnosed disorders were:

- Attention-deficit/hyperactivity disorder (6.8 Percent)
- Behavioral or conduct problems (3.5 Percent)
- Anxiety (3 percent)
- Depression (2.1 Percent)
- Autism spectrum disorders (1.1 Percent)[10]

About 4.7 percent of adolescents aged twelve to seventeen had an illicit drug use disorder in the past year, 4.2 percent had an alcohol abuse disorder in the past year and 2.8 percent had cigarette dependency in the past month. The overall suicide rate for persons aged ten to nineteen years was 4.5 suicides per 100,000 persons in 2010.[11]

There has not been specific surveillance of adoptees. However, there are parent reports from the 2007 National Survey of Adoptive Parents.[12] The National Survey of Children's Health (NSCH) is a nationally representative survey of US children under age eighteen. The National Survey of Adoptive Parents (NSAP) was an add-on module to the 2007 NSCH. The survey includes parent reports on children adopted from the foster care system, intercountry adoptions and private domestic adoption (of mostly infants). It does not include step-parent adoptions. The majority of adoptees, regardless of the type of adoption, were physically as well as psychologically and emotionally healthy. Only a small minority of adopted children have ever been diagnosed with an attachment disorder, depression, Attention Deficit Disorder or Attention Deficit Hyperactivity Disorder (ADD/ADHD) or behavior or conduct disorder. However, compared to the general population of children, adopted children are more likely to have been diagnosed with, or have moderate to severe symptoms of, depression, ADD/ADHD or behavior/conduct disorder. According to NSAP: "…9 percent of adopted children ages 2 and older have ever been diagnosed with depression, compared with 4 percent of children in the general population. Additionally, 26 percent of adopted children ages 6 and older have ever been diagnosed with ADD/ADHD, compared with 10 percent of children in the general population. A similar pattern of differences emerges for behavior/conduct disorder: 15 percent of adopted children have ever been so diagnosed compared with 4 percent of children in the general population."[13]

Children adopted from foster care are about twice as likely as those adopted privately or internationally to have been diagnosed with ADD/ADHD, behavior/conduct problems and about three times as likely to have been diagnosed with an attachment disorder. Depression is rare, regardless of the type of adoption.[14]

We are reluctant to offer a checklist, because parents then may compare the child's behavior to the checklist. If you are worried about your child's behavior, school performance or developmental functioning, start by consulting your pediatrician. Talk to other adoptive parents. Then find an adoption-sensitive mental health professional.

ADOPTION-SENSITIVE MENTAL HEALTH PROVIDERS

We are always amazed to hear from adoptive parents that they go to a professional to seek help for their adoption or their adoptee and one of the first recommendations they hear is to give the child back. This is completely unhelpful and offensive. Children are not merchandise; you don't "give them back" as the first intervention. Any professional who starts the conversation with this recommendation should be dismissed immediately.

Here is a list of questions to ask the mental health provider who you want to treat your child and work with your family:

- What is your background and training in child development? Did your training include adoption training? Tell me about your adoption training.

- If they have no specific training, ask them if they have ever recommended that an adoptive family give a child back. If so, this is not the therapist for you.

- Do you have a personal connection to adoption? If you do, are you willing to share your personal connection? The provider doesn't need a personal connection to adoption but having one helps.

- What do you know about entitlement and adoption? If she or he doesn't know the word, explain that entitlement is when adoptive parents claim their child as their own and the adoptee claims the adoptive parents as his or her own. Ask how you can help your child with the entitlement process.

- What do they think of the role of medication in treating children for mental health problems? Is this someone who wants to try interventions first before recommending medications or does this person seem overeager to recommend medications?

- Do you work with the entire family or only the adoptee? We want to be included in any treatment you give our child, so how can this happen? You should be clear that you can only support treatment if the family is involved in the child's treatment.

Even with these questions as a guide, you should be aware that finding a good child psychiatrist is difficult. There is often a waiting list or long periods of time to get appointments. Some hospitals use medical students and medical fellows to provide services. This is problematic for two reasons: One, they often don't have the training or the professional experiences that a parent or child requires if they need child psychiatry. Two, continuity of care is critical—you don't want your child to have to start a new relationship every year or so as medical professionals in training leave. You need someone who can have a long-term relationship with your adopted child (and you). Rely on other adoptive parents to help you identify a child psychiatrist who not only understands child mental health but also understands adoption.

ADOPTING A CHILD WITH KNOWN MENTAL HEALTH PROBLEMS

Some parents choose to adopt a child diagnosed with Autism, Fetal Alcohol Syndrome or other problems. Like any decision, you should go into the adoption knowing everything you can about the problem and develop resources in your community to support yourself as a parent. If you don't have these resources in your community or cannot easily access resources, you should reconsider adopting this child. Adoptive families and children do best when they are strongly supported in their network of family and friends as well as with professionals who can help support and guide them. Before placement, get all the professional resources in place. It is much better to do it early rather than waiting for a crisis. Follow any recommendations given to you at the time of adoptive placement in order to assure a successful transition and stability after placement.

Often there are "red flags" alerting us to problems a child may be experiencing. Obvious signs may include changes in eating or sleeping patterns, problems with peer relations, changes in family dynamics and in school or other settings. Anyone can have a bad day, but if you notice a pattern of concerning behaviors or your child's daily functioning is becoming negatively impacted, talk to your child or others (teachers, family) in your child's life to find out more. If the problem continues or worsens, you may want to speak with a qualified professional with adoption experience, at least for a consultation. In some instances, an emerging problem is not so obvious. Parents are typically in tune enough with their child to pick up on concerns. Building trust, facilitating attachment and maintaining open communication will encourage children to share their concerns. These qualities are the bedrock of a healthy parent-child relationship and will serve to resolve problems and build resiliency.

Even when children have a propensity for developing a mental health issue, the adoptive family can be a powerful force for diminishing the impact of genetic forces or pre-adoptive experiences on the development of some types of mental health problems, according to Holly C. Wilcox and associates.[15] That doesn't mean problems should be ignored or minimized. Rather, keep in mind that the reason that adoption is so wonderful is because it is often a tremendously improved situation for the child and can help a child recover from early negative experiences.

Adoptive families can be, in and of themselves, a healing influence on children. However, for some children, the healing power and love of the adoptive family is not enough and you will need to obtain professional services from psychiatrists, psychologists, social workers and others to help them adjust and prosper in their new family.

CHAPTER 16

Physical Health

It is important that adoptive parents obtain as much information as possible about their child's medical history. Children adopted at an older age may have health problems related to a history of abuse or neglect while children adopted from most low-resource countries are at a higher risk of conditions common to children living in poverty or in orphanages in that country. This includes developmental problems, sensory problems, exposure to diseases such as hepatitis and general poor health.

Parents adopting domestically should be able to obtain their child's complete medical records from the placing agency. In the United States, laws pertaining to agency requirements for disclosing a child's medical history vary by state. For example, in some states agencies must provide adoptive parents with copies of medical records as opposed to a written summary of the records. Even if policies vary, you have a right to obtain all the medical records of your child. It is usually easier to obtain them before placement. You might have to sign a form indicating that you received all the medical records from the placing agency.

In general, adoption agencies are required to perform due diligence in collecting and disclosing a child's health and medical history. The American Academy of Pediatrics recommends which records your agency should be able to provide to adoptive parents.[1] This list includes prenatal test results for the biological mother, gestational age, birth weight, length and head size, Apgar scores, history of abuse or neglect, reason for placement, nutritional history, immunizations and allergies. View the list online for more information.

If you feel there are gaps in your child's medical history, ask your adoption caseworker about why there are gaps and how you can obtain additional information. Agencies and adoptive parents may not be able to obtain all of the child's medical records due to confidentiality issues. Your adoption attorney and your child's pediatrician may be able to help you obtain records you are having difficulty accessing.[2]

Parents who adopt children from another country may have a more difficult task obtaining their child's complete medical history. Although Hague Convention countries are required to provide adoptive parents with a translated medical report, often this report is incomplete or even inaccurate. Non-Hague Convention countries may supply even less background information. You should request the complete medical record of your child in the language of the country where your child resides and not accept just an extracted record or summary. Even if there are additional costs and delays in the process, you may be well served to obtain the complete record and then have it translated. Otherwise, you will receive an extracted record that could be completely accurate or completely inaccurate. The information recorded reflects what the person who summarized (i.e., extracted) the information judges to be important. Some countries use their own medical jargon and you will need help deciphering the terms.

Find a qualified pediatrician before placement. The pediatrician can review the records you have and develop a preliminary plan for when she or he sees your child the first time.

THE INITIAL HEALTH SCREENING

Parents adopting a child from another country will want to consult a pediatrician before they bring their child home to discuss what they have learned about the child's medical history. Show the doctor photos or videos of the child and get his or her opinion on any conditions or diseases you have been told the child has.[3] The doctor will need to see your child in person to confirm what conditions he does or does not have. Parents adopting domestically may be able to bring their child to a pediatrician during the visitation period, before adoptive placement. Ask your agency what the rules and procedures are in regard to taking your child to a pediatrician during the pre-adoptive phase.

Children adopted internationally will receive a health screening and possibly immunizations (depending on the receiving country's requirements) before they leave the country. The US Department of State (DOS) requires all children to see a DOS-designated physician prior to entering the United States and obtaining travel documents from the country of origin to the United States.

Before traveling to another country, adoptive parents must ensure that their own vaccinations and the vaccinations of their children and other members of the household who travel with them are up to date. Children adopted from other countries may not be immunized or have immunization failure, making them more susceptible to various diseases, the CDC advises.[4] Children who are adopted domestically may also lack immunizations, so try to obtain accurate immunization records from the child's former pediatrician or school. Once your child's new pediatrician determines which immunizations your child needs, she will schedule your child for a visit or explain to you when your child will receive the necessary immunizations. Sometimes pediatricians will conduct blood tests to determine the immunizations needed; sometimes they will repeat particular immunizations.

Most children adopted from the foster care system will be covered by public health insurance (Medicaid). Hopefully, your child's foster parents have taken your child to the doctor for annual check-ups and other health needs. If you need to find a new pediatrician for your child who accepts public insurance or your own private insurance, your agency may be able to refer you to a pediatrician specially qualified in treating children who have been in foster care. You may also want to ask your agency to refer you to a clinic in a hospital or medical center that specializes in serving adopted children. Once you find a pediatrician with whom you are comfortable, have your child's medical records transferred to the new pediatrician as soon as possible to avoid delays in getting an appointment.

All older children adopted domestically or from another country should see their new pediatrician within two weeks of coming home. Share with the pediatrician all the information you have about your child's health history, including his history of neglect or abuse, trauma, developmental delays, fetal alcohol or drug exposure and mental health. Ask the doctor to complete a comprehensive health evaluation that includes a hearing and vision screening as well as assessments for physical developmental delays. If your pediatrician identifies a problem, ask the pediatrician to refer you to an occupational therapist, physical therapist, mental health professional or speech therapist if she believes more specialized evaluation is needed. Also, ask her to refer you to a pediatric dentist.

If you are using Medicaid, some service providers do not accept it as insurance. You have several options. One, add children to your private medical policy. Some policies will not let you add children until the adoption is finalized. Two, contact the agency or county from which you are adopting and ask for a special subsidy or contract to cover these costs (often this is difficult to negotiate). Three, ask other parents who adopted older children domestically who they went to for services and make sure they understand that you are using Medicaid. Many have figured out where to go and can be invaluable in helping you find the correct health or mental health service provider.

With intercountry adoptions, have the new pediatrician repeat laboratory tests and do a second comprehensive health screening, even if the child was seen by a physician in his country of origin. Make sure the doctor screens for conditions and diseases prevalent in your child's country of origin.[5] Also, ask the doctor to evaluate your child's chronological age. Birth records provided to adoptive parents in some countries may not be entirely accurate. It may take a year or so for the pediatrician to determine your child's true age.[6]

Children adopted from another country may never have been to a doctor before or had terrible experiences with healthcare personnel; they may be very anxious before their first experience. Before a visit to a doctor in the child's country of origin, ask a translator to explain the purpose of the visit to your child. Once you bring your child home you may still want to have a translator explain what tests and procedures are going to be conducted before the child's first few visits to the new pediatrician.[7] Talk to the pediatrician about your child's anxiety and ask her to be patient and use humor during the visit.

During the initial health screening, your child's doctor may discover previously undetected health problems and discuss any concerns he has about your child's current health. If your child's doctor suspects that your child has a condition or disease that must be confirmed by laboratory tests or further evaluation, ask him what symptoms or behavior you should be watching out for. Find out what symptoms or behavior should be immediately reported to the physician.

THE GENERAL HEALTH OF ADOPTED CHILDREN

Generally, children adopted domestically or internationally are in good physical health but they do exhibit higher rates of certain medical conditions than other children. Matthew D. Bramlett, Laura F. Radel and Stephen J. Blumberg compared health indicators of adopted (at any age) and non-adopted children included in the National Survey of Children's Health conducted in 2003.[8] Overall, they reported adoptees have more health problems, learning disabilities, developmental delays or physical impairments. Adopted children had higher rates of asthma. Children adopted from foster care and adopted internationally were at a greater risk of having been exposed to lead. Both groups of children had more dental problems caused by poor dental hygiene as well as poor nutrition early in life.

While older adoptees usually have more health problems, once adopted they receive more preventive medical care than non-adopted children. Adopted children are more likely than biological children to receive needed mental health care and to receive care in the home; they are more likely to have consistent health insurance coverage and are less likely to live in households in which someone smokes. So while adoptees may have more health-related difficulties, being adopted gives them better access to preventive and remedial health care. Adoptive parents are doing a good job making sure their child's healthcare needs are being met.

The 2007 National Survey of Children's Health, supplemented by a new National Survey of Adoptive Parents, yielded additional information about the physical health of adopted children in the United States. This study followed children adopted at birth, children adopted from another country and children adopted from foster care. The vast majority of the adoptive parents (85 percent) rated their children in very good or excellent physical health. However, 26 percent of adoptive parents compared to 10 percent of non-adoptive parents reported their child had moderate or severe health problems including a learning disability, mental health problem or behavioral disorder (e.g. ADHD). According to the survey, children adopted from foster care had more health problems as compared to those adopted internationally or privately as infants.[9]

Similar to the 2003 findings, the 2007 survey also showed adopted children had more consistent healthcare insurance than non-adopted children. They had similar rates of adequate coverage and adopted children were slightly more likely to receive sensitive, family-focused care.

Having adverse/stressful/traumatic experiences early in life leads to health problems and the more negative experiences a child has, the more risk for problematic health outcomes.[10] However, adoption is a powerful intervention that allows children to recover from early problematic experiences, van IJzendoorn and Juffer report.[11] It does not erase but can mitigate the effects of many negative early experiences.

DEVELOPMENTAL DELAYS

It is well documented that many children adopted from another country who grow up in institutions enter their adoptive families with significant developmental delays. When the children are young, most parents and physicians are attuned to making sure they are assessed for developmental problems. However, if a child is older, developmental delays are often undiagnosed. Since so much of development builds on previously accomplished skills, if a child doesn't build that skill or ability he will have developmental delays. Fortunately, because the children who lived in orphanages are survivors, they can compensate for many delays as they get older. But compensation is not the same as if development happened on schedule and sequentially.

Professionals often miss that older children still have some significant delays. It may not be in gross motor skills—walking, running, jumping, etc.—but it may be in fine motor or language skills. If children do not develop language skills in their first language, they may have problems developing language skills in a second language.

For children adopted from foster care, their developmental delays may have been discovered or missed. Children who were young when entering foster care and lived there for a period of time are at developmental risk, according to Christopher Lloyd and Richard Barth.[12] Also, in sibling groups, the older children may help hide that a younger sibling has some delay. Part of being a sibling is to help out siblings who may be delayed and since the children are always together as a group, a delay in one child may go unnoticed.

Never assume your child is developmentally appropriate. As part of your visits with a pediatrician during the first year, make sure there is an assessment of development. Your child might have developmental delays that could benefit from participation in physical, occupational or language therapy.

Placement stability through adoption and parental commitment are major positive forces in promoting development, but you may need to access services to help your child maximize his or her development, according to Henrietta Bada et al.[13] The sooner you know and the sooner you obtain services, the better the prognosis.

SENSORY PROBLEMS

Children raised in deprived environments have difficulty with processing sensory information—that is, with sight, sound, smell, touch, texture or movement. They can show either under-reactions or over-reactions to sensations.[14]

Two main factors contribute to problems in sensory integration. One is caregiving environments that are deprived of adequate stimulation and result in sensory difficulties. The second is a lack of significant persons to rejoice in the responses of infants/young children and encourage them to continue to explore, according to Sharon Cermak and Victor Groza.[15] While most of the research has focused on children entering families through intercountry adoption, children in foster care share similar experiences and are at risk for sensory problems. Probably the most undiagnosed group of children with sensory problems is children adopted from foster care.

One way this first comes up is around the issue of food. Typically, older children have acquired preferences for specific tastes, textures and smells. If you offer them something they don't know, they might reject it. Not even willing to taste it, they will tell you when they first look at the food that they don't like it. They may have a reaction to new food that is odd or upsetting. Particularly if the adoptive placement is new and when anxiety is already high, they may be unwilling to be adventuresome in their eating.

Some children will come into their adoptive families with terrible eating habits. Unwillingness to eat something new or different is not a behavior problem; it may actually be a sensory problem. The look, the smell or almost anything can lead them to turn away from something you consider healthy and nutritious. You should introduce new foods slowly and patiently.

There are other sensory difficulties like over-reaction to the experience of being touched, avoidance of oral activity such as brushing the teeth, fearfulness or over-reaction to sudden body movement and over-sensitivity to noise, light or sound. For most people, sensory integration occurs automatically, particularly when placed in a loving, stable, committed family. But for some children this is not enough and they need help with sensory integration. Sensory integration problems are often not noticeable, so unless the problem is severe, it may be overlooked or misinterpreted by people not trained in this area.[16] Children with sensory issues have problems with how the brain processes sensory information. Occupational therapy is one professional intervention that helps children with sensory problems. Sensory integration issues are "relatively" minor problems in that they are not life threatening. However, these problems can have a negative impact on the lives of children and their families if ignored and left untreated.

PRECOCIOUS PUBERTY

According to the Mayo Clinic, precocious puberty is when a child's body begins changing into that of an adult (going through puberty) too soon.[17] Puberty that begins before age eight in girls and before age nine in boys is considered precocious puberty. There is some evidence that children who experience extreme deprivation and then are adopted may be at increased risk for precocious puberty. Precocious puberty affects one in five thousand children and is ten times more common in girls, according to Sandra Cesario and Lisa Hughes.[18] Girls adopted from low-resource countries often have early or precocious puberty.[19] If children enter puberty too early, they may grow quickly at first and be tall compared with their peers but then often stop growing earlier than usual. It stunts their growth potential. Also, children who begin puberty long before their peers may be extremely self-conscious about the changes, which can lead to self-esteem problems and mental health difficulties.

There is not clear evidence as to why some children enter puberty early and others from similar situations do not. Older age at adoption increases the risk for premature onset of puberty; both intercountry and domestic adoptees may have precocious puberty, according to Grete Teilmann et al.[20] Jean-Claude Carel and Juliane Leger found that in about half of the cases of precocious pubertal development, pubertal manifestations will regress or stop progressing and no treatment is necessary.[21] Parents need to be aware that this might happen and, if it does, find appropriate resources to help them deal with it.

HEALTH CONCERNS IN INTERNATIONALLY-ADOPTED CHILDREN

Children adopted from countries with underdeveloped healthcare systems most likely did not receive adequate prenatal care and are more likely to have been exposed to pre and post-natal toxins as well as infectious diseases.[22] The CDC recommends that all internationally-adopted children also be screened for HIV, hepatitis, syphilis, tuberculosis, anemia and other infectious or inherited diseases prevalent in certain regions.

Don't assume that your internationally-adopted child is going to have a serious disease or condition. More frequently, they will have a less serious condition that is easily treatable. Children who have spent years in understaffed orphanages may have physical problems related to a lack of exercise or physical activity. Children who have spent too much time in cribs or beds or who do not have adequate space to play and exercise may have muscle or bone problems. Children with such issues may need physical and/or occupational therapy to improve their muscle tone and the range of motion in their joints.

Some children end up in orphanages because they were born with a disabling condition or disease. Either their parents were unable to care for a child with such medical needs or in some cases parents abandon their children, because they are ashamed to have a child with such a condition. They live in a culture where there is a stigma against children with disabilities. Many of the conditions and illnesses children who are adopted from low-resource countries have are easily treatable in countries where modern medicine and surgery are widely available. Adoption can literally save children's lives and offer them futures of hope and promise.

Time is the enemy for many children born with serious diseases or disabilities. In some countries, children with special healthcare needs are moved out of orphanages and into institutions if they are not adopted by a certain age. In these institutions, their conditions will almost certainly grow worse and they are vulnerable to abuse and neglect.[23] Rachel, one mother we spoke to who adopted a girl close to the age of four from a Ukrainian orphanage, said her child would have been sent to an institution for the disabled if she wasn't adopted by the age of five, because she had blindness and epilepsy.

Gayle, another mother we interviewed, adopted three children with her husband: a twenty-month-old from Belarus, a seven-month-old from Guatemala and a six-year-old from Ukraine. The six-year-old was born with arthrogryposis, a rare condition that develops in utero causing a child to have joint stiffening and curvature and/or abnormally developed muscles. Treatment options include physical and occupational therapy, splints and surgery. Gayle described many moments of pain for her child as well as the significant improvement in range of motion and strength she has experienced with treatment. In the following blog posts written by Gayle, note the importance of communication in the relationships and in the parent's ability to help her child:

> *While the boys were out, us girls took a nice long tub together.*
>
> *It also gave me a chance to talk to Sara again.*
>
> *I asked her if the medicine I gave her helped her feel better, she said yes.*
>
> *I asked her if the medicine I gave her was yucky, she said no.*
>
> *I asked her if mommy or daddy got mad at her for hurting, she said no.*
>
> *I asked her if mommy came to get her when I heard she was hurting, she said yes.*
>
> *I asked her if mommy and daddy helped her get better, she said yes.*
>
> *I asked if we let the doctor hurt her, she said no.*
>
> *I asked her if we told her what was going on so she would know, she said yes.*
>
> *I asked her if her feet still hurt, she said no.*
>
> *I asked her if she now understands that mommies and daddies take care of their kids, especially when they hurt, and she very softly said yes.*
>
> *I asked her if mommies and daddies can help their kids' booboos if they don't know about them, she said no.*
>
> *So I tried to wrap it up with a lesson.*
>
> *She hugged me and kissed me and told me she loved me.*
>
> *I could tell she was exhausted, so we all laid down to watch a holiday movie.*

> *Older child adoption is very different from adopting a young child. In some ways it is easier and in some ways it is much harder. It has been harder to bond with Sara, just being honest. She can be very*

moody, she is hard to read, she is so closed up. I had a very hard night last night. I was so sad to realize that we still had so far to go till she really trusts us. I was so hurt that she could not tell me she was hurting, but told pretty much everyone else at school. I thought it was a reflection on us.

These past three weeks have been tough on all of us. I am so glad we are getting past the physical part of it. This pain she has been in has really closed her off to all of us. I just did not see it coming. We tried to explain to her that this would be part of a bigger plan, getting her more mobile. Four months is a long time to a six-year-old and we do understand that. But because she doesn't complain you tend to forget.

Now if we could just get that darn walker so she can get more mobile I think she would feel so much better!

She did sleep well last night and was in a much better mood today. I had her wear slipper boots to school instead of shoes to give her feet a break. She came home happy.

I asked her how her feet were and she said much better. I did check them to make sure the red puffiness was gone and it is!

The kids were so happy to go swimming! This is Sara's first time all in and standing in a long time!!!

I think I finally see the twinkle coming back!

Children adopted from other countries bring some unique health issues to their adoptive families. In addition to their primary pediatrician, families should be working with physicians who have expertise in intercountry adoption to assure their child's healthcare needs are met.

EFFECTS OF MALNUTRITION IN EARLY LIFE

Neglect is the most common form of maltreatment worldwide. It occurs in biological families, in institutions and sometimes in foster family care. In a previous chapter, we discussed adopting a child who experienced neglect. In addition to the psychosocial issues, there are health consequences from experiencing neglect.

Children who were neglected may be malnourished. Once they gain access to food, they may not have developed the internal sensors that let them know when they are full. Children who are not provided with balanced meals and dietary supervision may be at a higher risk of obesity, diabetes and even high blood pressure or heart disease as they age. A physician experienced in treating children will know for which nutritional deficiencies to screen. He will tell you what type of diet is best for your child and which supplements he should be taking.

Learn all you can about your child's eating habits before he comes home. Speak to former foster parents about your child's favorite foods. Speak to the orphanage staff. If your child had a favorite food that is particularly healthy, make sure you keep it well stocked in your home! You may also want to learn how to cook food and dishes your child is used to if he is from a different culture or country.

Talk to your child's pediatrician about his past eating habits and what effects a diet high in sugar or fat may have had on your child. Your child's doctor may recommend that he goes on a specific diet or begins an exercise routine. In subsequent visits to the doctor, talk to her about your child's eating habits at home. Let the doctor know if he is hoarding food or refusing to eat the food you prepare for him. She may offer suggestions to assist you in helping your child improve his eating habits.

Your child should be learning the basics about healthy eating at school but there are ways you can reinforce these lessons. Instill in your child an enjoyment of eating healthy food. Cook healthy meals with your child or create fun vegetable or fruit salad dishes. You might also cultivate a vegetable garden with your child. If you do not have a yard in which to do so, find out where you and your children can get involved in a community garden. It might even be fun for you to host a fresh fruits and vegetables sale at your home or in the community. If you live in an apartment building, find out if your children can set up a vegetable stand right in the lobby!

The long-term consequences of early deprivation and malnutrition are not yet fully understood.[24] There is a growing body of evidence to which parents should pay attention and also inform the medical professionals with whom they are working. It is not something to obsess about but it *is* something to which every parent should pay attention.

ALCOHOL AND DRUG EXPOSURE

Some pregnant mothers use alcohol and other drugs to suppress the pains of hunger. Some use them recreationally before they know they are pregnant. Some use them because they are addicted and unable to stop during pregnancy. The most common drug used during pregnancy is tobacco. Each drug has different effects on the developing fetus. The one that has been most widely studied is alcohol.

Fetal alcohol spectrum disorders (FASD) is a term used to describe a range of problems caused by prenatal exposure to alcohol. FASD includes Fetal Alcohol Syndrome (FAS), Alcohol-Related Neurodevelopmental Disorder (ARND), Alcohol–Related Birth Defects (ARBD) and behavior difficulties assumed to come from prenatal alcohol exposure.[25] Physical FASD can result in birth defects, epilepsy, vision problems, poor muscle control, a lack of coordination, heart defects, problems with other internal organs, dental problems, hearing problems, growth issues and problems with brain development.

FAS is the most serious FASD. Children diagnosed with FAS can have profound physical, neurological, cognitive and growth problems. According to the Centers for Disease Control, children diagnosed with FAS have facial feature abnormalities including wide-set or narrow eyes, growth problems and nervous system issues that may or may not affect the brain structure. Children diagnosed with FAS often exhibit profound delays in cognitive, social and/or emotional functioning.

Your adoption agency may be able to tell you if your child's biological parents had substance abuse problems. If the biological parents did abuse drugs or alcohol, ask if your child was ever evaluated for FASD. Parents adopting internationally are less likely to get accurate information about their child's biological parents' lifestyle choices and health. Some adoptive parents do not know for certain that their child was exposed prenatally to drugs or alcohol but suspect he or she was. If you are worried about prenatal exposure of your child and cannot live without knowing, you may not want to consider intercountry adoption.

FASD problems are manageable with physical and occupational therapies, special education and medication, but FASD is not curable. Children diagnosed with FASD may have profound challenges throughout their lives. If your child has been diagnosed with FASD, stay current with the latest research about treatment, join a support group, visit one of the websites recommended in the appendix of this book and maintain an open dialogue with your child's doctors, therapists, psychiatrist and teachers about how your child is doing.

Children exposed prenatally to illicit or even legal drugs that are harmful to a developing fetus could also exhibit social, emotional, cognitive or physical delays or disabilities as they develop. You may be able to get some information from a domestic adoption agency about the biological mother's history of drug abuse, but the full extent of her problem may not be known.

Researchers have difficulty separating out the effects of neglect, low birth weight, premature birth and other socioeconomic disadvantages from the long-term effects of prenatal drug exposure. The good news is that most researchers believe that careful monitoring by pediatricians and sound parenting practices can help children who have been exposed to drugs prenatally lead healthy lives. Notably, the research studies conducted by Stacy Buckingham-Howes et al have shown that a majority of the children born to cocaine-addicted mothers in the 1980s did not grow up with the profound difficulties that were expected.[26] In fact, as many media reports, including Susan Okie's in *The New York Times*, have illustrated, most of these children have grown up to be productive, happy, functional adults.[27]

In an ideal world, no child is exposed to alcohol, drugs or toxins while in utero or has to live in a family that neglects or abuses him or her. Yet this is reality for thousands of children, including children available for adoption. Our intent in mentioning these problems is not to frighten you, but to make you aware of all the possible difficulties you might encounter. While there is cause for concern, and you deserve information as complete and accurate as you can get, in life there are no guarantees. You might adopt a child who had prenatal alcohol exposure and suffers no effect or you might adopt a child with no known prenatal alcohol exposure who has some difficulties in her life. All you can do is deal with the hand you were dealt and work at creating the best life for you and your family.

CHILDREN WITH SERIOUS ILLNESSES AND CONDITIONS

There are angels who walk among us disguised as parents, who adopt children with serious health conditions and diseases. Some of them may even adopt children whom they know have a short life expectancy but they want to provide the children with as much love as possible during their short time on earth. These parents deserve our utmost respect and admiration.

Children eligible to be adopted may be designated as having special medical needs if they have serious conditions such as HIV, cancer, kidney problems, lung problems, Down Syndrome, blood disorders, muscular disorders, bone deformities or cerebral palsy. Families who adopt children with special medical needs often receive additional public subsidies. They may also be able to receive financial and other support from private organizations that specialize in helping families care for sick children at home or that support families that adopt children with special medical needs. (See the appendix for a list of organizations that may be able to help you.)

CHAPTER 17

Development and Learning

Trauma from abuse, neglect or institutionalization can have a profound impact on a child's cognitive, emotional and social development, as can prenatal exposure to toxins such as drugs or alcohol. Trauma and developmental delays can impact learning. Frequent changes in school settings may also impede a foster child's ability to focus at school and socialize with a consistent group of peers. Parents of older adopted children need to be aware of the effects of early trauma, school changes and prenatal toxic exposure on their children's development and ability to learn. Evidence-based interventions can help a child heal from trauma, positively impact development and enhance a child's learning ability. Obtain developmental and academic evaluations and appropriate services for your child early. Placement stability through adoption and parental commitment are major positive forces in promoting development and learning but your child may need professional services to help him reach his full potential.

IMPACTS OF EARLY MALTREATMENT ON DEVELOPMENT AND LEARNING

According to researchers Ann M. Easterbrooks, Jean-Francois Bureau and Karlen Lyons-Ruth, early neglect and trauma can adversely affect a child's social, cognitive and emotional development.[1] Examples of emotional neglect include when a baby cries and no one responds or when a child asks for help and no one answers. While early emotional neglect, inattention or under-stimulation are often associated with orphanages or other types of institutional settings, this type of neglect also occurs in homes. Examples of physical neglect of a child include not being fed, being left in dirty diapers or not being allowed to move about freely. All too often, children suffer from both emotional and physical neglect. Severe neglect can be devastating to a child's development.

Social and emotional (SE) development are inextricably linked and rooted, in part, in the interaction between caregiver and child during the earliest part of life. Rahil D. Briggs and associates found that caregiver-child interaction, specifically reliable and consistent emotional responsiveness, plays a large part in the SE competency of children.[2] The ability to appraise and manage emotions is greatly affected by the extent to which there was appropriate, sufficient and positive face-to-face interaction with a primary caregiver. The emergence of language development and formation of emotional competencies begins with the caregiver's emotional responsiveness to the infant. This is where nuances such as eye contact and facial expressiveness begin to imprint on an infant's brain to help him or her recognize and understand emotions and communication—both verbal and nonverbal. SE skills are so critical to an individual's success in life that the most effective preschool programs include a strong SE curriculum.

Children who have experienced neglect are at a higher risk of cognitive, social and emotional delays. Jack P. Shonkoff, renowned professor of Child Health and Development at Harvard University, and Susan N. Bales said emotional neglect can actually change the way the neural pathways of the brain are networked.[3] Emotional neglect may impact many areas of functioning, including social competencies, language development, emotion regulation and cognitive development. Children who have experienced neglect may have difficulty deciphering facial expressions, developing empathy, reading emotional signals and relating to others, noted Seth Pollak and associates.[4]

Children who have experienced abuse and other traumatic experiences may become hypervigilant (a heightened state of alertness) in response to repeated stress and fear. The central nervous system may be more easily aroused, triggering the fight or flight response, in which case the child may perceive a threat where there is none. In the classroom, a hypervigilant child may be missing out on learning critical information due to this heightened arousal state, being "on guard" and watchful of threats. The child is more apt to notice negative facial expressions and emotions while missing positive emotions, as well as misinterpreting social cues. For example, a child may not respond to humor appropriately or may misread nonverbal gestures. As a result, there can be confusion, frustration, conflict and overall disenchantment with social relations and school involvement, having little to do with actual academics.

When the brain is preoccupied with fears and concerns about safety, even when those threats are no longer present, this can take up cognitive resources and limit the child's ability to focus, attend to new information long enough to store in short-term memory, access stored long-term information or perform well on challenging cognitive tasks. On the surface, certain issues can be confused with learning disabilities, when in fact there is a psychological issue. Parsing out differences may require a specialist who can properly assess your child. Any time you observe a pattern of concern in learning or any area of functioning and you have attempted different strategies at home, it may help to get an evaluation. Children can benefit from counseling or educational services. When in doubt, talk to a professional.

There are several important factors to consider as you look at the consequences of exposure to neglect or abuse. First is the age at which the maltreatment first occurred; usually earlier exposure has a more negative impact. Second is the duration of exposure: a one-time incident usually has a different impact from something that occurs over a long period of time. Third is the severity of the mistreatment. All of this must also be considered in the context of the temperament of the child. Some children are affected greatly by very minor incidents while others seem to tolerate a great deal without long-lasting negative effects. It is important to think about your child's degree of resilience or vulnerability to adverse experiences as you consider professional and parental interventions.

DEVELOPMENTAL AGE

Parents and educators must not rely solely on the child's chronological age when making decisions about behavior, development and ability. The child may have a different "developmental age." For example, a five-year-old may act and play more like a toddler. A nine-year-old may have the social skills of a four-year-old. A child's history of trauma, including abuse and neglect, may have frozen her development at a specific point in time. Skills acquired at a certain age during the period of a major traumatic event in the life of the child may have to be relearned or the child may need help advancing to the next stage of social or emotional development. When parenting children, take into consideration the developmental and emotional age of the child rather than targeting chronological age.

As previously noted, many children who grow up in orphanages have significant developmental delays. In older children, these delays are often undiagnosed. For instance, children who did not develop language skills in their first language may have problems with their second.

Barbara discussed the frustrating experience of not realizing that the problems her adopted children were experiencing were a result of incongruence between chronological and developmental age:

I wish that I had been told our boys' developmental ages and that I should treat them as that age even though they might protest or it might seem silly—even if they seemed to act like their bio ages. It was after almost a year that they were with us that I was told that our then four-and-a-half-year-old was developmentally at eighteen to twenty-four months! Had I been told from the beginning to play peek-a-boo, give infant massage, cuddle him like a baby, feed him, etc., we might be much more ahead managing their developmental issues than we are.

I wish that I had understood the differences between our two boys, realizing now how affected our youngest was by not having any mother figure for the most important first two-and-a-half years of life. He had no one to bond to and trust and he is in major catch-up mode. This affects his ability to understand others verbally and non-verbally, to manage his emotions, to maintain any sense of calm, to play, eat, be independent. Our older son had someone taking care of him for his first years and he manages relationships with others in a fairly typical way.

More has to be noted about neglect and should be as important as reports of abuse. Abuse is typically the scarier word and is reported upon, but neglect may be worse as it strips away the foundation for psychological, physical and intellectual growth. My youngest began retaining memories at about six and a half years. He still has problems remembering names and numbers even as he repeats kindergarten.

It is best not to assume that your adopted child's developmental abilities match her chronological age. As part of your initial visits with a pediatrician, be sure to obtain an assessment of development to find out whether your child is behaving according to her age or whether there are developmental delays. Your child may benefit from intervention services in the areas of physical, occupational, speech or mental health therapy.

CHILDREN'S BELIEFS ABOUT THEIR OWN INTELLIGENCE

Learning is closely related to development. The ability to learn and acquire information is about much more than a set amount of intelligence that people are "born with." The process of acquiring and applying knowledge is influenced by biological, social, emotional and physical development. An individual's genetic predisposition, combined with prenatal exposures and the postnatal environment (e.g., family dynamics and societal influences), affects development and development affects how a child interacts with his or her environment, according to renowned psychologist Urie Bronfenbrenner and Stephen J Ceci.[5] Disrupted development is a risk factor for academic issues but academic problems are not inevitable. Often children simply lose faith in their ability to perform academically, developing a self-defeating attitude when it comes to school.

According to leading social psychology researcher Carol Dweck, professor of psychology at Stanford University, the way children think about their abilities or intelligence (implicit assumptions or "self-theories") can dictate to what extent they are able to overcome fears of failing and triumph through academic difficulties or other cognitive tasks.[6]

Children who believe that intelligence and ability are *malleable* or flexible (able to be changed and grow) have far greater success in their lives compared to those who possess a self-theory that intelligence and ability are *fixed* (not changeable). Children with a malleable orientation are more likely to persist in the face of failure; they keep trying and don't give up as easily. This mindset leads to mastery learning.

Children with a fixed orientation tend to believe that people's intelligence or ability is limited to what they are born with, for example, believing they are "not good in math." This fixed mindset lends itself to giving up when encountering difficulties. Failure is perceived as a weakness or indicator that the task is above the individual's abilities, whereas a child with a flexible mindset sees failure as a challenge to keep trying and perceives mistakes as part of the learning process.

When observing your child performing a particular task (e.g., a school project, sport, practicing an instrument), offer feedback to encourage the actions they are taking to master the task ("You've been practicing your clarinet a lot and I can hear improvement. Keep it up!" or "I like how you kept trying until you figured out how to solve the problem!"). Dr. Dweck cuations against praising children for their intelligence rather than process and mastery. It is crucial to be specific. "Praise the process, not the person," which is to say, focus on the effort, determination, persistence and improvement, not the child's general ability (avoid generalizations, such as "Good job," which doesn't specify anything about how the child is learning).[7] By targeting feedback toward specific efforts or specific tasks and encouraging persistence, parents can help children learn to make the connection between the amount of effort exerted and the amount of learning achieved.

Cultivate and encourage a growth mindset by demonstrating and reinforcing the idea that competency can be developed and that discipline leads to productive effort. In academic success, self-discipline matters twice as much as intelligence, according to Angela L. Duckworth and esteemed psychologist Martin E. P. Seligman.[8] Lack of self-discipline is a major reason for underachievement and falling short of one's potential and it is suspected that self-discipline matters more than the kind of teacher a student has, the textbook and the class environment.[9]

Children with increased levels of resilience are ultimately better equipped to focus on learning and they have amassed the resources to persist through cognitive challenges. Resilient children bounce back quicker after setbacks. When their self-esteem takes a hit, they believe they can overcome difficulties. From the moment children wake up they are being challenged in many ways—cognitively, physically, emotionally, socially. The more of these strengths they possess, the better the chance they will make it through the day feeling hopeful. Fostering resilience in children is an ongoing and involved process that becomes part of daily functioning and can be evident in the way a parent discusses challenges with the child, how a parent responds to the child's perceived or real barriers and how a parent serves as a liaison with the school and other services. Building resilience becomes part of the whole parenting package.

SCHOOL INTERVENTIONS

Make an effort to understand the type of educational experiences your child had prior to being adopted. Children adopted from another country may not have had the best educational preparation. Institutions vary widely both within a country and between countries. According to Emily C. Merz and associates, one way to classify them is socially depriving vs. globally depriving.[10] In socially-depriving institutions, there is a lack of individual interaction. Individual efforts to learn are not rewarded or noticed. Because there is no individual attention, learning gaps are not identified. The group experience is the basis for living, with no emphasis on the individual. In globally-depriving institutions, there is not even educational programming. In these settings, you can expect delays in learning and children from these settings may be more prone to learning difficulties as the learning experience starts late. Regardless of the type of institution, any experience in institutional living places children at risk for learning problems, according to The Bucharest Early Intervention Project's study on the impact of neglect.[11]

Children who grow up in foster care may have experienced multiple moves to different families and between schools. There are now laws in place to help child welfare agencies access the educational records of children in their care.[12] The goal of these new laws is to improve educational outcomes for children in foster care. Adoptive parents should speak to their adoption caseworker about their child's school records and what is known about the child's educational successes and challenges.

According to well-respected neuroscientist Charles A Nelson III et al, children who are moved from an institutional placement into foster care experience cognitive gains, yet children in foster care still exhibit a high degree of academic problems.[13] Fortunately, once adopted, children tend to perform at or above average in reading or math.[14] Regardless of a child's level of academic functioning, forming an alliance with the school and other sources of support will increase chances for school success.

Caring teachers and a supportive school environment can lessen or alleviate the effects of early trauma adversity and improve outcomes for learning and development. It is important to establish developmentally appropriate (not necessarily age-matched) academic goals to achieve realistic outcomes. Effective educational programs aim to teach children within prominent Russian psychologist Lev Vygotsky's "Zone of Proximal Development," which is the optimal range of learning potential (not too easy, not too difficult).[15] However, in typical classrooms, teachers are not able to teach every child at his or her optimal range of learning. Thus, children who are not sufficiently challenged or are overly challenged are at risk of failing from boredom or frustration.

Scaffolding is a technique to guide the learner to achieve optimal learning with strategic support to help the child overcome challenges. Over time, the "scaffolds" are removed as the child's competency increases.

Parents and teachers should maintain open communication about the child's school performance and functioning. It is not uncommon for children to receive rave reviews from their teachers yet exhibit problems at home or vice versa. When parents and teachers are in regular communication about the child's school experience, problems can be prevented or remedied before they escalate. Bring in additional preventive or remedial services as needed.

Academic outcomes are not necessarily independent of peer experiences and actually have been found to be linked. A child who is ostracized does not fare well and peer rejection is associated with educational underachievement, according to Michael M. Criss and colleagues.[16] Being in tune with your child's school experiences is necessary for his or her success. Children are not always eager to tell parents about problems at school; therefore, it is a parent's responsibility to find out by maintaining an open dialogue with the child, teachers and relevant school staff. Part of this alliance includes attending parent-teacher conferences and becoming involved. Parent participation is a predictor of a child's success in school, according to respected developmental psychologist Urie Bronfenbrenner.[17]

Children who experience significant social delays or challenges connecting with peers may benefit from extra services, such as social skills training (SST) sessions to help them build skills and gain confidence or cognitive-behavioral therapy (CBT). Talk with professionals at school to learn about available assessments (e.g., Thomas M. Achenbach's Child Behavior Checklist) if more information is needed about specific areas of concern.[18]

For instance, when starting your child at a new school, take steps to prepare him mentally by making early introductions with teachers and staff. Find out about orientation programs if there is an opportunity to gradually introduce your child to the school. When that is not possible, for instance when school is already in session, talk with school personnel, including any specialists, and discuss your plans, goals and any concerns you or your child might have and seek other opportunities to lessen the stress and increase chances for success.

OBTAINING INDIVIDUALIZED SERVICES

Navigating the terrain of educational and specialized services can be a daunting task for parents. You may find yourself becoming immersed in knowledge of the school's policies, student and family rights, state and federal laws and regulations and protocols for obtaining services. Whether your child has been referred for services or you identified an area of concern, you will want to learn as much as possible to provide your child with the most effective services and best possible outcomes. All parents would like the process of obtaining services to go smoothly. When it doesn't, parents must be strong advocates for their children and learn as much as possible to achieve a successful outcome.

Listed below are just a few of the many possible areas of discussion related to your child's individual needs. This is not comprehensive by any means, nor does it pertain specifically to adopted children. It is simply a snapshot of topics that may warrant discussions between parents, teachers, school administrators, service providers or others:

- Learning issues
- Behavioral issues
- Classroom strategies
- Special accommodations
- IEP (Individualized Education Program)
- Academic or social support
- Tests and evaluations
- Special education services
- ESL (English as a Second Language)
- Inclusion
- Supplementary aids
- Assistive technology
- Roles and responsibilities
- Progress reports
- Extended school year
- Transitions
- Retention
- Implementation of services

When school districts oversee the process of providing special services to eligible students, there are set procedures such as the implementation of an IEP (Individualized Education Program). In public schools, for children in kindergarten and above, an IEP is created to document special needs and services beyond typical classroom practices, such as special education and therapies. The IEP is a customized plan for the child and all of those who are involved in the decision-making process and carrying out the plan. It includes a history of the child's development, parent reports, progress reports, test results, evaluations and anything else relevant to the plan. In addition to the parent and child, the team may consist of teachers, service providers and school administrators. Parents are expected to attend all meetings.

Evaluations are conducted through the school district or external providers to determine needs. IEP meetings are held to discuss specifics and to form an action plan. Criteria have to be met for students to be eligible to receive services at no cost to the family. Typical services include speech therapy, occupational therapy, physical therapy, mental health therapy and special education services. Families who are declined can appeal the decision, seek services out-of-pocket on their own or check with their private healthcare insurance for coverage.

Parents can initiate the process for obtaining services or the school might offer a recommendation based on teacher feedback or standardized testing. Examples include speech therapy for expressive or receptive language delays, physical therapy for gross motor delays, mental health services for disruptive behavioral problems or occupational therapy for weak fine motor skills. In instances where there is a clear need for services, the process tends to progress more smoothly (though speed and ease vary based on school districts and the paperwork pipeline). Typically, a referral is made, parents provide permission for formal assessments, then the child's levels of functioning are formally measured and documented. If the results show the child meets at least the minimal criteria to receive services, the paperwork and meetings are more of a formality. Parents monitor progress, but they don't necessarily have to "fight" for their child to receive services. Problems may still arise, such as issues with the quality, duration or consistency or services; however, the initial process itself tends to be more straightforward when it appears obvious that a child would benefit from services.

Whereas certain developmental issues are clear-cut, others are not so apparent. Parents (or teachers) may have valid concerns and proceed to request an evaluation for services. It is possible that a child falls under the radar of the set criteria while still displaying concerning behaviors or symptoms. However, if the child's level of functioning does not meet the criteria for services through assessments administered by the school, a parent may want to request external evaluations. Parents may observe a mild concern and request services as a preventive measure but, unfortunately, public funds are typically not available for preventive purposes. It's also possible that a parent's requests for initial or continued services are met with resistance due to policies, regulations, limited funding, the district's excessive caseload or incompetence. Whatever the reason, there are occasions when parents have to work harder to obtain services for their child. In those instances, it will be beneficial for the parents to formulate a solid plan with clear goals and objectives.

Listed here are some proven strategies to increase your chances of a successful outcome as you advocate for your child:

- Before meeting with anyone, formulate a plan that helps you organize your thoughts about the issue and how to proceed. Do research, if necessary, and gather your thoughts. Have notes in front of you for the phone call or meeting.
- Consider these elements proposed by Pamela and Pete Wright as you organize your plan: your vision, mission, goals, strategies and timelines.[19]
- Become educated about the specific topics, procedures, processes and regulations in your school district.
- Maintain an organized record-keeping system where you can file documents and refer back for correspondence, action steps, progress and any other important details.
- Keep a record of contacts and relevant facts such as dates, times, names, discussion points and action plans.
- Follow up with anyone you have not heard back from in a reasonable amount of time (ask up front about when to expect responses, decisions, services, etc.).
- Try to remain calm when emotions get heightened.

- Practice effective skills in communication, conflict resolution, decision-making and collaboration.
- Bring a helpful person with you for emotional support or knowledge so you can be more confident and relaxed at meetings.
- Never assume there is a "meeting of the minds" where everyone understands each other precisely. To ensure accuracy and follow-through, reflect and summarize key points during meetings and discussions, then follow up afterward in writing as a reminder of the key points and action plan.

Students and their families have a right to equal education opportunities and to receive services for unique or special needs. Federal laws dictate standards and regulations of educational practice and protections, though states and school districts may vary in specific criteria and procedures. Becoming acquainted with the school's policies, student and family rights, relevant state and federal regulations or laws and school district procedures and processes can help you navigate the hurdles. Learn the jargon and acronyms so that you can understand the terms being used and talk with those involved to develop realistic expectations.

Parents can find an abundance of information online and elsewhere on advocacy, legal issues and the educational system. The US Department of Education provides a great deal of information, such as the "Individuals with Disabilities Education Act" (IDEA) guide.[20] There you can find a chapter on IEP regulations among numerous other topics, such as procedures for determining learning disabilities. Concerns about the privacy of educational records can be found in the Family Educational Rights and Privacy Act (FERPA).[21] Private entities also offer assistance and guidance. For instance, WrightsLaw offers books, online resources, services and referrals.[22] Parent support services and forums may be available online or in your community.

As your child's best advocate, preparing yourself with relevant knowledge about your child's needs and arming yourself with effective strategies will improve your chances of preempting problems and addressing difficulties effectively as they arise.

EXTERNAL SERVICES

When your child's academic and learning difficulties have become too complicated to resolve at home or in the schools, you should seek outside support. There is a variety of services available for learning and academics, from the widely known franchises to an individual provider. The key is to become informed and have your child properly assessed. You might begin with the school or primary care doctor, perhaps get a referral for a psychologist, neuropsychologist or other relevant specialist depending on your areas of concern. There are numerous providers that could be helpful (speech, OT, PT, mental health, etc.) depending on the nature of the problem.

CHAPTER 18

Parenting Methods to Build Your Child's Resilience and Enhance Behavioral Functioning

There are proven strategies to build upon your child's strengths and consider their efforts, persistence and ways to overcome obstacles. Parents are a child's emotional "scaffold" and primary source of support during challenging times.

Provide your children with developmentally-appropriate activities to help them strive toward attainable goals. This will help develop their self-confidence. Give children opportunities where they can feel empowered to take initiative and engage in fulfilling activities that build self-efficacy (belief in oneself). Examples include horseback riding, karate, team sports, dance and art. Reinforce their mastery efforts and offer feedback. Focus on positive behaviors in order to encourage optimal functioning at home and use effective strategies for achieving target behaviors, recommends Alan E. Kazdin, world-renowned clinical child psychologist, professor of Psychology and Child Psychiatry at Yale University and director of the Yale Parenting Center.[1]

Nurturing a child's learning and development entails a multifaceted approach, and it begins with the parent-child relationship. Be involved with the school and supportive of any other contexts in which your child becomes involved (church, community, sports). Your enthusiasm toward your child's efforts will show how much you care.

As noted earlier, children with healthy social-emotional skills and a resilient mindset fare better in life. The confidence they experience and build within themselves serves as a buffer to the adversity faced at school and in life. Similarly, parenting styles that focus on strengths and positive behaviors are more likely to set up children for success. Effective "positive parenting" styles promote a healthy, secure attachment between child and parent, have a high rate of success and reduce parenting stress. The opposite is true of punitive methods which increase aggression, have a high failure rate, increase parental stress and deteriorate the parent-child bond.

LOCUS OF CONTROL

There are two types of perceived control: internal and external. Those who feel they possess an internal *locus of control* (LC) are more inclined to find fulfillment and satisfaction in life. They focus on the things they have control over and attribute positive outcomes to their actions. An external LC refers to the belief that we have an inadequate amount of control in our lives and a feeling of powerlessness. While it may be entirely appropriate for a child to feel an external LC when he has little or no effect on his or her existence, this perspective yields poorer psychological outcomes.

The loss of parents, separation anxiety and stress of parental absence and the ambiguity of a new living environment can make a child vulnerable to negative outcomes and a sense of powerlessness. Living in an institution or in the foster care system places children at the mercy of those in charge and may leave them feeling that they have little or no control over their circumstances.

Children who possess a greater amount of psychological resilience may perceive themselves to have some degree of control even when there is very little. Either through their imagination or in small meaningful ways, they affect change, such as through interactions with others, for example by making someone laugh or learning a new skill. However, the trauma they experience can decrease their resilience and sense of control over events. Older children waiting to be adopted, particularly those who have endured lengthy delays or experienced multiple failed placements, may struggle with the lack of control in their lives.

Being active participants in our own lives is an important part of living a fulfilling and healthy existence. An internal locus of control drives us to achieve, accomplish and take actions toward our goals. Children who lack a feeling of control over their lives begin to feel helpless. Parents and others in the child's life can do specific things to help the child develop an internal locus of control. Provide the child with opportunities for choices throughout the day. For younger children this may be as simple as offering a choice between wearing a red or blue shirt to school, then a choice between eggs or cereal for breakfast, what music to listen to in the car, etc. For older children, decisions can be presented in more complex and meaningful ways. For example, you might ask your teenager to choose from a list of dinner options, school activities, friends to visit or vacation destinations. More opportunities for making choices give children control in their lives. This approach may also reduce power struggles. It helps children who already present oppositional behaviors or severe behavior problems; however, in these cases, it is best to discuss effective strategies as part of an overall behavior plan.

LEARNED HELPLESSNESS

Achieving goals involves motivation to perform the task, volition to follow through and the belief that one can do the work (self-efficacy). Children who have repeatedly experienced disappointments, abuse, neglect or betrayal may have been unwittingly conditioned to give up when facing a new challenge at school or at home. They may feel a sense of loss of control in their lives (external locus of control). The idea proposed by Martin E.P. Seligman and associates that "nothing I do matters" best sums up learned helplessness (LH) and also exemplifies the kind of affect that accompanies depression.[2] To combat LH and feelings of inadequacy or pessimism, it is important to promote skills that demonstrate optimistic thinking and resilience (see the next section). We need to understand what LH is and how it looks before we can reverse it.

Unlike a tantrum or outburst, where the child is showing an overt emotion, children who exhibit learned helplessness (not a diagnosis, but rather a constellation of symptoms) tend to shut down emotionally and relinquish their control to outside forces. Perhaps they have lost interest in activities for which they previously expressed enthusiasm. Feelings of despair, loss of hope, grief, anger, sadness and guilt may be at the core of LH, and while some children act out and externalize their anger by displaying aggression, others internalize it and turn their pain inward on themselves. Typically, LH children may appear lethargic, socially withdrawn or depressed.

Adopted children's early experiences can put them at greater risk of LH in a variety of ways. Neglected children may come to feel that their voices do not matter; therefore, they may be inclined not to speak up to have their needs met and to avoid sharing opinions. Abused children may have come to learn that speaking up results in violence or punishment, so they shut down for their own protection. Multiple failed placements can deplete the child of hope or motivation about the future. Children who believe that the people in their lives repeatedly give up on them may also give up on themselves.

A belief that things will not improve can lead to self-defeating behaviors and maladaptive ways of coping; for instance, externalizing behaviors, blaming others and task avoidance can lead to a cycle of failure and even contribute to learning disorders. These self-preservation responses made sense when children were forced to find ways to cope as a function of their dysfunctional environments. They might have learned that trying hard and playing by the rules does not necessarily result in fair outcomes.

Once children are placed into a healthy, functioning home with emotionally responsive parents, they need to relearn beliefs and expected behaviors. This process may not be easy, and typically children are unaware of these dynamics. What appears to be a behavior problem might simply be a learned response to the previous way of functioning prior to placement. Even when former "coping" methods no longer work for their new environment, children may not be aware of the distinction and they might not know how else to function. Parents and schools can help children adjust and acclimate to their new environments by setting

limits, explaining rules, responding consistently, demonstrating empathy and warmth and becoming predictable. It may take a while for some
children to believe that things have improved, so do not be surprised if
your efforts are met with resistance or disbelief. There might be a lot of
thinking to "undo."

The beliefs and behaviors that represent LH may signify a deeper
issue such as depression; therefore, further evaluation may be needed.
Regardless, it will benefit the child to promote resilience. Learned helplessness can be reversed by learned optimism.[3] Teaching children the skills
of optimism, bolstering resilience and encouraging mastery learning will
help combat feelings of learned helplessness.[4]

PROMOTING RESILIENCE AND PROTECTIVE FACTORS

In general, taking a preventive approach (e.g., building resiliency) will
serve as a buffer to risk factors. In this regard, give children as many
developmentally-appropriate opportunities as possible to exercise control and take action. By demonstrating a belief in our children's abilities,
we cultivate resilience.

Psychological resilience is the flipside of learned helplessness. It has
been defined in various ways, but most commonly it refers to an individual's ability to overcome challenges despite adversities. The concept
applies to all children, not just those at risk, as defined by Suniya S. Luthar
et al.[5] Resilience is about the child's ability to cope with everyday challenges in an effective way. Those challenges may include getting along with
friends, working with others cooperatively on academic tasks, dealing
with setbacks, bouncing back from disappointments and unmet expectations, accepting influence from parents and coping with trauma or any
degree of stress. Children who are encouraged to find ways to solve problems effectively are better able to manage life's challenges.

Children are born with varying degrees of resilience and vulnerability
to adverse conditions. For children awaiting adoption, the very experience
of being separated from their parents and home tends to be traumatic.
Other pre-adoptive risk factors may include poverty, maltreatment, injury
and illness, social deprivation, repeated traumatic events, grief and loss.
These stressors have a cumulative effect, cognitive-behavioral therapy

pioneer Donald Meichenbaum postulates.[6] As the risk factors pile up over time, children may become less capable of coping and the accumulation puts them at risk of chronic trauma. Without adequate emotional support, children will be at risk. Bolstering resilience can help a vulnerable child survive or a resilient child to thrive.[7] Avenues to resilience include developing specific skills in optimism and empathy or the constructed narrative (story) the child tells himself in the aftermath of trauma.[8]

According to the Administration on Children, Youth and Families, "protective factors are conditions or attributes in individuals, families, communities or the larger society that, when present, mitigate or eliminate risk in families and communities and that, when present, increase the health and well-being of children and families."[9] Protective factors can be infused into the child's life in a number of ways to buffer the effects of adversity.

In addition to having parents and family who care about them, other protective factors for children include a positive school environment, community support, extended family and relatives who are invested in the child's well-being and other sources of social support such as team sports, extracurricular activities and positive peer relations. Anyone in the child's life can serve as a protective factor. Those who spend the most time with the child on a regular basis, such as teachers and parents, will have more opportunities to boost a child's resilience and create opportunities for success. Simply providing an empathic response and individualized support buffers children from the effects of failure and helps them cope. Distant supportive members of the child's network—those who have sporadic contact—also can make a positive difference.

AUTHORITATIVE PARENTING

One effective style of parenting is *authoritative parenting*, which focuses on balancing warmth and setting firm limits in a consistent manner. This evidence-based approach acknowledges the parent-child relationship as reciprocal, not equal. The authoritative style proposed by clinical and developmental psychologist Diana Baumrind views child-rearing as a form of education. It respects the child as an individual with his or her own ideas and a certain amount of freedom, yet needing structure and clear boundaries.[10]

Unlike a top-down approach, where the parent expects blind compliance and obedience, the authoritative parent modifies expectations based upon a child's characteristics and uniqueness, such as resilience, developmental variations and temperament.[11] Therefore, the style entails a certain amount of flexibility on the parents' part; however, it is not a permissive or "laissez faire" approach. Parents using this approach seek to build their children's strengths while managing behavior.

While there is no "one-size-fits-all" approach, authoritative parenting is one of the more effective styles that emphasizes a developmentally-appropriate strategy, allows children to exert some influence and control and sets limits while preserving the emotional bond. When a parent is met with opposition, he or she acknowledges the child's position but adheres to the request or consequences. Consistent parenting teaches the child what to expect and makes the parent predictable. This is especially important for children who have experienced trauma and inconsistency.

EMOTION COACHING

Another evidence-based style of parenting is *emotion coaching*, developed by John Gottman and Joan DeClaire.[12] This style is empathy-based and designed to nurture a positive parent-child relationship, develop resilience and foster emotionally intelligent children. There is an undercurrent of respect and reciprocity, similar to the other positive parenting methods discussed elsewhere in this chapter. Emotion coaching is about acknowledging your child's emotions and being okay with the negative ones but still setting limits on behaviors (e.g., "It's okay to feel angry, but we don't throw things.").

Parents tend to expect a lot from their children—the way they think and behave, what they value and believe, how they express their emotions and their choices about future goals. These are quite common expectations. No parent would decline fewer tantrums, less opposition, more compliance and enhanced skills all around. However, simply training children to be obedient will not achieve the complex goals we set for our children. If parents strive to give their children the greatest chance for success in life, first they need to be realistic about their child's development. Second, they need to consider what goes into developing emotional regulation, self-confidence, compassion toward others and carving out a purposeful and meaningful life—all of these have been identified as outcomes of the emotion coaching method.[13]

Emotion coaching (EC) takes advantage of the many moments where children are expressing heightened emotions and provides parents with the tools to connect with children during those times to influence how children perceive and manage their emotions. In EC, parent-child interaction is based upon a foundation of empathy. Parents teach their child, through modeling and strategically responding to their child's emotions, the essential skills that promote positive social and emotional development.

A connected parent-child relationship is the core of EC. There are many benefits shown in emotion-coached children. They do better academically, behaviorally, socially and emotionally, show greater self-motivation, have fewer infectious illnesses due to a better immune system and display more resilience.

John Gottman and Joan DeClaire proposed five key steps toward developing emotionally-intelligent children.[14] Keep in mind that as you help your child work through his or her emotions, resist the temptation to complete the steps for him or her. You will be a supportive "coach" and guide your child in developmentally appropriate ways (according to developmental level of comprehension and ability) to do each step. The steps are:

The Five Key Steps to Emotion Coaching

1. Become aware of the child's emotions—this requires parents to understand their own emotions and increase their awareness and comfort level with those emotions so they can serve as nonjudgmental coaches.
2. Recognize emotional expression as an opportunity for intimacy and teaching—parents use empathy and modeling to convey to their

child that negative emotions are acceptable and not threats to their authority, nor something they (parents) have to fix or deny. Parents act as their child's ally, helping him navigate challenging emotions together.

3. Listen empathetically and validate a child's feelings—observe your child and take his perspective to understand his emotional state. Listen, reflect on what is heard and be empathic. Try to avoid probing and asking questions to which you already know the answer. Be cautious about damaging your child's trust in you by the way you talk or behave. Even if you do not agree with your child's emotional reaction to a situation, accept his emotions and don't make him deny them.

4. Help your child find words to label his emotions—offer supportive help in identifying and labeling your child's feelings without telling your child how he should feel. When reflecting emotional labels, offer specifics and don't be surprised if your child is experiencing contradictory emotions.

5. Set limits while helping your child solve the problem—this final step has five components:

    5.1. Set limits on your child's behaviors. Children need to know that it's okay to have negative emotions. We are allowed to feel bad but we are not allowed to hit, throw, break, punch, etc. Accept her emotions. Your child is entitled to her feelings. Encourage her to verbalize her feelings but establish boundaries on behaviors that are not appropriate (e.g., "You can be angry, but you can't hit.").

    5.2. Identify goals. Seek to understand your child's goals and help her articulate her needs. Give her emotional support as she explores what is going on behind her feelings.

    5.3. Think of possible solutions—empower your child to come up with solutions and try to resist coming up with all the answers. You're teaching her to problem-solve.

    5.4. Evaluate the proposed solutions based on your family's values— help her think about which ideas might work best.

    5.5. Help your child choose a solution—encourage her to make a choice.

THE KAZDIN METHOD

The Kazdin Method is an evidence-based approach to parenting and child behavior management devised by Alan Kazdin, which focuses on building positive behaviors and improving parent-child interaction. A central theme is to "catch your child being good" or, in other words, pay attention to the good behaviors and enthusiastically reinforce those behaviors rather than waiting for a problem. This strength-based approach may seem counterintuitive at first, since as parents we tend to naturally focus on problem behaviors. However, sometimes the most effective method is not the one that feels intuitive.[15]

Whether dealing with everyday, normal behaviors and challenges or more severe behaviors, The Kazdin Method (KM) can be implemented as a whole package or applied to specific target behaviors. The tools and concepts are designed to encourage a healthy parent-child relationship and secure attachment, build and maintain pro-social behaviors and prevent or treat problem behaviors. This system also fits well with other "positive parenting" approaches, such as Diane Baumrind's Authoritative Parenting style and Gottman's Emotion Coaching.[16] KM is a good fit for a wide range of behaviors, such as whining, yelling, tantrums, difficulty with transitions, noncompliance, aggression, sibling conflicts, hitting, vandalism, stealing, etc. Built into KM are protective factors and resilience: supportive parenting, control over choices, developing empathy and encouraging effective problem solving. Given the utilitarian nature of these techniques, we will provide details to help you get started.

The main techniques are designed to prompt and shape behaviors, build compliance throughout the day and reinforce positive interaction through consistent and precise methods. While not complicated, the techniques do require some practice, just like any new skill, until they become automatic.

Some of the main features of KM are as follows:

1. Effective *praise* increases desired behaviors.
2. Effective *prompting* elicits desired behaviors that the child is not initiating or that don't occur naturally.
3. *Practice* the desired behaviors.

4. The *ABCs* of shaping:
   A = Antecedent: this is what occurs prior to the behavior, for example, when you prompt the behavior by making a specific request
   or by establishing nonverbal setting events that cue the behavior
   (e.g., dim the lights to indicate bedtime routine),
   B = Behavior: the desired behavior
   C = Consequence: this is what follows the behavior, such as praise.
5. Reward with point charts to systematically and strategically shape
   desired behaviors.

Highlights of the main principles and techniques are:

EFFECTIVE PRAISE is composed of three main elements:
1. Enthusiasm—when your child performs the behavior, you use an
   excited voice and facial expressions like a cheerleader to show your
   verbal and nonverbal enthusiasm immediately after the behavior is
   performed.
2. Specificity—What behavior are you targeting? Praise the exact behavior using words that describe that specific behavior.
3. Touch the child gently (hug, high five, pat on shoulder, etc.), because
   physical contact is a reinforcer.

These three components also need to happen for PRAISE to be
effective:
1. Praise immediately after the behavior occurs.
2. Praise needs to be contingent upon the behavior (in response to the
   specific behavior).
3. Praise frequently, at least during the first week. Catch as many occurrences of the behavior as possible.

EFFECTIVE ANTECEDENTS

Prompting is one form of antecedent which occurs before the behavior. Prompting helps to get the behavior to occur when the child does
not initiate the behavior on her own.

An antecedent is also a setting-up event that gives your child a clue that the behavior is expected, such as turning off the TV and dimming the lights to indicate the start of the bedtime routine. This "primes the pump," so to speak, by creating an opportunity for the behavior to happen so that it can be praised.

1. Request the behavior calmly in a warm tone and start with "Please..."
2. Be specific.
3. Be close to your child when asking.
4. Make it a statement. Don't end with "Okay?"
5. Deliver effective praise after your child complies.

Antecedents are incredibly important in getting the behavior to happen, according to Kazdin.[17] Setting up the situation ("setting events") helps to establish environmental or contextual cues to influence the behavior that is expected. This sets the stage for behaviors and consequences, sort of like a trigger that kicks off a chain reaction. When practicing (simulating) the sequence of expected actions, you would choose a set of events that ultimately will become a sequence that gets triggered by the first event. A setting event can be something that is cued in the setting (e.g., dimming the lights for bedtime), externally by a person (e.g., a verbal request to put on pajamas) or by an internal state (e.g., feeling tired is the antecedent to going to bed).

You want to establish operations that build upon the setting event. For example, you tell your child using a calm voice that she can choose the Lady Bug pajamas or the Butterfly pajamas (antecedent). She makes a choice (behavior) and you lavish her with specific praise (consequence), "You made a choice! I'm proud of you!" and extend a high five. Then you prompt her to choose a book for story time and give her a choice, then when she chooses, you praise, etc. By practicing this sequence of steps, you can create an established chain of behaviors that gets triggered by the very first antecedent (the initial verbal prompt). Eventually, with practice and consistency, the steps become more automatic, just like your own bedtime or wake-up routine.

Practicing (simulation) is critical to establishing operations. In the same way that an actor rehearses all his lines before the play begins or a musician practices her instrument before the concert, children benefit from practicing expected behaviors prior to the moment the parent makes the request.

For example, imagine a parent planning a trip to the grocery store with a child who tends to act out in public places. Picture the child screaming in the aisles, kicking the parent who is dragging him through the store, begging for candy and throwing a tantrum at every turn. The parent can plan things in advance and make it a game at home on a day when there will not be a grocery store trip. In a calm manner, when there is "peace" and quiet (when your child is not being lured by other temptations or stimulated by games or TV), when there are no interruptions, explain to your child that you will be playing a game and he will earn points for playing. Set up the scene of going shopping and how he can make choices (push the cart, pick out two favorite fruits; keep the choices simple). Walk him through the steps and make it fun: "Let's play a game where we pretend we're going shopping together and you get to pick out two items!" Specify the items, set up the events in sequence and keep the simulation fun with lots of enthusiasm and specific praise: "I like the way you walk beside me!" and "Great choice—I like cherries too!" At the end of the "game" you offer him a sticker and tons of effective praise (see that section for proper delivery of praise).

Examples of establishing conditions to create a bedtime routine are:

1. Give a five-minute verbal prompt that bedtime will begin soon and that you will set the timer for five minutes. (If this step is too challenging for your child, you can start by setting the timer at five minute intervals for fifteen minutes, announcing the remaining time at each interval: fifteen minutes, ten minutes, five minutes.)
2. After time is up, dim the lights.
3. Turn off the television set and other electronics.
4. Calmly and clearly prompt your child to go to the bathroom to use the toilet, brush teeth, wash up or take a bath and put on pajamas. This step is primarily to get your child to the bathroom, where you will present more setting events.
5. Read a book with your child.
6. Give good-night hugs and kisses.

While this may seem like many steps, practicing these steps and repeating the sequence in the same order sets the stage for the future. You can make a game of the bedtime routine (not at bedtime but during the day when you have a few calm moments). Eventually, through repetition, the first step will trigger the entire sequence automatically and your child will transition through each step with greater compliance and less prompting.

CREATING A POINT CHART

A point chart can help establish behaviors when used in conjunction with the above strategies (remember the ABCs, especially practicing and praising). When using point charts, never take away points or privileges the child has previously earned. This is a positive experience that is supposed to be used with enthusiasm.

1. **Point Chart**—the success of the point chart is not based on how pretty it looks but rather on how it is *employed*. Be creative, but stick to the specific tenets outlined here to carry out the plan effectively.

2. **Redeeming Points** for rewards—every time your child performs the specific behavior you targeted, he earns points that can be used to "buy" items you already chose based on his likes. Price rewards reasonably. Make the point system attainable so he can buy something daily. If he can only earn a maximum of 20 points a day, there should be a few items worth less than that so he has choices.

3. **Timing** between the behavior occurring and earning points should be quick. Reinforcements are most effective when they occur immediately or soon after the behavior.

4. **Reward Menu**—Contrary to popular belief, you don't have to break the bank to buy toys nor risk a sugar high by offering sweets. You can have a "grab bag" of inexpensive items; just be sure you choose rewards that the child genuinely likes or this system may not work effectively. You know best, but you can also give your child choices that are free or inexpensive, such as going to the park, baking together, reading an extra book before bed, staying up fifteen more minutes.

5. **Explain** the program—Once you identify the "positive opposite" behavior (the opposite of the undesired behavior), teach your child how the point system works and be very specific. "Each time you do what I ask the first time I ask you, you get five points on this chart. Does that make sense? [Pause, repeat:] Every time you do what I ask right away, without waiting for me to ask again, you get five points. Then you can use your points to choose from these items."

6. **Practice!** This is a very important part of the program. Give your child the opportunity to go through the entire sequence, from responding to your request to practicing the target behavior to earning a point for practice. Reward liberally and adjust your point and menu system accordingly. Early on, co-author Gloria made the mistake of offering high point values for compliance and pricing the rewards too cheaply, so the rewards ran out quickly and it was like the child hit the jackpot for doing very little.

7. **Routine**—Establish a sequence of events to cue your child to the behavior (the "antecedent" of the ABCs). These cues can be verbal and contextual. You could have a poster or pictures showing the order of the routine to trigger the process and link the steps. For example, the bedtime routine. You can establish conditions for the morning routine as well. This is very important for making requests and only asking once; otherwise, the link becomes you asking a hundred times, then yelling, then threatening and a downward spiral of punishment.

If appropriate behavior still doesn't occur with prompting and points, do not give your child attention for noncompliance. Instead, in a neutral and calm voice simply tell your child you are not able to give her points for the behavior (be specific) but that you will try again later. Break eye contact and walk to another room or begin a task to discourage dialogue or attempts to negotiate. The key to achieving the desired outcomes is practice and praising all instances of the desired behavior. Simulating the techniques during calm times gives the parent and child opportunities to master the skills, reinforces the desired behaviors and fosters positive interaction.

The Kazdin Method replaces the ineffective, negative things parents tend to resort to (yelling, making repeated demands, nagging, coercion, threats, punishment). It's easy to be fooled into thinking something like yelling works because sometimes it looks like it "works," but the risk is that there is a tendency for hostility and aggression to escalate when met with noncompliance. When a child does comply, it is short- term, does not change or teach new behaviors and typically is to avoid something negative (fear, unpleasant interactions, additional punishment).

Punishment is widely misunderstood and does not teach the child anything valuable. Threats and other forms of punishment tell the child what NOT to do rather than what TO do. Punishment has harmful, negative side effects, increases aggression with peers and offers no substitutes for desired behaviors. A maladaptive pattern can lead to a downward spiral of escalation (heightened emotions, yelling, power struggle, verbal and physical aggression). The increase in hostility and aggression creates a negative pattern that damages the parent-child relationship over time. The child learns to avoid or escape the parent. Parents who are operating without an effective plan are at risk of falling into this "punishment trap," particularly at times when there are more pressures, heightened emotions or time constraints.

The Kazdin Method eliminates these risks, primes parents to notice positive behaviors, and offers levels of support for the most challenging behaviors. It's like a plan with several backup plans and a safety net.

If we think about children's strengths in terms of self-esteem and imagine this as poker chips, children begin the day with a certain number of "chips." Parents and protective factors can add to those chips, but the typical challenges of everyday life—sibling rivalry, academic challenges, responding to the demands of school and home—gradually subtract from those chips. Foster children or orphans living in institutions might not have any chips at all, perhaps for a long time, so they are not able to take the chances and learning risks that children need to take to grow. For some children, it is too scary to expose their vulnerabilities. Raising a hand in class takes courage and confidence in one's ability to speak up. Approaching a classmate can feel daunting to the child whose chips haven't been replenished in a long time. When a child only has one chip, deciding where to "spend" it is not an easy choice.

If children were struggling emotionally for survival in their pre-adoption homes, perhaps hungry, lonely, scared, forgotten or abused, their cognitive and emotional resources were tapped out even before leaving the house. School might have been a respite for children who feared going home. When school was not a source of comfort, these children may have felt despair, as if they had nowhere to turn.

As pointed out previously, it may take time to convince your child that he or she is emotionally and physically safe. Implementing new strategies may not seem easy at first but over time, with practice and consistency, your child and family will be on a trajectory toward improved functioning and healthy development.

PART IV

adoptive parents' problems

CHAPTER 19

The Strengths of Adoptive Parents

We have been moved by the strength, resilience, creativity, patience and absolute dedication of the parents we have interviewed. People who dedicate themselves to children who have already faced unthinkable trauma and challenges during their short lives are truly everyday heroes. Some adoptive parents of older children have a long and difficult road, while others face fewer challenges, but one thing they have in common is that they have opened their hearts and homes to children in need of loving families.

CREATING NEW DEFINITIONS OF "FAMILY"

Some people continue to hold deep cultural or religious beliefs that family can only be formed through birth or marriage. Inflexible notions of family can make adoptive families feel marginalized in certain cultures and communities. But adoptive families have a unique opportunity to prove through their lived experiences that love, not blood, defines a family.

Adoptive parents reimagine parenthood. They know that they love their adopted children as much as they would a biological child. Adoptive mothers and fathers show every day that they are "real" parents through their hard work and dedication to their children.

Adoptive families also create new definitions of extended family. Adoptive family kin—their child's biological family members—often become part of the extended family. They are accepted and welcome to celebrate the child's milestone events, join in holiday celebrations and be part of the child's life. Though some of these relationships can be contentious, often the adoptive kin network becomes an essential part of the fabric of their child's and, therefore, their own lives.

PERSONAL GROWTH

Adoptive parenting presents opportunities for personal growth. Many adoptive parents develop resilience as they encounter people who either disapprove of their choice to adopt or who adopt themselves. Adoptive parents also grow stronger as they fight for the resources, support and assistance their children and families need. During the journey, adoptive parents may begin to feel greater empathy for people or communities they previously dismissed or judged. As Betsy Smith and associates describe this potential change, "...Their love for a child not born to them may open their hearts to a love for other people and other communities that they never felt before."[1]

Parents of children from a different culture or race also may experience considerable personal growth. As they come to see the world through their children's eyes, they may develop a greater appreciation of how other ethnic or racial groups are marginalized or discriminated against. They may need to learn to navigate difficult terrain where race or culture becomes a barrier for their children or for themselves. White parents of African-American children may come to view discrimination or prejudice in a more personal way.

Raising a child from a different cultural background can provide adoptive parents an opportunity for growth. They may come to appreciate other cultures' histories and contributions to society or develop interests in cultural activities and practices different from their own. The experience of intercountry adoption may also influence parents to develop more interest in global issues. Parents of adoptees from different cultures may also gain a greater understanding of the multicultural society and world their child will eventually need to navigate as an adult.[2]

CHARACTERISTICS AND APPROACHES OF SUCCESSFUL ADOPTIVE PARENTS

Most parents who adopt older children domestically or from other countries come to understand that they will need to be creative in their parenting approach. They know that many of the traditional tricks of the trade of parenting are not going to work with a traumatized child. They come to realize that forming a close, loving relationship with their child will take time, patience and understanding. Adoptive parents also come to develop a sixth sense about how to best raise their child.

Research can help us understand characteristics of adoptive parents that are helpful in raising children from difficult backgrounds. Several studies suggest flexibility and adaptability are important characteristics of adoptive parents.[3] In their study, Jocelyn Johnstone and Anita Gibbs found that adoptive parents who were able to help children cope with past grief and current stress and who were adaptable to occurrences of changing behavior and situations developed closer relationships with their children.[4]

According to several research studies and our own interviews with parents, it seems many adoptive parents come to adoptive parenthood with strong notions about adoption that may help them succeed. For example, Pamela Clark found in her study that many successful adoptive parents believe in their child's right to be cared for.[5] As reflected in several research studies and our own interviews, many adoptive parents also come to older child adoption with the belief that parents must be highly committed to both the adoption and the child.[6] Along with being committed, some parents from the study said adoptive parents must place the needs of their children before their own.

CHAPTER 20

The Importance of Social Support and Community

Having access to a supportive social network is a protective factor for all families, especially single-parent families, according to Karne Benzies and Richelle Mychasiuk.[1] Social support networks are, as defined by James Garbarino, the interconnected relationships that provide long-lasting interactions, interpersonal relations, nurturing and reinforcements for coping with daily life.[2] The people and organizations that make up your network provide supportive behaviors such as approval, guidance, kindness, love, caring, emotional help, information and concrete aid. Concrete aid may mean cash when you run short, helping fix something when it breaks down, child caregiving when you need a break or are ill, giving you a ride, bringing over a meal to share or anything tangible that helps you or your family. Within the network structure, people make demands and request help. If it works well, it is reciprocal—sometimes you need help, sometimes they do.

Adoptive families generally have two types of support networks: informal and formal. Informal networks include family, friends, work associates, clergy, school colleagues and neighbors. When people need help, the first sources of assistance are usually those in the interpersonal or informal networks, according to Benjamin H. Gottlieb.[3] The second type of support network many adoptive families have is, according to Gerald Caplan, more formal and includes social workers, psychologists, teachers, doctors, lawyers and other professionals.[4] Families tend to be more reluctant to involve the formal system in solving problems.

Successful adoptive families get a great deal of support for the adoption from family and friends. This support remains consistently high over time. Unfortunately, some adoptive parents come to realize that certain members of their informal support network are less than supportive and enthusiastic about their decision to parent children adopted at an older age from the foster care system or another country. Adoptive parents may find that family or friends are avoiding spending time with them, because they disapprove of the adoption or because the child's behavior is disruptive. When family and friends no longer provide the support and understanding an adoptive parent needs, the parent should seek out others who approve of her decision to adopt, understand the unique challenges in raising the child and appreciate her steadfast commitment to the child. Resilient adoptive parents will seek out people who make their parenting journey easier, not harder. They will look for those who support and believe in what they are doing.

Many families will contact members of their clergy before they venture into the formal system.[5] Often families are hesitant to enlist the help of their formal support network because they feel they should be able to handle their family challenges on their own or with the help of their informal network. They also may feel more comfortable with relationships that are reciprocal. With formal supports there is a lack of reciprocity and families may feel that they are dependent people who can't meet their own needs.

An important part of a family's social network is members of the community, including individuals from clubs/social groups, organizations, churches/temples, work, school, friends and/or neighbors. In addition, many adoptive families have contact with other adoptive families. These contacts are social in nature—a meal, play dates, school events or church functions.

Most adoptive families use a combination of formal and informal networks.[6] Adoptive families with children who have both major emotional/behavioral disturbances and physical disabilities use more formal support networks. Support system interventions that help adoptive families to find and use formal and informal supports can minimize stresses.

Through our research and interviews, we have discovered that many adoptive parents of older children are expert networkers and community builders. They form communities online, through their agencies and in their communities. Involvement in advocacy can be an important form of community building and peer support. The communities we have had contact with and observed during the writing of this book reflect the deep understanding that adoptive parents can have for one another and the lengths to which they will go to support one another.

Some parents turn to adoptive parent support groups when they are confronting parenting challenges and need empathy/support. Parent-to-parent support groups perform the important function of helping parents cope with the stress. These support groups can offer emotional reinforcement and understanding as well as a forum for sharing first-hand experiences and information. They also afford parents opportunities for collective advocacy, sharing information and offering assistance. The appendix has a list of online support groups for adoptive parents of older children as well as websites that can help you locate in-person support groups. Justine, an adoptive mother of one boy and foster mom to four other children, writes:

> I have an online support network that helps me very much when I am struggling emotionally. I would love to have more of a "real life" support network, maybe through our agency—but I think it would be hard to develop the same type of relationships as online, since so many things we say or do could easily be taken out of context and shared with the agency.

Support groups may focus on a particular topic, such as bad behavior, sibling rivalry, issues with grandparents, overprotectiveness, disagreements between parents regarding childrearing, painful experiences and child development. While parents acknowledge the value of information and support, they also appreciate the normalization of issues, according to Richard Louv.[7]

SOCIAL SUPPORT NEEDS OF NON-TRADITIONAL PARENTS

Certain groups of adoptive parents of older children may benefit from additional or specialized support. Gay and lesbian, single and older parents as well as relative caregivers redefine parenthood in many ways and deserve the utmost respect and support from the community. Sometimes, that support can be less than forthcoming because of marginalization. Nevertheless, non-traditional adoptive parents are sometimes the most resilient of all and have formed even stronger informal networks than traditional two-parent adoptive families out of necessity and/or to offer others facing similar challenges support and understanding.

GAY AND LESBIAN PARENTS

Until recently, families headed by gays or lesbians have had to operate without a legal framework to protect them and often without wider community support. Even with more acknowledgment that these families should have legal rights to marry and pursue second-parent adoption, these rights are not yet universal. Many gay and lesbian parents often seek out people to be part of their lives who will love and support them without ridicule or condemnation. Many build a strong social network of people who support and love them for who they are prior to adopting children. Their social networks continue to be supportive after adoption. Some friends and family members may not be supportive of their decision to adopt and parent or feel odd being connected to a family that is now occupied with raising children. Yet gay or lesbian-headed families will find new supports in adoption support groups and professionals who accept their family without judgement.

SINGLE PARENTS

Some adoptive parents are single by choice while others become single after they adopt, through divorce or the death of a spouse. Many people grow up in single-parent households and some of the strongest families are single-parent families. Single parents are amazingly resourceful and are managers as good as most business executives. They know how to make the most of their resources. Single parents are often very independent but need support as much as any other parent. In some major metropolitan areas there are support groups for singles who adopt, but almost all adoptive parent support groups have both singles and couples.

KINSHIP CAREGIVERS AND ADOPTIVE PARENTS

When grandparents, aunts, uncles or other extended family members adopt a child related to them, they may need additional support to adjust to their new roles as primary caregivers. Family members may have little time to adjust to the idea of caring for a child related to them, because often children are placed very quickly with family members after a crisis situation. Family members may feel resentful that they have suddenly been pushed into the role of caregiver while others welcome the opportunity to care for and protect a child they know to be suffering from abuse or neglect at home.

Relative caregivers and adopters can benefit from adoptive parent groups geared toward their unique needs. (Some of these groups are listed in the appendix.)

CHAPTER 21

Adoptive Parents' Self-Care

Self-care is critically important for success in adoption. Each parent must take care of him or herself. You are only as good a parent as you are good to yourself. Every parent needs some time away from parenting. Self-care is about taking time to renew and refresh so you can be the best parent possible.

One of the ways you can take care of yourself is to reflect on all you have accomplished as a parent. Every parent will have bad days; on these days, think about all the good days you and your child or children have had. Every family is going to have bad days as well; on these days, recall the good times your family has had after your child was adopted and how many fun and happy occasions lie ahead such as birthdays, holidays and vacations. The bad days for parents and families can, for a time, eclipse the positive aspects of family life and parenting, because your child's negative behavior may leave a residue of stress and anxiety. When you find that you cannot return to hopeful or happy thoughts, talk to your spouse or partner or another adult about what you are feeling and perhaps they can help you refocus your energy.

Think about everything you have done for your child. Don't expect that your child will express gratitude for all you've done for him. This is just not something a young child or even a teenager has the capacity to do or should be expected to do. But during your own times of reflection and in conversations with friends, think about and talk about all of the progress, big and small, your child has made since coming home. Even if your child is struggling in his day-to-day life to adjust to his new family, perform at school, get along with siblings, make new friends or even function in basic ways, think about how much harder it would be for him if he was still in an orphanage, a foster home he did not like or with abusive or neglectful parents. Your child has been through a lot and may not be able to express his love or appreciation until he is an adult, but you know the difference you are making and it's okay to give yourself a pat on the back every now and then.

You also need to give yourself permission to not be a perfect person or a perfect parent. Sometimes you will just be a "good enough" parent and that's okay. The theme of the AdoptUSKids public service campaign is: "You don't have to be perfect to be a perfect parent." The idea behind this campaign is, "Youth in foster care don't need perfection; they need the commitment and love a permanent adoptive family can provide."[1] It is true, no one else is perfect and neither are you, but by providing a safe, permanent home and family to your child you are making a profound difference in his life. Some days you will doubt your ability to be an effective parent. On these days, give yourself permission to make mistakes. One day your child will hopefully understand that you're not just Super Mom or Dad but a real human being with needs, fears and feelings too!

TOOLS FOR SELF-CARE

Every parent should have a self-care plan—a written list of what they are going to do for themselves and when they are going to do it. At some point you need to stop thinking about how and when you will take care of yourself and just do it! Some activities that might help you refocus and refresh include:

- Exercise
- Going to the movies
- Going out to eat

- Meditation
- Yoga
- Attending a spiritual retreat
- Doing an arts and crafts project
- Hiring a babysitter and going out with your spouse, partner or friends
- Writing in a journal or blogging
- Involving your child in a playgroup so she can make friends and do fun activities while you get to spend time with other parents
- Learning to play a musical instrument
- Taking a class
- Shopping (don't get too crazy!)
- Spending time in nature

You and your spouse or partner might choose one night a week when one parent regularly stays home with the kids while the other goes out. If this is not realistic or you are a single parent, hire a babysitter one regular night a week so you have some time to yourself. Alternatively, you can arrange to have your child spend time with a friend or family member on a specific night each week so you can get some alone time. Don't be afraid to ask for help and support from others—all parents, especially adoptive parents of older children with special needs, deserve time to care for themselves and their needs.

CHAPTER 22

Help for Adoptive Parents Dealing with Serious Issues

Parenting is hard work, but when you have a child who is dealing with loss, grief, a history of abuse or neglect and other traumas, parenting can seem unbearable at times. But there is help. When you feel like you can no longer cope with the stress of parenting, know that there is always someone who wants to help you, whether it be another adoptive parent, a therapist, a clergy member, a family member or a friend.

We spoke to Carol, a parent who adopted three children from the public child welfare system in the United States. She described to us how at some moments she and her husband felt they were going to crack up. It's worth noting that today she is highly satisfied with her decision to adopt and can't imagine life without her four beautiful children.

Many of our challenges were similar to those birth families face: Adjustment, attachment, post-partum depression (the adoptive parent version), feelings of regret and inadequacy and fear of failure among others. Other challenges after transition were based on my issues. I am an intelligent, articulate, confident woman and these little humans reduced me to a crying, irrational mess on more occasions than I care to admit. However, I admit it often in the hopes of letting other crying-in-a-corner parents hope for the future. I'm not sure how this is different from my bio-parent friends who go some level of crazy after bringing home their little bundles. I think we all share a similar challenge in that way.

GRIEF AND LOSS

Not only are some adoptive parents trying to help their children work through their grief and loss, but they are also trying to work through their *own* grief and loss. Adoptive parents build their families through adoption with many hopes, dreams and anxieties. The first way to build success is to understand these feelings. You wouldn't become an adoptive parent unless you wanted to have the experience of parenting. Yet, the experience can be bittersweet. On one hand, you get to be the mom or dad you always dreamed of becoming. On the other hand, for many families, due to primary or secondary infertility or because you are in a relationship where having a biological child is not possible or practical, you have to deal with feelings of loss from not having a biological child. Parents try to minimize or deny these feelings when it is better to recognize and manage them. It is typical and acceptable to love parenting but mourn or feel sad that you are not biologically connected to your child. Having these feelings doesn't diminish your love. In fact, denying the feelings may negatively impact you and your family.

Every parent has dreams of the child or children they will love and parent. The "wish child" or "dream child" is a part of the experience of readying for parenthood. Yet, the ideal child of your dreams is usually not the child you end up parenting. Sometimes the difference is so dramatic that you wonder what you were thinking. You may think your child will be grateful to you for "saving him." Then you are disappointed when he's actually ungrateful, disrespectful or even claims he does not want you to be his parent. Sometimes you might regret the decision you made.

You worry that the actual work of parenting is very different from what you thought it would be. Many parents have these worries. Adoptive parents have the added challenge of parenting a child with a prior family experience. Your fantasy child dream may explode while you try to help your child pick up the pieces of his life, recover from trauma and move forward. All of this is hard work (both for you and your child) and it may bring feelings of loss as the life you envisioned gives way to something different. But remember that each of us walks our own path. Your parenting journey may be more difficult or frustrating than others' but there are opportunities for growth and ultimately joy down every path.

One of the parents we interviewed said that adoptive parents of children with difficult pasts must remember where their children came from and trust that their hard work will make a difference. To parents who are struggling, she offered this advice:

> *Seek help and, more importantly, talk with other families who are also struggling or who have been there—get a network! Try to understand the pain and trauma your child has gone through and the resultant feelings of fear and lack of trust. When I step back and imagine being our daughter or the children we hoped to adopt before the adoption disrupted, it makes it easier to see why it was hard for them to trust us and even easier to see their reactions as what they were.*

> *Remember that children do not need to be rescued from what happened or situations that may have occurred because of their behaviors. We cannot change what happened to them and they need to learn (not be sheltered) from their errors.*

> *Love is necessary but not always enough. Love is a start for us to give them, even when they cannot understand it or give it back, but more important is an understanding of where they have been—all children who are adopted have had trauma and loss—and what they need to heal from that early pain.*

Even without a traumatic history, an older child comes into the family with her own values and ways of solving problems, including behaviors that help her survive in difficult situations. You may not match on temperament, problem-solving styles or values—this is the process of reconciliation. You cannot make a square fit into a circle but you can create an entirely new image that blends the circle and square. This is a reconciliation process; some parents call it a struggle and other parents call it constant conflict. It is not a linear process but it is the way adoptive families work. It requires everyone to blend into a new type of family, bringing your history and experiences together to create something new.

Some adoptive parents may experience grief and loss due to a prior adoption disruption. When an adoption is disrupted, that means it is never legally finalized and the child has left the pre-adoptive home. It is important to deal with these feelings of grief and loss related to an adoption disruption before seeking to adopt another child. One of the parents we spoke to said she and her husband were grief-stricken when the child they wanted to adopt domestically, who had lived with them for several months, decided he did not want to be adopted by them. The couple was disappointed that the agency never offered them support in dealing with their grief. In time they were able to move on and adopt a special needs child from another country. The mother explained that although their adoption journey took several unexpected turns, she believes it all worked out the way it was supposed to. It is common to hear adoptive parents say they believe they were destined to adopt their child.

WHEN YOUR FAMILY IS STUCK

Some adoptive parents may feel stuck. Their child has been home one or even two years and they are still dealing with difficult behavior, the child's persistent anger or lack of acceptance of her new family. Arleta James describes how the adoptive family can be caught in a state of suspended animation where everyone is just trying to cope with the day-to-day realities of living with a difficult child and, in effect, failing to nurture their relationships with each other.[1]

Older child adoption can place stress on a relationship or marriage. When there is disagreement about how to manage the child's behaviors, relationships can suffer. When the child plays one parent off of the other, this can also cause relationship stress. Couples must approach the task of adoptive parenting as a team and remember their relationship with each other is as important as each parent's relationship with the child. Couples must not blame each other for a child's worsening behavior. Rather they should work together to come up with new approaches to managing the behavior and helping the child heal. Couples therapy may be needed to help parents develop new patterns of coping and managing family stress.

DEPRESSION

Some people have so much stress in their lives that it can trigger a mental illness. Parents need to know the signs of clinical depression in themselves. Parents may have grief, loss, anxiety, stress and a host of other feelings but are still able to function at work and home, maintain friendships and pursue their interests. If you feel that your energy is nonexistent and you have persistent thoughts of sadness, guilt, regret or anger that are affecting your ability to function, you must seek help from a mental health professional. Loss of appetite, sleep difficulties, a loss of interest in friends and family and an inability to concentrate at work could be indicators of clinical depression and/or another mental health disorder.

Some adoptive parents can even become severely depressed soon after adopting. Although post-partum depression is often triggered by hormonal changes after a woman gives birth, something that adoptive mothers will not experience, depression is a real possibility for adoptive parents after a child comes home. Adoptive mothers or fathers can develop intense sadness at having lost their freedom, their previous lifestyles, their ideal notion of parenthood or may simply be so overwhelmed by the stress of adopting that they develop clinical depression.

Again, do not hesitate to consult a mental health professional if sudden feelings of anxiety or sadness overwhelm you in the first days, weeks or months after adopting an older child. These feelings are nothing to be ashamed of and you can get help, including therapy and/or medication, to treat an episode of clinical depression.

DEALING WITH YOUR OWN TRAUMA
HISTORY OR VICARIOUS TRAUMA

Memories of adoptive parents' own trauma histories could be triggered by listening to their children describe past abuse, neglect or other traumatic events they have experienced. Parents who never dealt with their own past traumas could be at risk for a number of health problems. The ACES study conducted in the 1990s showed that adults who suffered one or more childhood traumas were at a higher risk for disease, addiction, being in abusive relationships and even early death.[2] If parents feel their own traumatic history is being triggered by adopting a child with a traumatic background they should seek the help of a mental health professional.

The ACES study has produced an ACES score which measures an adult's risk for adverse effects from past traumas by adding up the number of traumatic events that person experienced. Go to http://acestudy.org/ to find out what your ACES score is and to learn more about the potentially life-altering negative effects of untreated childhood traumatic stress.

Parents may also suffer vicarious trauma and secondary traumatic stress symptoms upon hearing their child describe his own traumatic events. Parents can feel victimized themselves simply by hearing how their child was victimized. Symptoms of secondary traumatic stress may include anxiety, depression, hypervigilance, anger and/or mistrust of people or the world.

Parents whose daily functioning is impeded by secondary traumatic stress should seek professional help. Patricia, an adoptive parent whom we interviewed, agreed that parents experiencing traumatic stress reactions must reach out for help:

> *Reach out! Talking to other parents experiencing the same struggles is essential! Don't be afraid to get help for yourself. I have needed therapy for myself since adopting my son. The military knows that wives who live with soldiers with PTSD can develop secondary PTSD from living with the unpredictable mood swings and behaviors. That is also very, very true of parents living with kids who have experienced trauma.*

Parents who do not seek help for their secondary traumatic stress symptoms could end up distancing themselves from their children. They might become less effective parents or even become inadvertently angry at their children for creating a climate of sadness and anxiety in their home.

If you decide to seek therapy for a mental health problem, whether it be for anxiety, depression or to process childhood trauma, be sure you choose a therapist who understands adoption and adoptive families. If your therapist blames you for your child's problems or makes you feel you are failing as a parent, find someone else, Susan Smith recommends.[3] One parent, Nancy, had this to say about how therapy is helping her cope with raising a very difficult child:

> *Finding a therapist who understood was very important. She has coached me to "Detach from the outcome." I can provide my son with all of the opportunities to heal, but if he chooses to stay "stuck," I can't force him to get better. She tells me it will not be my fault if he does not succeed as an adult. Learning to accept that is still a work in progress.*

RESPITE AND OUT-OF-HOME CARE FOR YOUR CHILD

Some adoptive families will experience severe stress because of an adopted child's behaviors. If you are one of those families, you may need a temporary break from your child. If the child's behavior is dangerous to himself or others, you may need to place him in temporary out-of-home care. You need to explore your options.

We believe that adoptive parents should never consider *adoption dissolution* or "rehoming" their child. A very small number of adoptions are dissolved—that is, legally severed after finalization. "Rehoming" is an unprofessional practice whereby adoptive parents go online to find a new home for their child because they can no longer cope with his or her behavior or care for the child. Child welfare authorities are not notified that the parents are placing the child in a new home. Adoption dissolution and rehoming will, in our opinion, re-traumatize a child who has already experienced much adversity. There are other possibilites for parents who feel they can no longer cope, including sending their child to a therapeutic school or treatment facility or getting *respite care.*

When parents need a temporary break from their child, respite care may be available through your adoption agency or a respite care organization. This may involve an out-of-home visit with caregivers for several hours or even a weekend. Respite care allows adoptive parents to rest, regroup and spend time with their other children or partners. (See the appendix for respite care resources.)

If your child has a mental health problem, behavioral disorder or substance abuse problem that is impacting his ability to live at home, residential treatment may be an option. One scenario in which residential treatment may be needed is when your child poses a danger to himself or other members of the household. You should contact your adoption agency, pediatrician, mental health provider and/or health insurance company for a referral to a facility. Choose a facility that takes your insurance and has the capacity to treat your child's specific disorder or problem.

A final out-of-home care option is a residential treatment school or a therapeutic boarding school that enrolls children with behavioral or other mental health problems. These schools offer children structure and specialized educational services. Your school district or mental health provider may be able to refer you to a special residential school for your child.

STAYING COMMITTED TO YOUR CHILD

You may be having difficulties coping with the stress of living with your child or need to get her temporary or long-term out-of-home care. This does not mean you are any less committed to her. One thing we have learned in conducting research for this book is that adoptive parents rarely give up, even when they are faced with overwhelming stress and adversity. They stay committed to their children and go to painstaking lengths to get their children the right help they need to heal and recover.

In rare instances, a child may need to live at a residential facility on a long-term basis. As we learned from Tracy, an incredibly resilient parent, just because an adopted child may not be able to live at home does not mean his parents are any less committed to him or are abandoning him:

> *Honestly, I never seriously considered not adopting Justin. I never really felt that I had a choice in the matter. I always felt so strongly called to adopt a waiting child. I had fostered five kids before him, all of whom went back to their bio-families. Justin was my son from the moment I met him. As infuriating as he can be, I have always felt that he is better off with me as his mom than anybody else. I tell him that I am the most stubborn person he will ever meet and no matter what he does I will always be his mom. That does not mean he will always*

live with me. I have looked into residential treatment programs and boarding schools. I still haven't completely ruled out something like that. I work with adults who have developmental disabilities and live in group homes. I understand that even though they are in residential care, their families still play a very important role—and I want to always be that for Justin, even if I eventually decide I can't have him living with me. Especially after I learned how much of his story had been covered up—I felt that there was no one else who ever could or would advocate for him as well as I can. I understand how he thinks and how his brain works. I understand that the reason he appears lazy is because he believes there is no point in trying and I understand why he believes that. I have seen how much pain is beneath all of his difficult behaviors. I absolutely believe that the only thing harder than parenting him is being him. His life will never be easy. Inside his head is the scariest place I can imagine. It is infuriating when the behaviors are still there and still constant after so much time and effort. But no one else will ever put in that effort for him. I spend a lot of time trying to remember where he came from and why—it is the only thing that keeps me compassionate when I am burning out.

Conclusion

Many parents choose to adopt due to infertility, often having delayed childbirth until there are too many risks and/or because they are led by their faith/beliefs or from a long-standing humanitarian desire to parent a child without a family. Whatever the motivation, you need to fully participate in the process of contemplating, questioning and fantasizing. You need to think about your motives, attitudes, convictions and beliefs about biological parents, adoptive parents, adoptees and other members of the adoption constellation.

New, sad, negative or positive information may cause you to pause and rethink what you are doing; again, this is good. You need to keep evaluating and thinking about what this experience will mean. It will change your life and the lives of those around you forever.

Adoption is a lifelong process. It begins before finalization of the adoption and continues to have an impact on you, the adoptee, the biological parent and all members of the adoption constellation for years to come. Adoption even impacts future generations. It is different from having a child by birth but remember, different is not deficit. It means it is an experience that has unique components. Soul searching is a vital part of the adoption process.

BE PREPARED FOR YOUR ADOPTION JOURNEY

One thing pre-adoptive parents have difficulty doing is questioning their agency if the agency says something that is not consistent with parents' understanding or starts to behave in a way that is not child-centered. Although you are the client or consumer of an agency, adoption should always be about what is in the best interests of the child and which family best meets the needs of the child (not which child you want).

You have a right and an obligation to raise questions. If you are with an agency that refuses to answer questions or threatens you, this is not the agency for you. You want an agency that is transparent and willing to rethink what they are saying or what they are doing. You want an agency that will help you work through your questions, not ignore them. You want an agency that is responsive and accountable. Aside from the adoption itself, choosing an agency that is right for you is the most important step in the process.

While the adoption agency you choose may provide you with some information, don't rely solely on what they give you or tell you. Be a critical consumer. You cannot spend enough time reading, thinking and planning. Work to take away the blinders that don't let you hear or read problematic or negative information—it is as important as the positive information. If you don't prepare for the adoption, there is little you can do after the placement is made. Families who report feeling prepared for their adoption have the most mastery over experiences after adoption.

For those who have not yet adopted, a great deal of this book is about helping you recognize and begin to evaluate information so you are prepared to deal with issues, should they arise. You might not encounter many of the issues explored in this book but, if you do, then you are prepared—at least somewhat. While you still may be stressed and shocked to experience certain issues, at least you have a head start in developing resources and managing these feelings. You can quickly create a plan for what you will do to manage the situation.

No amount of reading, thinking or talking prepares you for the reality of adopting and parenting. But you will be far ahead of others if you take the time to prepare for the adoption of an older child.

Remember, as part of your preparation, don't rely solely on your agency or the Internet. Go to community forums about adoption, watch adoption programs and visit the library to check out books and articles. This is one of the most important decisions of your life, so reading, thinking and evaluating are important parts of your process. It is time well-spent.

RALLY YOUR RESOURCES BEFORE PLACEMENT

When you are adopting an older child, you need many of the same types of medical care as if you are adopting an infant—a pediatrician, a dentist, etc. But you also may need additional medical resources like a physical therapist, speech therapist, occupational therapist and adoption sensitive psychiatrist/psychologist/therapist. You may need tutoring and educational testing. If you adopt from another country, you should consult with a physician who has specialized training in intercountry adoption health.

It is helpful to create a file of potential providers so you are ready. It is less stressful to have the information prepared and easy to obtain than to try to research it among the tasks of daily parenting. In the era of the Internet, not only can you find providers, but you can consult discussion boards and services where people have given feedback about those providers.

Tap into adoptive parent networks. Don't wait until placement to begin meeting other adoptive parents—do it early. They are one of the best sources for information, advice and concrete support. They can be mentors and respite providers. In much of the adoption research, social contact with other adoptive families and support groups and with other adoptive parents is evaluated as the most helpful—even more helpful than professional services!

SEEK SUPPORT AND ADVICE FROM
OTHER ADOPTIVE PARENTS

One of the best things you can do is attend adoptive parent support groups, either face-to-face or virtually on the Internet. These other parents will give you an education and also can be your best supports before, during and after placement. According to the North American Council on

Adoptable Children, by bringing together people who have been touched by adoption, a parent group can:

- Validate parents' experiences and frustrations
- Celebrate the joys and triumphs unique to adoptive parenting
- Enable parents to share resources, suggestions and success stories
- Identify and solve problems
- Guide parents to a better understanding of adoption's impact on child development
- Reduce feelings of isolation and self-doubt or guilt when problems arise in the family

Most importantly, parent groups offer encouragement and hope.[1]

Social support system theory proposes that the ways people believe, act and feel are affected by the people with whom they are interconnected in various ways. Adoptive parent groups are an important component of social support. This support can help adoptive families as they integrate a child with a history and life story that precedes assimilation into an adoptive family. Feeling supported and cared for buffers the negative effects of stressful life events; parenting is stressful! For adoptive families, the uniqueness of their situation may leave them feeling isolated. With a lack of appropriate role models for what an adoptive parent is supposed to be like, adoptive parents may feel lost. Interaction with other adoptive families can reduce isolation and give adoptive families and adoptees a forum for discussing issues they face with others in similar situations.

We believe that regardless of the age of the child you adopt, adoptive parent groups increase your successes. Sometimes you just need a listener who understands the journey you have undertaken and the frustrations that you will inevitably encounter, without judgment or criticism. Find or build your network of adoptive families who become part of your social support network. Over time, after you have obtained support, you will become the adoptive parent or family that can give support to others who are in a different part of their journey.

PURSUE PROFESSIONAL HELP SOONER
RATHER THAN LATER

Adoptive parents often have perfection paralysis. After having gone through home study, a matching process and placement and post-placement supervision, they are often reluctant to discuss their real issues or problems. They feel that they should know how to handle the child or children placed with them. Some fear that if they talk about their problems, the child will be taken away.

Remember you are adopting children with different genetics and histories and trying to merge them into a new and different family. Some children enter their families having experienced a great deal of trauma. Some children enter with genetic predispositions that may make them more prone to certain physical, mental or learning problems. Getting professional help during different phases of your adoption journey is normal and should be expected.

Even if you are an anxious parent, err on the side of caution. Don't let anyone discount your feelings or concerns. If you think there might be a problem, don't let it fester. Get an assessment. An assessment is more than just a conversation with a pediatrician or other professional. It should not be only office-based; children behave differently in different environments. An assessment can begin or end in an office but it should also be conducted at day care or at school and in the home. You want a credentialed person to see the behaviors in the contexts in which they occur to help you determine whether or not you need professional help. If you disagree with the assessment, work with the professional to reach a mutually-agreed-upon assessment and plan for your child. After all, you are the person with the legal authority for your child and you know your child better than anyone else.

Earlier intervention is better for a number of reasons. One, you can ascertain if there are problems that you will need to manage short-term or long-term. Two, it can stop the problem from worsening or slow down the progression. Three, it gives you professional support and all adoptive families benefit from a combination of informal and professional support.

BENEFITS OF OLDER CHILD ADOPTIONS

Claiming the child as your own is a process that families go through, usually quicker than the child claiming the adoptive family as his or her family. It is not bad to have high expectations, but be ready to change your expectations to match the potential of the child you have adopted.

While families can wait up to a decade to adopt an infant, you can adopt older children more quickly. Whether you adopt from the public system or from another country, families adopting older children receive quicker placement. There are thousands and thousands of older, wonderful children waiting for a family.

The cost of adopting older children is considerably less than adopting an infant. Most older children from the public child welfare system come with an adoption subsidy that is used to help meet the child's needs. There often are discounts for intercountry adoption of older children.

You can immediately begin doing fun activities with older children. You may see changes occur quickly and each new event can be as thrilling for you as it is for the child.

Though we offer many caveats and concerns about older child adoption in this book, we want to conclude by stressing the benefits. We believe in adoption. We believe in the healing power of families. We believe that adoption is the most powerful and best intervention for children without families.

As the late Dave Thomas, one of America's biggest adoption proponents, said: "People ask me, 'What about gay adoptions? Interracial? Single Parent?' I say, 'Hey, fine, as long as it works for the child and the family is responsible.' My big stand is this: Every child deserves a home and love. Period."

Recommended Resources by Chapter

PART 1: THE ADOPTION PROCESS

CHAPTER 1: DECIDING TO ADOPT AN OLDER CHILD

What adoption means to them...

- A young man adopted from Ukraine talks to orphans about his initial misconceptions about being adopted by Americans and how adoption changed his life for the better:
  http://www.1blessing2another.blogspot.com/2012/08/andrews-video-for-older-orphans.html
- Children discuss their journeys through foster care and what finding a permanent family has meant to them, AdoptUSKids:
  http://www.adoptuskids.org/meet-the-children
- Family stories about adoption and foster care, AdoptUSKids:
  http://www.adoptuskids.org/join-the-conversation/real-foster-care-and-adoption-stories/families
- Adoptive parents describe why they decided to pursue older child adoption, AdoptUSKids:
  http://adoptuskids.org/for-families/how-to-adopt/deciding-to-pursue-adoption

- Adoption public service announcements from the Dave Thomas Foundation for Adoption (if you view just one, watch the last one, *Say Yes*, but make sure you have a tissue close by):
http://www.davethomasfoundation.org/free-adoption-resources/educational
-videos-and-psa/
- Adoption stories around the nation (audio), National Resource Center for Adoption:
http://www.nrcadoption.org/map/
- Digital stories from the field (audiovisual), National Resource Center for Permanency and Family Connections:
http://www.nrcpfc.org/digital_stories/index.htm
- We Have Room: an extraordinary story of adoption (documentary recommended by one of our families):
http://www.fourthwatchentertainment.com/

Dave Thomas Foundation for Adoption

- Domestic adoption success stories:
http://www.davethomasfoundation.org/about-foster-care-adoption/success
-stories/
- Common myths about domestic older child adoption:
http://www.davethomasfoundation.org/about-foster-care-adoption/myths
-and-misconceptions/
- Free adoption guides in English, Spanish and French:
https://www.davethomasfoundation.org/free-adoption-resources/adoption
-guides/

Child Welfare Information Gateway

- State Adoption Information Websites:
https://www.childwelfare.gov
- Adoption options:
https://www.childwelfare.gov/pubs/f_adoptoption.pdf
- Foster parents considering adoption, factsheet for families (2012):
https://www.childwelfare.gov/pubs/f_fospar.cfm

Other:

- Learn about your state's public adoption policies and requirements, AdoptUSKids:
http://www.adoptuskids.org/for-professionals/state-adoption-and-foster-care
-information

- *Labor of the Heart: A parent's guide to the decision and emotions in adoption* by Kathleen L. Whitten: http://books.google.com/books?id=gym8dttbD4EC&dq =labors+of+the+heart+decisions+adoption&source=gbs_navlinks_sna
- *Adoption Today* magazine: http://www.adoptinfo.net/
- Adopting the older child, online course for people considering older child adoption, Adopting Learning Partners: http://www.adoptionlearningpartners.org/ catalog/courses/adopting-the-older-child.cfm

CHAPTER 2: WHO CAN ADOPT AN OLDER CHILD?

- *Who May Adopt, Be Adopted or Place a Child for Adoption?*
  Child Welfare Information Gateway, (2012) comprehensive state-by-state information about age, residency and sexual orientation status requirements: https://www.childwelfare.gov/systemwide/laws_policies/statutes/parties.pdf
- *Retirees who choose to adopt*
  NBC Nightly News segment aired May 20th, 2013:
  http://www.nbcnews.com/video/nightly-news/52051170#52051170
- Read more about single parent adoption and locate resources for single adoptive parents on Child Welfare Information Gateway:
  https://www.childwelfare.gov/pubs/single_parent.pdf

Recommended resources for LGBT singles or
couples interested in older child adoption:

Web resources:

- LGBT Parents in Child Welfare—a list of resources, mostly geared toward professionals but with some information that would be useful to adoptive parents, from the National Resource Center for Permanency and Family Connections, Silberman School of Social Work at Hunter College:
  http://www.nrcpfc.org/is/LGBT-Parents-in-ChildWelfare.html
- Frequently Asked Questions From Lesbian, Gay, Bisexual and Transgender (LGBT) Prospective Foster and Adoptive Parents (Child Welfare Information Gateway, 2011):
  https://www.childwelfare.gov/pubs/factsheets/faq_lgbt.cfm
- Permanency Planning Today (2010)—an issue of the National Resource Center for Permanency and Family Connections' quarterly newsletter that features excellent resources and articles for LGBT adoptive and prospective adoptive parents:
  http://www.nrcpfc.org/newsletter/ppt-summer-2010.pdf

- Second Parent Adoption Laws (map)—Family Equality Council: http://www.familyequality.org/get_informed/equality_maps/second-parent_adoption_laws/
- Second Parent Adoption—an overview of laws pertaining to second parent adoption, Human Rights Campaign (HRC): http://www.hrc.org/resources/entry/second-parent-adoption
- All Children: All Families Project—a list of parenting resources for LGBT adoptive families, HRC: http://www.hrc.org/resources/category/parenting
- Adoptive Families Circle discussion forum for LGBT prospective and current parents: http://www.adoptivefamiliescircle.com/groups/topics/LGBT_Parents1/

Audiovisual:
- Cliff's Story—a brief audiovisual presentation by a gay father of three adopted children, from the National Resource Center for Permanency and Family Connections: http://www.nrcpfc.org/digital_stories/FAFP_Cliff_L/index.htm
- Daddy and Papa—an award winning documentary about gay fathers including adoptive fathers: http://daddyandpapa.com/
- Foster Care's Invisible Youth—seven LGBTQ foster youth share their stories, In the Life Media: http://www.youtube.com/watch?v=nuSikwpqazA
- LGBT-Headed Foster and Adoptive Families: Youth Perspectives—A 90-minute webinar sponsored by AdoptUSKids: http://video.adoptuskids.org/v/Webinar/lgbt-headed-foster-and-adoptive-families/lib/playback.html
- Living Adoption: Gay Parents Speak—a documentary about LGBT adoption by HRC and PhotoSynthesis Productions: http://www.hrc.org/resources/entry/living-adoption-gay-parents-speak1
- William and Estevan, adoptive fathers of three and foster parents of many, talk about their love of children and family, Family Equality Council: http://www.youtube.com/watch?v=gHW1bQuateM
- *Adoptions by Lesbians and Gay Men: A New Dimension in Family Diversity* (2012) edited by David M. Brodzinsky and Adam Pertman: http://www.amazon.com/Adoption-Lesbians-Gay-Men-Dimension/dp/0195322606

Kinship Care and Adoption

- GrandFacts: A website for grandparents raising grandkids, American Association of Retired People (AARP)—comprehensive website with state fact sheets that include information about specific programs and supports, articles and other resources:
http://www.aarp.org/relationships/friends-family/info-12-2011/grandparent-raising-children-resource.html
- Grand Successes: Stories of lives well raised (2012), Generations United—tells the stories of prominent persons raised by grandparents and other relatives: http://www.gu.org/LinkClick.aspx?fileticket=0iTKo-4Hf1E%3D&tabid =157&mid=606
- Kinship Care Policies (2007), Casey Family Programs State Child Welfare Policy Database—look up state-by-state policies governing kinship care including licensure options and guardianship policies (interactive map): http://www.childwelfarepolicy.org/maps/single?id=8
- Placement of Children with Relatives (2010), Child Welfare information Gateway, State Statutes—provides state-by-state information about the laws pertaining to kinship care and adoption: https://www.childwelfare.gov/systemwide/laws_policies/statutes/placement.cfm
- Guardianship, Child Welfare Information Gateway—resources describing the benefits of and process of getting legal guardianship of a related child: https://www.childwelfare.gov/permanency/guardianship.cfm
- Center for Law and Social Policy—"Is Kinship Care Good for Kids?" (Conway & Hutson, 2007):
http://www.clasp.org/resources-and-publications/files/0347.pdf

Recommended resources for military families interested in adoption:

- The Child Welfare Information Gateway—a comprehensive list of resources for military families interested in adoption:
https://www.childwelfare.gov/adoption/adoptive/military_families.cfm
- AdoptUSKids—a service of the US Children's Bureau (US Department of Health and Human Services) offers assistance to military families interested in adopting including a number of resources available:
http://www.adoptuskids.org/for-families/who-can-foster-and-adopt/adoption-resources-for-military-families

- Wherever my family is: that's home!—geared toward adoption professionals wishing to better serve military parents interested in adopting but includes a wealth of resources that will be useful to prospective adoptive parents at the end: http://www.adoptuskids.org/_assets/files/NRCRRFAP/resources/wherever -my-family-is-thats-home.pdf
- Vida Adoptions—an intercountry adoption agency that places children, including hard to place American children, with families all over the world including US military service members living abroad: http://www.vidaadoptions.org/
- AdoptAbroad—full-service adoption agency that specializes in working with American citizens living abroad and military service members and diplomats stationed abroad interested in adopting internationally or from the US foster system: http://www.adopt-abroad.com/military.htm

Recommended resources for US citizens living abroad or non-citizens interested in adoption:

- The National Council for Adoption—provides a list of useful information for American citizens, including military families, interested in adopting US and non-US citizens: https://www.adoptioncouncil.org/publications/adoption-advocate-no-49 .html
- Adoption by Non-US Citizens Living in the United States—The US Department of State provides information pertaining to this population of prospective adoptive parents on its intercountry adoption site: http://adoption.state.gov/adoption_process/who_can_adopt/residents.php

Resources for prospective adoptive parents of color:

- Minority specializing agency directory, AdoptUSKids: http://adoptuskids.org/_assets/files/NRCRRFAP/resources/minority -specializing-agency-directory.pdf
- PACT—Online discussion forums and support groups for adoptive parents of color: http://www.pactadopt.org/adoptive/services/support/adoptive_parents_of _color.html

- List of adoption agencies that specialize in serving African-American adoptive families, North American Council on Adoptable Children: http://www.nacac.org/howtoadopt/AAagencies.html
- Learn more about the complexities of disproportionality in a comprehensive research paper by the Center for the Study of Social Policy and The Annie E. Casey Foundation on behalf of The Alliance for Racial Equity in Child Welfare: http://www.cssp.org/publications/child-welfare/alliance/Disparities-and -Disproportionality-in-Child-Welfare_An-Analysis-of-the-Research-December -2011.pdf

CHAPTER 3: ADOPTING WITHIN (AND FROM) THE UNITED STATES

Learn how federal legislation impacts child welfare
service delivery in the United States:

- National Council for Adoption: Federal Laws (brief overviews): https://www.adoptioncouncil.org/current-laws/federal-laws.html
- Child Welfare Information Gateway: Major Federal Legislation Concerned With Child Protection, Child Welfare and Adoption (detailed factsheet): https://www.childwelfare.gov/pubs/otherpubs/majorfedlegis.pdf

Learn more about child welfare service delivery
and the child welfare system:

- National Child Welfare Workforce Institute: www.ncwwi.org
- Children's Bureau Express: https://cbexpress.acf.hhs.gov/

Read or listen to interviews with children and teens
who have spent time in the foster care system:

- *Advocating for America's Youth in Foster Care: Perspectives and Recommendations from Former Foster Youth* (2012). Adoption Advocate, No. 47. A publication of the National Council for Adoption: https://www.adoptioncouncil.org/images/stories/documents/NCFA _ADOPTION_ADVOCATE_NO47.pdf

- Digital stories from the field, The National Resource Center for Permanency and Family Connections—videos feature teens discussing their experiences in foster care and the importance of having a support system: http://www.nrcpfc.org/digital_stories/_youth/
- Children in Foster Care, AdoptUsKids—a ten-minute excerpt from a two hour documentary about foster and adoptive youth and families: http://www.adoptuskids.org/meet-the-children

Resources for foster parents and kinship caregivers considering adopting children in their care:

- State foster care information websites: https://www.childwelfare.gov/pubs/reslist/rl_dsp_website.cfm?rs_id =17&rate_chno=AZ-0002E
- Comprehensive resources for prospective and current foster parents: https://www.childwelfare.gov/outofhome/resources_kinship/resources_ foster_families.cfm
- Factsheet for foster parents considering adoption: https://www.childwelfare.gov/pubs/f_fospar.pdf
- State statutes governing placement of children with relative caregivers: https://www.childwelfare.gov/systemwide/laws_policies/statutes/placement.pdf

Choosing an agency:

- Searchable database of public and private agencies: https://www.childwelfare.gov/nfcad/
- Listing of state child welfare agency websites: https://www.childwelfare.gov/pubs/reslist/rl_dsp.cfm?rs_ID=16&rate_chno =AZ-0004E
- Searchable database of manuals and guides published by state child welfare agencies as well as information about public adoption, child protection, kinship care, licensing and more: https://www.childwelfare.gov/systemwide/sgm/
- How to assess the reputation of licensed, private adoption agencies: https://www.childwelfare.gov/pubs/twenty.cfm

- National Council for Adoption searchable database of member agencies (private): https://www.adoptioncouncil.org/members/

Recommended websites for learning more about older child adoption within or from the United States:

- www.Adoptivefamilies.com—national magazine, section of website on older child adoption that includes blogs, articles and resources
- www.foreverparents.com—nice collection of blog posts, resources and advice for pre-adoptive and adoptive parents
- www.childwelfare.gov—Child Welfare Information Gateway, sponsored by the US Children's Bureau, one of the best sources of information about child welfare and adoption on the internet.
- www.AdoptUSKids.org—a service of the US Children's Bureau, provides photo-listing of waiting children in the United States and numerous resources for prospective and pre-adoptive parents interested in adopting children from the foster care system
- http://older-child.adoption.com/—section of comprehensive adoption.com website about older child adoption
- www.nacac.org—North American Council on Adoptable Children, organization that serves prospective adoptive parents adopting through the public child welfare system, be sure to check the "how to adopt" page, fact sheets and searchable database of over 900 adoption-related groups including parent support groups
- National Resource Center for Adoption—The National Resource Center for Adoption's vision is that every child and youth in the public child welfare system will have a permanent family that provides them safety, permanence and well-being: http://www.nrcadoption.org/
- National Resource Center for Permanency and Family Connections—The National Resource Center for Permanency and Family Connections at the Hunter College School of Social Work is a training, technical assistance and information services organization dedicated to help strengthen the capacity of state, local, Tribal and other publicly administered or supported child welfare agencies to institutionalize a safety-focused, family-centered and community-based approach to meet the needs of children, youth and families: http://www.nrcpfc.org/

Adoptive parent training:

- Foster Parent College—forty-four low-cost online courses for adoptive and foster parents and kinship caregivers; topics include adopting from the foster care system, the child welfare system and child development: http://www.fosterparentcollege.com/index.jsp
- Adoption Learning Partners online courses for pre-adoptive parents: http://www.adoptionlearningpartners.org/adopting/index.cfm
- National Photo Listings: http://www.adoptuskids.org/meet-the-children/state-photolists

Other

- For more information about interstate adoption, see the Child Welfare Information Gateway's page, Adopting Children from other States or Jurisdictions: https://www.childwelfare.gov/adoption/adoptive/states_jurisdictions.cfm
- See the Child Welfare Information Gateway factsheet on obtaining background information on your prospective adoptive child: https://www.childwelfare.gov/pubs/f_background.pdf
- Search for a Wendy's Wonderful Kids Navigator Program near you (United States and Canada) https://www.davethomasfoundation.org/what-we-do/wendys-wonderful-kids/program-sites/

Financial support for older child adoption and adopted children:

- Child Welfare Information Gateway resources, adoption assistance for children adopted from foster care: https://www.childwelfare.gov/pubs/f_subsid.pdf
- Adoption assistance by state: www.childwelfare.gov/adoption/adopt_assistance
- National Council for Adoption, provides a list of organizations that offer adoption grants and loans: https://www.adoptioncouncil.org/for-families/financial-resources.html
- The North American Council on Adoptable Children provides some of the best information on the internet about financial support for special needs and older child adoption: how to adopt: http://www.nacac.org/howtoadopt/howtoadopt.html adoption subsidy: http://www.nacac.org/adoptionsubsidy/adoptionsubsidy.html

- The Dave Thomas Foundation for Adoption provides a list of employers who offer adoption-related assistance to their employees: https://www.davethomasfoundation.org/what-we-do/adoption-friendly -workplace/adoption-friendly-employers-benchmarks/adoption-friendly -workplace-employers/

CHAPTER 4: INTERCOUNTRY ADOPTION

- Council on Accreditation: http://adoption.state.gov/hague_convention/agency_accreditation/agency _search.php
- National Council for Adoption, member attorneys: https://www.adoptioncouncil.org/who-we-are/attorneys.html
- US Department of State: http://adoption.state.gov/country_information.php
- Rainbow Kids: http://www.rainbowkids.com/
- Child Welfare Information Gateway, Intercountry adoption: where do I start: https://www.childwelfare.gov/pubs/f_inter/f_inter.pdf
- Child Welfare Information Gateway, state recognition of intercountry adoptions finalized abroad https://www.childwelfare.gov/systemwide/laws_policies/statutes/intercountry.pdf
- US Department of State, Child Citizenship Act of 2000: http://adoption.state.gov/adoption_process/faqs/child_citizenship_act_of _2000.php
- Online Hague-Compliant Training from the National Council for Adoption: http://about.hagueadoption.org/

Support Groups:

- *Adoptive Families* Magazine, searchable database: http://adoptivefamilies.com/support_group.php
- Adoptive Families Circle, country-specific discussion forums: http://www.adoptivefamiliescircle.com/groups/
- Adoption.com discussion forums: http://forums.adoption.com/international-adoption/

CHAPTER 5: POST-ADOPTION SERVICES

- Finding services for an adopted child:
  https://www.childwelfare.gov/adoption/adopt_parenting/services/
  https://www.childwelfare.gov/pubs/f_postadoption.cfm
  http://adoption.state.gov/adoption_process/how_to_adopt/postadoption.php
- Searchable database of post-adoption services by state:
  www.childwelfare.gov/adoption/postplacement/services/models.cfm#private
- National Foster Care and Adoption Directory Search (includes options for services):
  https://www.childwelfare.gov/nfcad/
- List of adoption services by state:
  https://www.childwelfare.gov/adoption/adopt_assistance/questions
  .cfm?quest_id=7
- North American Council on Adoptable Children, Post-adoption services:
  http://www.nacac.org/postadopt/postadopt.html
- Higher education assistance:
  https://www.childwelfare.gov/adoption/adopt_parenting/financial/
- Adoption Learning Partners:
  http://www.adoptionlearningpartners.org
- Foster parent College (includes training for adoptive parents as well):
  www.fosterparentcollege.com
- The Center for Adoption Support and Education (CASE):
  http://adoptionsupport.org/index.php/training-institute/

PART 2: ADOPTIVE FAMILIES

CHAPTER 6: WELCOMING YOUR CHILD HOME

- Adoption & Child Welfare Lawsite—summaries of state and federal statues, FAQS and a hotline:
  http://www.adoptionchildwelfarelaw.org/
- American Academy of Adoption Attorneys—searchable database of AAAA approved attorneys:
  http://www.adoptionattorneys.org/aaaa_directory
- Transitioning foster children to adoptive children:
  https://www.childwelfare.gov/adoption/adopt_parenting/foster/transitioning
  .cfm

CHAPTER 7: ADOPTIVE FAMILIES ARE "REAL" FAMILIES—
EDUCATING FAMILY AND FRIENDS ABOUT OLDER CHILD ADOPTION

- Dave Thomas Foundation for Adoption's Adoption Guide:
  https://www.davethomasfoundation.org/about-foster-care-adoption/
  adoption-guide/
- "Answering strangers' questions about adoption" (2007) by Deborah McCurdy,
  MSW (article):
  http://www.rainbowkids.com/ArticleDetails.aspx?id=509
- *W.I.S.E. Up! Powerbook* (2000) by Marilyn Schoettle—Helps children answer
  awkward questions about being adopted:
  http://www.adoptionsupport.org/pub/

CHAPTER 8: MULTICULTURAL AND MULTIRACIAL ADOPTIVE FAMILIES

- Adoption.com—Transracial adoption discussion forum:
  http://forums.adoption.com/transracial-adoption/
- *Adoptive Families* Magazine—List of cultural and heritage events by state:
  http://www.adoptivefamilies.com/calendar.php?cal=camp
- *Native American Transracial Adoptees Tell their Stories* By Rita James Simon and
  Sarah Hernandez:
  http://www.amazon.com/Native-American-Transracial-Adoptees-Stories/
  dp/0739124927
- "Nurturing racial-ethnic-cultural identities in adoptive families," an online
  article written by Jane Brown, MSW (2006):
  http://www.adoptedthemovie.com/nurturing-identities-in-adoptive
  -families/
- The Ties Program—Cultural travel opportunities for adoptive families:
  http://www.adoptivefamilytravel.com/
- *PACT* (nonprofit that serves adopted children of color)—Transracial adoption
  resources including videos:
  https://www.pactadopt.org/resources/transracial-adoption-interracial
  -adoption.html
- Baby Veronica case timeline:
  http://www.cnn.com/2013/08/13/justice/south-carolina-adoption-timeline/
  index.html

- National Indian Child Welfare Association (NICWA)—ICWA resources for families:
  http://www.nicwa.org/Indian_Child_Welfare_Act/#resources
- NICWA curriculum module—Indian extended family and foster family care:
  http://www.nicwa.org/resources/curriculum/?p=Curriculum_05
- Native American Rights Fund—ICWA guide to adoption:
  http://narf.org/icwa/faq/adoption.htm

CHAPTER 9: SIBLING RELATIONSHIPS

- Ten Myths and Realities of Sibling Adoption:
  http://www.adoptuskids.org/_assets/files/NRCRRFAP/resources/ten-myths
  -and-realities-of-sibling-adoptions.pdf
- Camp to Belong—Summer camp for siblings placed in separate foster care or adoptive homes:
  http://camptobelong.org/
- Siblings and Adoption, *Adoptive Families* magazine:
  http://www.adoptivefamilies.com/siblings
- Child Welfare Information Gateway, Sibling issues in foster care and adoption:
  https://www.childwelfare.gov/pubs/siblingissues/

Recommended books:
- *Brothers and Sisters in Adoption* (2012) by Arleta James
- *The Family of Adoption* (2005) by Joyce Maguire Pavao
- *Siblings in Adoption and Foster Care: Traumatic Separations and Honored Connections* edited by Deborah N. Silverstein and Susan Livingston Smith (Dec 30, 2008)
- *Welcoming a new brother or sister through Adoption* by Arleta James, 2013

CHAPTER 10: NAVIGATING BIOLOGICAL FAMILY RELATIONSHIPS AND UNDERSTANDING ADOPTION

- The Adopted Child's Changing View—includes information about how children view adoption at each developmental stage:
  http://www.adoptionsupport.org/res/timeline.php

- Post adoption contact agreements between birth and adoptive families, Child Welfare Information Gateway: https://www.childwelfare.gov/systemwide/laws_policies/statutes/coopera-tive.pdf
- *Making Room in Our Hearts: Keeping Family Ties through Open Adoption* (2006) by Micky Duxbury

PART 3: UNDERSTANDING YOUR CHILD

CHAPTER 11: THE TRAUMATIZED CHILD

Getting professional help for your traumatized child:
- American Psychological Association:
  www.apa.org
  1–800–964–2000 (toll free)
- National Alliance for the Mentally Ill:
  www.nami.org
- National Child Traumatic Stress Network:
  http://www.nctsnet.org/about-us/network-members
  http://www.nctsn.org/resources/get-help-now
  (310) 235–2633
- Resources for Parents and Caregivers:
  http://www.nctsn.org/resources/audiences/parents-caregivers
- Empirically Supported Treatments and Promising Practices:
  http://www.nctsn.org/resources/topics/treatments-that-work/promising-practices
- Definitions of Child Abuse and Neglect (by state):
  https://www.childwelfare.gov/systemwide/laws_policies/statutes/define.pdf
- *Nurturing Adoptions: Creating Resilience After Neglect and Trauma* by Deborah D. Gray

CHAPTER 12: GRIEF AND LOSS IN ADOPTED CHILDREN

- American Adoption Congress, Grief and Loss (Silverstein & Kaplan, 2007):
  http://www.americanadoptioncongress.org/grief_silverstein_article.php
- Child Welfare Information Gateway, Helping adopted children cope with grief and loss:
  https://www.childwelfare.gov/adoption/adopt_parenting/helping.cfm

- PACT, Grief and loss in adoption:
  https://www.pactadopt.org/resources/grief-and-loss-in-adoption.html
- Adoption Learning Partners, Finding the missing pieces (audiovisual):
  http://www.adoptionlearningpartners.org/catalog/courses/finding-the
  -missing-pieces.cfm
- Older Child Adoption Support, Grief and loss in adoptive families (Ward,
  2009):
  http://www.olderchildadoptionsupport.com/grief-and-loss/

CHAPTER 13: ATTACHMENT AND ADOPTION

- *Attaching in Adoption: Practical Tools for Today's Parents* by Deborah Gray
- Older Child Adoption Support, Learning about Attachment:
  http://www.olderchildadoptionsupport.com/attachment/
- "Bent but Not Broken: Building Resilient Adoptive Families" (2003) by Dee
  Paddock:
  http://library.adoption.com/articles/bent-but-not-broken.html

Possible Therapies for Attachment Problems
- Play Therapy
- Filial Therapy
- Attachment Therapy (e.g., Theraplay)
- Cognitive-Behavior Therapy (CBT)
- Problem Solving Skills Training (PSST)
- Parent Management Training (PMT)
- Family-Based Interventions (e.g., MST, MTFC)
- Eye Movement Desensitization and Reprocessing (EMDR)
- Creative Arts Therapy (e.g., DMT)
- Bio-Feedback Therapy
- Rational-Emotive Behavior Therapy (REBT)
- Psychopharmacological Approaches
- Parent-Child Interaction Therapy (PCIT)

CHAPTER 14: EMERGING SENSE OF SELF

- *We can do better* (DVD)—(includes downloadable video segments on transracial
  adoption and adoptees' sense of identity):
  http://www.adoptedthemovie.com/companion-dvd/

- Tools to Support LGBTQ Youth in Care (2013):
  http://www.lambdalegal.org/publications/getting-down-to-basics#families
- Caring for LGBTQ children and youth—A guide for child welfare providers (useful for parents as well):
  http://www.hrc.org/files/assets/resources/HRC_Caring_For_LGBTQ_Children_Youth.pdf

CHAPTER 15: MENTAL HEALTH

- *Adoption Voices* Magazine, "Adoption Issues and Self-Harm: Suicidal Thoughts in Adopted Children" (2013):
  http://adoptionvoicesmagazine.com/adoptive-parents/adoptee-self-harm/#.U01O0U1OU3E
- National Alliance on Mental Illness (NAMI):
  www.nami.org
- Child Welfare Information Gateway, Choosing therapy for adopted children and youth:
  https://www.childwelfare.gov/adoption/adopt_parenting/services/therapy.cfm

CHAPTER 16: PHYSICAL HEALTH

- American Academy of Pediatrics—On their council on foster care, adoption and kinship care page, you can find a pediatrician in your area who specializes in providing services to foster and adopted children:
  http://www2.aap.org/sections/adoption/index.html
- Centers for Disease Control and Prevention, Fetal Alcohol Spectrum Disorders Treatment:
  http://www.cdc.gov/ncbddd/fasd/treatments.html
- Fetal Alcohol Spectrum Disorders Center for Excellence (US DHHS, SAMHSA):
  http://fasdcenter.samhsa.gov/
- Adopting and Fostering Children with Fetal Alcohol Spectrum Disorders:
  http://www.fasdcenter.samhsa.gov/documents/WYNK_Adoption.pdf
- The Physical Effects of Fetal Alcohol Spectrum Disorders:
  http://fasdcenter.samhsa.gov/documents/WYNK_Physical_Effects.pdf
- New Alternatives for Children—a program that helps families adopt and care for children with serious medical conditions:
  http://nackidscan.org/what_we_do/programs_fostercare_fostercare.php

PART 4: ADOPTIVE PARENTS' PAINFUL PROBLEMS

CHAPTER 19: THE RESILIENCE OF ADOPTIVE PARENTS

- Expert Beacon, "Build resilience strategies with your adoptive or foster family" by Betsy Keefer Smalley:
  http://expertbeacon.com/build-resilience-strategies-your-adoptive-or-foster-family/#.U2mfsPldWQx
- Child Welfare Information Gateway, Parental Resilience:
  https://www.childwelfare.gov/can/factors/resilience.cfm

CHAPTER 20: THE IMPORTANCE OF SOCIAL SUPPORT AND COMMUNITY

- Searchable databases of support groups for adoptive families, *Adoptive Families* Magazine:
  www.adoptivefamilies.com/support_group

Online discussion forums for adoptive parents
(not affiliated with specific agencies):
- Yuku discussion forum:
  www.olderchildadoption.Yuku.com
- *Adoptive Families* Magazine:
  http://www.adoptivefamiliescircle.com/groups/group/Older_Child_Adoption1/
- Adoption.com:
  http://forums.adoption.com/
- Yahoo Groups:
  http://groups.yahoo.com/neo/groups/A_O_K/info
- Forever Parents:
  http://forums.foreverparents.com/

CHAPTER 21: ADOPTIVE PARENTS' SELF-CARE

- Moms Find Healing:
  www.momsfindhealing.com
- Read this blog entry about taking care of yourself:
  http://momsfindhealing.com/index.php/blog/put-your-own-oxygen-mask-first/

- North American Council on Adoptable Children, Self-care barriers and basics for foster/adoptive parents (article): http://www.nacac.org/adoptalk/selfcare.html

CHAPTER 22: HELP FOR ADOPTIVE FAMILIES DEALING WITH SERIOUS ISSUES

- American Adoption Congress, "Grief and Loss" (Silverstein & Kaplan, 2007): http://www.americanadoptioncongress.org/grief_silverstein_article.php
- ARCH National Respite Network: www.archrespite.org 919–490–5577
- Fact sheet on respite care for adoptive families: www.archrespite.org/images/docs/Factsheets/fs_33-adoptive_families.pdf
- Respite services to support grandparents (fact sheet, 2010): http://archrespite.org/images/docs/Factsheets/FS_45-Grandparents _Grandchildren.pdf
- Calculate your Adverse Childhood Experiences (ACE) Score: http://acestudy.org/yahoo_site_admin/assets/docs/ACE_Calculator-English .127143712.pdf
- National Association of Therapeutic Schools and Programs: http://natsap.org/
- About Post-adoption Depression: https://www.childwelfare.gov/adoption/adopt_parenting/depression.cfm

Notes

INTRODUCTION

1. US Department of Health and Human Services, Administration for Children and Families, Children's Bureau. *The AFCARS Report*. Adoption and Foster Care Analysis and Reporting System, Preliminary FY 2012 Estimates as of November 2013, No. 20, 1-6. (2013), accessed June 12, 2014 http://www.acf.hhs.gov/sites/default/files/cb/afcarsreport20.pdf

2. "Orphans," UNICEF Press Centre, accessed June 16, 2014, http://www .unicef.org/media/media_45279.html.

3. Harris Interactive. *National Foster Care Adoption Attitudes Survey: 2013 Executive Summary and Detailed Findings* (for the Dave Thomas Foundation on Adoption, 2013), accessed June 15, 2014. http://dciw4f53l7k9i.cloud-front.net/wp-content/uploads/2013/07/DTFA-HarrisPoll-REPORT-USA -FINAL1.pdf.

4. Harris Interactive, "Attitudes Survey."

5. Susan Smith, Keeping the Promise: The Critical Need for Post-Adoption Services to Enable Children and Families to Succeed," *Evan B. Donaldson Adoption Institute* (2010), accessed June 13, 2014. http://adoptioninsti-tute.org/publications/keeping-the-promise-the-critical-need-for-post -adoption-services-to-enable-children-and-families-to-succeed/.

CHAPTER 1

1. Lois Wright and Cynthia C. Flynn, "Adolescent Adoption: Success Despite Challenges." *Children and Youth Services Review* 28, no. 5 (2006): 487-510.
2. Ibid; US Department of Health and Human Services, Administration for Children and Families, Children's Bureau, "A Report to Congress on Barriers and Success Factor in Adoption from Foster Care: Perspectives of Families and Staff," (2007), accessed June 16, 2014 http://adoptuskids .org/_assets/files/NRCRRFAP/resources/barriers-and-success-report -to-congress.pdf. Ibid; US Department of Health and Human Services, Administration for Children and Families, Children's Bureau, "A Report to Congress on Barriers and Success Factor in Adoption from Foster Care: Perspectives of Families and Staff," (2007), accessed June 16, 2014 http://adoptuskids.org/_assets/files/NRCRRFAP/resources/barriers-and -success-report-to-congress.pdf.
3. Children's Bureau, "A Report to Congress."
4. Wright and Flynn, "Adolescent Adoption."
5. Cynthia Flynn, Wendy Welch and Kathleen Paget, "Field Initiated Research on Successful Adolescent Adoptions: Final Report." *The Center for Child and Family Studies, College of Social Work, University of South Carolina*, (2004), accessed June 18, 2014, http://centerforchildwelfare2.fmhi.usf.edu/kb/ bppub/SuccessfulAdolescentAdopt.pdf.
6. Wright and Flynn, "Adolescent Adoption."
7. Ibid.

CHAPTER 2

1. US Department of Health and Human Services, "AFCARS Report," 6, https:// www.childwelfare.gov/pubs/single_parent.pdf.
2. Ibid.
3. "Kinship Adoption: Meeting the Unique Needs of a Growing Population." *Child Focus, and North American Council on Adoptable Children* (2010), accessed June 13, 2014 http://childfocuspartners.com/wpcontent/uploads/ CF_Kinship_Adoption_Report_v5.pdf.
4. Ibid.
5. Judith McKenzie, John McKenzie and Rosemary Jackson, "Wherever My Family Is: That's Home! Adoption Services for Military Families, A Reference Guide for Practitioners," *AdoptUSKids*, accessed June 15, 2014, http:// www.adoptuskids.org/_assets/files/NRCRRFAP/resources/wherever -my-family-is-thats-home.pdf.

6. Ibid.
7. Human Rights Campaign, "Caring for LGBTQ Children and Youth," *Human Rights Campaign Foundation*, (2013), accessed June 13, 1014, http://www.hrc.org/files/assets/resources/HRC_Caring_For_LGBTQ_Children_Youth.pdf.
8. Ibid, 14-35.
9. Gary J Gates, M.V. Lee Badgett, Jennifer Ehrle Macomber and Kate Chambers, "Adoption and Foster Care by Gay and Lesbian Parents in the United States," The Williams Institute, and the Urban Institute (2007), accessed June 15, 2014, http://www.urban.org/UploadedPDF/411437_Adoption_Foster_Care.pdf (accessed June 15, 2014).
10. Ibid, 14.
11. Gary J. Gates, "LGBT Parenting in the United States." The Williams Institute, (2013), accessed June 15, 2014, http://williamsinstitute.law.ucla.edu/wp-content/uploads/LGBT-Parenting.pdf.
12. Gates, Lee Badgett, Macomber, Chambers, "Adoption and Foster Care."
13. Melissa Blauvelt, "Adoption Advocate No. 49: Adoption Resources for Americans Living Abroad." *National Council for Adoption*, (July 2012), accessed June 15, 2014, https://www.adoptioncouncil.org/publications/adoption-advocate-no-49.html.
14. "Intercountry Adoption, Adoptions by Non-US Citizens Living in the US," Bureau of Consular Affairs, US Department of State, last updated March, 2014, http://adoption.state.gov/adoption_process/who_can_adopt/residents.php.
15. Alicia Summers, Steve Wood and Jennifer Donovan, "Disproportionality Rates for Children of Color in Foster Care," *National Council of Juvenile and Family Court Judges*, Technical Bulletin, (2013), accessed June 15, 2014, http://www.ncjfcj.org/sites/default/files/Disproportionality%20Rates%20for%20Children%20of%20Color%20in%20Foster%20Care%202013.pdf.

CHAPTER 3

1. Harris Interactive, "Attitudes Survey," p. 7.
2. "History" US Department of Health and Human Services, Administration for Children and Families, Children's Bureau, accessed June 15, 2014, http://www.acf.hhs.gov/programs/cb/about/history.

3. "Major Federal Legislation Concerned with Child Protection, Child Welfare, and Adoption," Child Welfare Information Gateway Factsheet, last updated April 2012, https://www.childwelfare.gov/pubs/otherpubs/majorfedlegis .pdf.

4. E-mail from Sara Munson, National Child Welfare Workforce Institute, July 1, 2014.

5. US Department of Health and Human Services, "AFCARS Report, FY 2012 Estimates."

6. Ibid.

7. "How Many Children Were Adopted in 2007 and 2008?" Child Welfare Information Gateway Numbers and Trends, last updated September 2011, https://www.childwelfare.gov/pubs/adopted0708.pdf.

8. "Placement of Children with Relatives, "Child Welfare Information Gateway State Statutes Series, current as of July, 2013, https://www.childwelfare .gov/systemwide/laws_policies/statutes/placement.pdf.

9. US Department of Health and Human Services, "AFCARS Report, FY 2012 Estimates."

10. Ibid.

11. Ibid.

12. Chambers, Kate, Erica H. Zielewski and Karin Malm, "Foster Youths' Views of Adoption and Permanency." *The Urban Institute* (2008), accessed June 16, 2014, http://www.urban.org/publications/411609.html.

13. "How to Adopt," North American Council on Adoptable Children, accessed June 16, 2014, http://www.nacac.org/howtoadopt/howtoadopt.html.

14. Ramona W. Denby, Keith A. Alford and Jessica Ayala, "The Journey to Adopt a Child Who Has Special Needs: Parents' Perspectives." Small sample study in *Children and Youth Services Review* 33, no. 9 (2011): 1543-54.

15. David Brodzinsky, "Adoptive Parent Preparation Project Phase I: Meeting the Mental Health and Developmental Needs of Adopted Children," *Evan B. Donaldson Adoption Institute* (2008), accessed June 16, 2014, http:// adoptioninstitute.org/old/publications/2008_02_Parent_Preparation.pdf.

16. US Department of Health and Human Services, "AFCARS Report, FY 2012 Estimates."

17. "Federal Adoption Tax Credit," National Council on Adoptable Children, last updated April 2014, http://www.nacac.org/taxcredit/taxcredit.html.

CHAPTER 4

1. Elizabeth J. Ryan, "For the Best Interests of the Children: Why the Hague Convention on Intercountry Adoption Needs to Go Farther as Evidenced by Romania and the United States," *Boston College International & Comparative Law Review* 29, no. 353, (2006): 353-383; Peter Selman, "The Rise and Fall of Intercountry Adoption in The 21st Century," *International Social Work* 52, no. 5, (2009): 575-594; Jini L. Roby, "Human Rights, Politics and Intercountry Adoption: An Examination of Two Sending Countries," *International Social Work*, 52, no. 5, (2009): 661-671.

2. Peter Selman, "From Bucharest to Beijing: Changes in Countries Sending Children for International Adoption 1990 to 2006" in *International Advances in Adoption Research for Practice*, eds. Gretchen Miller Woerbel and Elsbeth Neil, (Hoboken, NJ: Wiley Publishers, 2009), 41-69.

3. Benyam D. Mezmur, "Adoção internacional como medida de último recurso na África: promover os direitos de uma criança ao invés do direito a uma criança," *Sur. Revista Internacional de Direitos Humanos*, 6, no. 10, (2009): 82-105, accessed April 14, 2014, http://www.scielo.br/scielo.php?script=sci_arttext&pid=S1806-64452009000100005&lng=en&tlng=en.10.1590/S1806-64452009000100005.

4. David M. Smolin, "Intercountry Adoption as Child Trafficking," *Valparaiso Law Review*, 3, no. 2, (2004): 281-335; Ethan B. Kaptstein, "The Baby Trade," *Foreign Affairs*, 82, no. 6, (2003): 115–25; Roby, "Human Rights"; Kelley Bunkers McCreery, Victor Groza and Daniel P Lauer, "International adoption and child protection in Guatemala: A case of the tail wagging the dog," *International Social Work*, 52, no. 5, (2009): 649-660.

5. "Hague Convention Text," Bureau of Consular Affairs, US Department of State, accessed June 16, 2014, http://adoption.state.gov/hague_convention/text.php.

6. Elizabeth Bartholet, "Inter-American Commission on Human Rights, Organization of American States, Hearing on Human Rights of Unparented Children and Related International Adoption Policies, 137th Ordinary Period of Sessions," (Written Testimony of Delegation November 6, 2009): 1, accessed April 14, 2014, www.law.harvard.edu/programs/about/cap/ia/testimonyfullnov09.pdf.

7. "Orphans," UNICEF Press Centre, accessed June 16, 2014, http://www.unicef.org/media/media_45279.html.

8. Bunkers McCreery, Groza and Lauer, "International Adoption."

9. "Intercountry Adoption from Hague Convention and Non-Hague Convention Countries," Child Welfare Information Gateway Factsheets for Families, (2009), accessed June 16, 2014 https://www.childwelfare.gov/pubs/factsheets/hague.cfm).

CHAPTER 5

1. Children's Bureau, "A Report to Congress."
2. Ibid.

CHAPTER 6

1. Conway and Hutson, "Kinship Care."
2. "Adoption Disruption and Dissolution," Child Welfare Information Gateway, Numbers and Trends, last updated June 2012, https://www.childwelfare.gov/pubs/s_disrup.PDF.
3. "Consent to Adoption," Child Welfare Information Gateway, State Statutes, current through April 2013, https://www.childwelfare.gov/systemwide/laws_policies/statutes/consent.pdf.

CHAPTER 8

1. "National Survey of Adoptive Parents," www.cdc.gov/nchs/slaits/nsap.htm.
2. Ibid.
3. Ruth G. McRoy, "Finding Permanency for African American Children in the Child Welfare System: Implications of MEPA/IEPA" (testimony presented to the US Commission on Human Rights for the Evan B. Donaldson Adoption Institute, September 21, 2007), accessed June 16, 2014, http://www.researchgate.net/publication/253528062_Finding_Permanency_for_African_American_Children_in_the_Child_Welfare_System_Implications_of_MEPAIEPA.
4. Debra Jo Clayton and Nadja Jones, "The Indian Child Welfare Act (ICWA) an Overview," (National Child Welfare Workforce Institute webinar presented Oct. 12, 2011), accessed June 16, 2014, http://vimeo.com/41022708.
5. McRoy, "Finding Permanency."
6. Charlotte Paulsen and Joseph R. Merighi, "Adoption Preparedness, Cultural Engagement, and Parental Satisfaction in Intercountry Adoption." Small sample study in Adoption Quarterly 12, no. 1 (2009): 1-18.
7. Ibid, 4.

CHAPTER 9

1. "Sibling Issues in Foster Care and Adoption," Child Welfare Information Gateway, Bulletin for Professionals (2013), accessed June 15, 2014, https://www.childwelfare.gov/pubs/siblingissues/siblingissues.pdf.
2. Ibid, 1.
3. Cherilyn Dance, Alan Rushton and David Quinton, "Emotional Abuse in Early Childhood: Relationships with Progress in Subsequent Family Placement." *Journal of Child Psychology and Psychiatry* 43, no. 3 (2002): 395-407.
4. Youth Leadership Advisory Team, "Siblings In Foster Care and Adoption," (2002) retrieved June 23, 2014, http://www.ylat.org/wp-content/uploads/2013/09/Position-Paper-Siblings1.pdf.
5. Arleta James, *Brothers and Sisters in Adoption: Helping Children Navigate Relationships When New Kids Join the Family* (London: Jessica Kingsley Publishers, 2012).
6. Amanda Baden and John Raible, "Sibling Relationships in Transracial Adoptive Families" in *Sibling Development: Implications for Mental Health Practitioners*, edited by Jonathan Caspi (New York: Springer Publishing Company, 2011): 289-321.
7. Harold D. Grotevant and Ruth Gail McRoy, *Openness in Adoption: Exploring Family Connections* (Thousand Oaks, CA: Sage Publishing, 1998).

CHAPTER 10

1. Monica Faulkner and Elissa E, Madden, "Open Adoption and Post-Adoption Birth Family Contact: A Comparison of Non-Relative Foster and Private Adoptions." *Adoption Quarterly* 15, no. 1 (2012): 35-56.
2. Ibid.
3. Michele Hanna, Kerri Tokarski, Dawn Matera and Rowena Fong, "Happily Ever After? The Journey from Foster Care to Adoption." *Adoption Quarterly* 14, no. 2 (2011): 107-31.; Wright and Flynn, "Adolescent Adoption."

CHAPTER 11

1. "What is Child Traumatic Stress?" National Child Traumatic Stress Network, accessed June 16, 2014, http://www.nctsnet.org/sites/default/files/assets/pdfs/what_is_child_traumatic_stress_0.pdf.

2. William W. Harris, Alicia F. Lieberman and Steven Marans, "In the Best Interests of Society," *Journal of Child Psychology and Psychiatry* 48, no. 3-4 (2007): 392-411.

3. Child Abuse and Maltreatment," National Institute of Justice.

4. "Physical Abuse," National Child Traumatic Stress Network, http://www .nctsn.org/trauma-types/physical-abuse, accessed June 23, 2014.

5. American Humane Association, http:/www.americanhumane.org/children/ stop-child-abuse/fact-sheets/emotional-abuse.html.

6. US Department of Health and Human Services, "AFCARS Report, FY 2012 Estimates."

7. "Child Maltreatment," World Health Organization Media Centre, last updated January 2014, http://www.who.int/mediacentre/factsheets/fs150/en/.

8. Ibid.

9. "What is Childhood Traumatic Grief?" National Child Traumatic Stress Network, last updated April, 2014, http://www.nctsn.org/trauma-types/ traumatic-grief/what-childhood-traumatic-grief.

10. UNICEF, http://www.unicef.org/media/media_41118.html.

11. "What is Child Traumatic Stress?" National Child Traumatic Stress Network, accessed June 16, 2014, http://www.nctsn.org/resources/audiences/ parents-caregivers/what-is-cts.

12. Alicia F. Lieberman and Kathleen Knorr, "The Impact of Trauma: A Developmental Framework for Infancy and Early Childhood," *Pediatric annals* 36, no. 4 (2007): 209-15.

13. Lieberman and Knorr, "Impact of Trauma;" "Symptoms and Behaviors Associated with Exposure to Trauma," National Child Traumatic Stress Network, accessed June 16, 2014, http://www.nctsn.org/trauma-types/ early-childhood-trauma/Symptoms-and-Behaviors-Associated-with -Exposure-to-Trauma.

14. Lieberman and Knorr, "Impact of Trauma."

15. Robert Anda, "The Health and Social Impact of Growing Up With Adverse Childhood Experiences, The Human and Economic Costs of the Status Quo," The Adverse Childhood Experiences Study, accessed June 16, 2014, http:// acestudy.org/files/Review_of_ACE_Study_with_references_summary _table_2_.pdf.

16. Julian D. Ford, "Neurobiological and Developmental Research," in *Treating Complex Traumatic Stress Disorders: An Evidence-Based Guide*, Eds. Christine Courtois and Julian Ford (New York: Guilford Press, 2009), 31-58; Cohen et al., 2010).

17. Anda, "Health and Social Impact."

18. Ibid.

19. Harris, Lieberman and Marans, "Best Interests of Society," 392.

20. "Tips for Finding Help: Recommendation from the National Child Traumatic Stress Network, accessed June 16, 2014, http://www.nctsnet.org/sites/default/files/assets/pdfs/tips_for_finding_help.pdf.

21. Lieberman and Knorr, "Impact of Trauma."

22. James, *Brothers and Sisters*, 369.

23. Ibid, 376.

24. Ibid, 492.

25. Brenda McCreight, *Parenting Your Adopted Older Child: How to Overcome the Unique Challenges and Raise a Happy and Healthy Child* (Oakland, CA: Harbinger Publications, 2002), 48.

26. Ibid.

27. RG Tedeschi and LG Calhoun, *Trauma and Transformation: Growing in the Aftermath of Suffering* (Thousand Oaks, CA: Sage, 1995).

CHAPTER 12

1. Elisabeth Kübler-Ross and David A Kessler, *On Grief and Grieving: Finding the Meaning of Grief through the Five Stages of Loss* (New York: Simon and Schuster, 2005).

2. David M. Brodzinsky, Daniel W. Smith and Anne B. Brodzinsky, *Children's Adjustment to Adoption: Developmental and Clinical Issues* (Thousand Oaks, CA: Sage Publications, 1998).

CHAPTER 13

1. John Bowlby, *Attachment and Loss: Vol. 3. Loss: Sadness and Depression* (New York: Basic Books, 1980).

2. Robert A. Hinde, *Ethology and Child Development* (New York: Wiley, 1983).

3. John Bowlby, *Attachment* (New York, Basic Books, 1969); Ibid.

4. Mary D. S. Ainsworth, *The Development of Infant-Mother Attachment* (Chicago: University of Chicago Press, 1973); John Bowlby, *A Secure Base: Clinical Applications of Attachment Theory* (London: Routledge, 1988).

5. Mary Main and Donna Weston, "The Quality of the Toddler's Relationship to Mother and to Father: Related to Conflict Behavior and the Readiness to Establish New Relationships," *Child Development*, 52 (1981): 932-940.

6. Neil W. Boris, N. W. Wheeler, Sheryl Scott Heller and Charles Zeanah "Attachment and Developmental Psychopathology: A Case Study," *Psychiatry* 63, no. 1 (2000): 74-83.

7. American Psychiatric Association, *Diagnostic and Statistical Manual of Mental Disorders, Fifth Edition, DSM-5* (Arlington, VA, American Psychiatric Publishing, 2013).

8. Femmie Juffer and Lizette Rosenboom, "Infant-Mother Attachment of Internationally Adopted Children in the Netherlands, *International Journal of Behavioral Development* 20, no. 1 (1997): 93-107.

9. Patrica M. Crittenden, Mary F. Partridge and Angelika Claussen, "Family Patterns of Relationship in Normative and Dysfunctional Families," *Development and Psychopathology*, 3, no. 4 (1991): 491-512; Femmie Juffer, René A. C. Hoksbergen, Marianne Riksen-Walraven and Geldolph A. Kohnstamm, "Early Intervention in Adoptive Families: Supporting Maternal Sensitive Responsiveness, Infant Mother Attachment, and Infant Competence," *Journal of Child Psychology and Psychiatry* 38 no. 8 (1997): 1039-1050; Marianne S. De Wolff and Marinus H. van IJzendoorn, "Sensitivity and Attachment: A Meta-Analysis on Parental Antecedents of Infant Attachment," *Child Development*, 68, (199):571-591.; H.H Goldsmith and Jennifer A. Alansky, "Maternal and Infant Temperamental Predictors of Attachment: A Meta-Analytic Review," *Journal of Consulting and Clinical Psychology* 55, no. 6 (1987): 805-816.

10. Charles H. Zeanah, "Disturbances of Attachment in Young Children Adopted From Institutions," *Developmental and Behavioral Pediatrics* 21, no. 3 (2000): 230-236.; N.W. Boris, E.E. Wheeler, S.S. Heller and Charles Zeanah, "Attachment and Developmental Psychopathology: A Case Study," *Psychiatry* 63, no. 1 (2000): 74-83.

11. Douglas M.Teti, Miyuki Nakagawa, Rina Das and Oliver Wirth, "Security of Attachment Between Preschoolers and Their Mothers: Relations Among Social Interaction, Parenting Stress and Mothers' Sorts of the Attachment Q-Set," *Developmental Psychology*, 27, no. 3, (1991): 440-447; K. Chisholm, "A Three Year Follow-Up of Attachment and Indiscriminate Friendliness in Children Adopted From Romanian Orphanages," *Child Development* 69, no. 4, (1998): 1092-106.

12. Brodzinsky, Smith and Brodzinsky, *Children's Adjustment to Adoption*.

13. Victor Groza, "Adoption, Attachment and Self-Concept," *Child and Adolescent Social Work Journal* 9, no. 2 (1992): 169-191.

14. Lois Ruskai Melina, *Raising Adopted Children: Practical Reassuring Advice for Every Adoptive Parent* (New York: HarperCollins Publishers, 1990).

15. California Evidence-Based Clearinghouse for Child Welfare, accessed June 23, 2014, http://www.cebc4cw.org/; Victor Groza, "Adoption, Attachment and Self-Concept," *Child and Adolescent Social Work Journal* 9, no. 2 (1992): 169-191.

CHAPTER 14

1. Smith, "Keeping the Promise," 11.

2. Leslie H.Wind, Devon Brooks and Richard P. Barth, "Influences of Risk History and Adoption Preparation on Post-Adoption Services Use in US Adoptions." *Family Relations* 56, no. 4 (2007): 378-89.

3. Flynn, Welch and Paget, "Field Initiated Research."

4. Gina Miranda Samuels and Julia M. Pryce, "What Doesn't Kill You Makes You Stronger: Survivalist Self-Reliance as Resilience and Risk Among Young Adults Aging Out of Foster Care," *Children and Youth Services Review* 30 (2008): 1198–1210.

5. Wright and Flynn, "Adolescent Adoption;" Hanna et al., "Happily Ever After."

6. McRoy, "Finding Permanency."

7. J.W. Berry, "Immigration, acculturation, and adaptation," *Applied Psychology: An International Review.* 1997;46:5–34.

8. Jeffrey Jensen Arnett, "Emerging Adulthood: A Theory of Development from the Late Teens to the Early Twenties," *American Psychologist* 55, no. 5 (2000): 469-480; Jeffrey Jensen Arnett, *Emerging Adulthood: The Winding Road from the Late Teens through the Twenties* (New York: Oxford University Press, 2004).

9. Arnett, *Emerging Adulthood: The Winding Road.*

10. Meredith O'Connor, Ann Sanson, Mary T. Hawkins, John W. Toumbourou, Primrose Letcher and Erica Frydenberg, "Differentiating Three Conceptualisations of the Relationship Between Positive Development and Psychopathology During the Transition To Adulthood," *Journal of Adolescence* 34 (2011): 475–484.

11. Peter Martin and Michael A. Stayer, "The Experience of Micro- and Macroevents: A Life Span Analysis," *Research on Aging*, 12 (1990): 294-310.
12. Arnett, "Emerging Adulthood;" Arnett, *Emerging Adulthood: The Winding Road*.
13. Erik H. Erikson, *Childhood and Society* (New York: W. W. Norton, 1950); Erik E. Erikson, *Identity: Youth and Crisis* (New York: Norton, 1968); Kenneth Keniston, *Youth and Dissent: The Rise of a New Opposition* (New York: Harcourt Brace Jovanovich, 1971); Daniel J. Levinson, *The Seasons of a Man's Life* (NY: Random House, 1978).
14. Arnett, "Emerging Adulthood;" Arnett, *Emerging Adulthood: The Winding Road*.
15. Arnett, *Emerging Adulthood: The Winding Road*.
16. Ibid.
17. Marinus H. Van IJzendoorn and Femmie Juffer, "Adoption as Intervention: Meta-analytic Evidence for Massive Catch-Up and Plasticity in Physical, Socio-Emotional and Cognitive Development. The Emanuel Miller Memorial Lecture 2006," *Journal of Child Psychology and Psychiatry* 47 (2006): 1128–1245.

CHAPTER 15

1. Anu Sharma, Matthew McGue and Peter Benson, "The Emotional and Behavioral Adjustment of United States Adopted Adolescents: Part I. An Overview," *Children and Youth Services Review* 18, no 1–2 (1998): 83-100; Brent C. Miller, Xitao Fan, Mathew Christensen, Harold D. Grotevant, and Manfred Van Dulmen, "Comparisons of Adopted and Nonadopted Adolescents in A Large, Nationally Representative Sample," *Child Development* 71, no. 5 (2000): 1458–1473.
2. Sharma et al, "The Emotional and Behavioral Adjustment."
3. Michael Wierzbicki, "Psychological Adjustment of Adoptees: A Meta-Analysis," *Journal of Clinical Child Psychology* 22 (1993): 447–454.
4. Ann E. Brand and Paul Brinich, "Behavior Problems and Mental Health Contacts in Adopted, Foster, and Nonadopted Children.," *Journal of Child Psychology and Psychiatry* 40, no. 8 (1999): 1221-1229.
5. Linda van den Dries, Femmie Juffer, Marinus van IJzendoorn and Marian Bakermans-Kranenburg, "Fostering Security? A Meta-Analysis of Attachment in Adopted Children." *Children and Youth Services Review* 31 (2009): 410-421.

6. Miller, et al, "Comparisons of Adopted;" Femmie Juffer and Marinus van IJzendoorn, "Behavior Problems and Mental Health Referrals of International Adoptees: A Meta-Analysis," JAMA 293, no. 20 (2005):2501-2515.

7. Gail Slap, Elizabeth Goodman and Bin Huang, "Adoption as a Risk Factor for Attempted Suicide During Adolescence," Pediatrics 108, no. 2 (2001), accessed June 24, 2014, doi:10.1542/peds.108.2.e30; Anders Hjern, Frank Lindblad and Bo Vinnerljung, "Suicide, Psychiatric Illness, and Social Maladjustment in Intercountry Adoptees in Sweden: A Cohort Study," The Lancet, 360, no. 9331 (2002): 443-448.

8. David Brodzinsky, "Children's Understanding of Adoption: Developmental and Clinical Implications," Professional Psychology: Research and Practice 42, no. 2, (2011): 200–207.

9. Centers for Disease Control, " Mental Health Surveillance Among Children— United States, 2005-2011, Supplements May 17, 2013," 62, no. 2 (2013), accessed June 18, 2014 http://www.cdc.gov/mmwr/preview/mmwrhtml/su6202a1.htm.

10. Ibid.

11. Ibid.

12. Sharon Vandivere, Karin Malm and Laura Radel, "Adoption USA: A Chartbook Based on the 2007 National Survey of Adoptive Parents," Child Trends, and the U.S. Department of Health and Human Services, Office of the Assistant Secretary for Planning and Evaluation, last updated November 2009, http://aspe.hhs.gov/hsp/09/nsap/chartbook/index.cfm.

13. Ibid, 36.

14. Ibid.

15. Holly C. Wilcox, Janet Kuramoto, David Brent and Bo Runeson, "The Interaction of Parental History of Suicidal Behavior and Exposure to Adoptive Parents' Psychiatric Disorders on Adoptee Suicide Attempt Hospitalizations," American Journal of Psychiatry, 169 (2012):309-315.

CHAPTER 16

1. Veronnie F. Jones, Pamela C. High, Elaine Donoghue, Jill J. Fussell, Mary Margaret Gleason, Paula K. Jaudes, David M. Rubin and Elaine E. Schulte, "Comprehensive Health Evaluation of the Newly Adopted Child," Pediatrics 129, No. 1 (2012):e214 -e223, accessed June 18, 2014, doi: 10.1542/peds.2011-2381.

2. Ibid.

3. Ibid.

4. Cynthia R. Howard and Chandy C. John, "Chapter 7, International Travel with Infants and Children," in *CDC Health Information for International Travel*, accessed June 18, 2014 http://wwwnc.cdc.gov/travel/yellowbook/2014/chapter-7-international-travel-infants-children/international-adoption.

5. Ibid.

6. Jones et al., "Comprehensive Health Evaluation."

7. Ibid.

8. Matthew D. Bramlett, Laura F. Radel and Stephen J. Blumberg, "The Health and Well-being of Adopted Children," *Pediatrics* 119, no. supplement 1, (2007): S54-S60, accessed June 18, 2014, DOI: 10.1542/peds.2006-2089I.

9. Vandivere et al., "Adoption USA."

10. Emalee Flaherty, Richard Thompson, Alan Litrownik, Adrea Theodore, Diana English, Maureen Black, Traci Wike, Lakecia Whimper, Desmond Runyan and Howard Dubowitz, "Effect of Early Childhood Adversity on Child Health," *Archives of Pediatrics & Adolescent Medicine*, 160, no. 12 (2006):1232-1238.

11. Van IJzendoorn and Juffer, "Adoption as Intervention."

12. Christopher Lloyd and Richard Barth, "Developmental Outcomes After Five Years for Foster Children Returned Home, Remaining In Care, or Adopted," *Children and Youth Services Review* 33 (2011): 1383-1391.

13. Henrietta Bada, Jean Twomey, Charlotte Bursi, John Langer, Linda LaGasse, Charles Bauer, Seetha Shankaran, Barry Lester, Rosemary Higgins and Penelope Maza, "Importance of Stability of Early Living Arrangements on Behavior Outcomes of Children with and without Prenatal Drug Exposure," *Journal Of Developmental and Behavioral Pediatrics* 29, no. 3 (2008): 173-182.

14. Cermak, 1994; Sharon A. Cermak and Lisa A. Daunhauer, "Sensory Processing in the Postinstitutionalized Child," *American Journal of Occupational Therapy* 51, no. 7 (1997): 500-07; Gail Haradon, Barbara Bascom, Christiana Dragomir and Virginia Scripcaru, "Sensory Functions of Institutionalized Romanian Infants: A Pilot Study," *Occupational Therapy International* 1, no. 4 (1994): 250-260; Jane K. Sweeney and Barbara B. Bascom, "Motor Development and Self-Stimulatory Movement in Institutionalized Romanian Children," *Pediatric Physical Therapy* 7, no. 3 (1995): 124-32.; Sharon Cermak and Victor Groza, "Sensory Processing Problems in Post-Institutionalized Children: Implications for Social Work," *Child and Adolescent Social Work Journal* 15, no. 1 (1998): 5-37.

15. Cermak and Groza, "Sensory Processing Problems."

16. Ibid.

17. "Precocious Puberty," The Mayo Clinic, accessed June 24, 2014, http://www.mayoclinic.org/diseases-conditions/precocious-puberty/basics/definition/con-20029745.

18. Sandra Cesario and Lisa Hughes, "Precocious Puberty: A Comprehensive Review of Literature," *Journal of Obstetric, Gynecologic, & Neonatal Nursing,* 36, no. 3 (2007), 263-274.

19. T Tuvemo, B Jonsson, J Gustafsson, K Albertsson-Wikland, AS Aronson, A Häger, S Ivarson, et al., "Final Height after Combined Growth Hormone and GnRH Analogue Treatment in Adopted Girls with Early Puberty," *Acta Paediatrica* 93, no. 11 (2004): 1456-62.

20. Grete Teilmann, Carsten B. Pedersen, Niels E. Skakkebæk and Tina Kold Jensen, "Increased Risk of Precocious Puberty in Internationally Adopted Children in Denmark," *Pediatrics* 118, no. 2 (2006): e391-e99.; Leandro Soriano-Guillén, Raquel Corripio, José Ignacio Labarta, Ramón Cañete, Lidia Castro-Feijóo, Rafael Espino and Jesús Argente, "Central Precocious Puberty in Children Living in Spain: Incidence, Prevalence, and Influence of Adoption and Immigration," *Journal of Clinical Endocrinology & Metabolism* 95, no. 9 (2010), 4305-13.

21. Jean-Claude Carel and Juliane Leger, "Precocious Puberty." *New England Journal of Medicine* 358, no. 22 (2008): 2366-77.

22. Jones et al., "Comprehensive Health Evaluation."

23. O. Gavrilovici and Victor Groza, "Incidence, Prevalence and Trauma Symptoms in Institutionalized Romanian Children," *International Journal of Child and Family Welfare* 10, no. 3-4, (2007): 125-138.

24. Magnus Landgren, Marita Andersson Grönlund, Per-Olof Elfstrand, Jan-Erik Simonsson, Leif Svensson and Kerstin Strömland, "Health before and after Adoption from Eastern Europe." *Acta Pædiatrica* 95, no. 6 (2006): 720-25.; Laurie Miller, Marybet Kiernan, Michelle Mathers and Marisa Klein-Gitelman, "Developmental and Nutritional Status of Internationallya Adopted Children, *Archives of Pediatrics and Adolescent Medicine* 149, no. 1 (1995): 40-44; David Skuse, "Extreme Deprivation in Early Childhood - II. Theoretical Issues and a Comparative Review," *Journal of Child Psychology and Psychiatry* 25, no. 4 (1984): 543-572.

25. "About FASD," Fetal Alcohol Spectrum Disorders Center for Excellence", accessed June 24, 2014, http://fasdcenter.samhsa.gov/aboutUs/aboutFASD .aspx.

26. Stacy Buckingham-Howes, Sarah Shafer Berger, Laura A. Scaletti and Maureen M. Black, "Systematic Review of Prenatal Cocaine Exposure and Adolescent Development," *Pediatrics* 31, no. 6 (2013): e1917-36, accessed June 24, 2014, doi: 10.1542/peds.2012-0945.

27. Susan Okie, "The Epidemic that Wasn't," *The New York Times*, Jan. 26, 2009, accessed June 24, 2014, http://www.nytimes.com/2009/01/27/ health/27coca.html?pagewanted=all&_r=0; Susan FitzGerald, "Crack Baby' Study Ends with Unexpected but Clear Result," *The Inquirer*, July 22, 2013, accessed June 24, 2014, http://articles.philly.com/2013-0722/ news/40709969_1_hallam-hurt-so-called-crack-babies-funded-study.

CHAPTER 17

1. Ann M. Easterbrooks, Jean-Francois Bureau and Karlen Lyons-Ruth, "Developmental Correlates and Predictors of Emotional Availability In Mother–Child Interaction: A Longitudinal Study From Infancy To Middle Childhood," *Development and Psychopathology* 24, no. 1 (2012): 65-78.

2. Rahil D. Briggs, Ellen J. Silver, Laura M. Krug, Zachary S. Mason, Rebecca Schrag, Susan Chinitz and Andrew D. Racine, "Healthy Steps as a Moderator: The Impact of Maternal Trauma on Child Social-Emotional Development." *Clinical Practice in Pediatric Psychology* 2, no. 2 (2014): 166-75.

3. Jack P. Shonkoff and Susan N. Bales, "Science Does Not Speak For Itself: Translating Child Development Research for The Public and Its Policymakers," *Child Development*, 82, no.1 (2011): 17-32.

4. Seth Pollak, Dante Cicchetti, Katherine Hornung and Alex Reed, "Recognizing Emotion in Faces: Developmental Effects of Child Abuse and Neglect," *Developmental Psychology* 36, no. 5, (2000): 679-688.

5. Urie Bronfenbrenner and Stephen J Ceci, "Nature-Nuture Reconceptualized in Developmental Perspective: A Bioecological Model," *Psychological Review* 101, no. 4 (1994): 568.

6. Carol Dweck, *Self-Theories: Their Role in Motivation, Personality, and Development. Essays in Social Psychology* (New York: Psychology Press, 1999).

7. Ibid.

8. Angela L. Duckworth and Martin E. P. Seligman, "Self-Discipline Outdoes IQ in Predicting Academic Performance of Adolescents," *Psychological Science* 16, no. 12 (2005): 939-94.

9. Ibid.

10. Emily C. Merz, Robert B. McCall and Victor Groza, "Parent-Reported Executive Functioning in Postinstitutionalized Children: A Follow-Up Study," *Journal of Clinical Child and Adolescent Psychology* 42, no. 5 (2013): 726-733.

11. "The Impact of Neglect," The Bucharest Early Intervention Project, accessed July 1, 2014, http://www.bucharestearlyinterventionproject.org/; "British-Chinese Adoption Study," BAAF Adoption & Fostering, accessed July 2, 2014, http://www.baaf.org.uk/ourwork/bcas; http://www.socialsciences.leiden.edu/educationandchildstudies/adoc/research/adoptionresearch-in-the-netherlands.html; "The English and Romanian Adoptee (ERA) Project," King's College London, accessed July 2, 2014, https://www.kcl.ac.uk/iop/depts/mrc/research/PreviousResearch/theenglishandromaniandoptee(era)project.aspx.

12. "Brief: Education Records of Children in Foster Care," State Policy Advocacy and Reform Center and First Focus, accessed July 2, 2014, http://childwelfaresparc.org/education-records-of-children-in-foster-care/.

13. Charles A Nelson III, Charles H. Zeanah, Nathan A. Fox, Peter Marshall, Anna Smyke and Donald Guthrie, "Cognitive Recovery in Socially Deprived Young Children: The Bucharest Early Intervention Project," *Science*, 318, no. 5858 (2007): 1937-1940; Marinus van IJzendoorn, Femie Juffer, Caroline Poelhuis and Caroline W. Klein, "Adoption and Cognitive Development: A Meta-Analytic Comparison of Adopted and Nonadopted Children's IQ and School Performance." *Psychological Bulletin* 131, no. 2 (2005): 301-316; Andrea Zetlin, Lois Weinberg and Nancy M. Shea, "Caregivers, School Liaisons, and Agency Advocates Speak Out About the Educational Needs of Children and Youths in Foster Care," *Social Work* 55, no. 3 (2010): 245-254.

14. Caprice A. Knapp, Lindsey Woodworth and Mehda Ranka, "Parental Perceptions of Adopted Children's Educational Outcomes," *Adoption Quarterly*, 16, no.2 (2013): 85-96.

15. L.S. Vygotsky, *Mind in Society: The Development of Higher Psychological Processes* (Cambridge, Massachusetts: Harvard University Press, 1978).

16. Michael M. Criss, Gregory S. Pettit, John E. Bates, Kenneth A. Dodge and Amie L. Lapp, "Family Adversity, Positive Peer Relationships, And Children's Externalizing Behavior: A Longitudinal Perspective On Risk And Resilience," *Child Development*, 73, no. 4 (2002): 1220-1237.

17. Urie Bronfenbrenner, *The Ecology of Human Development: Experiments by Design and Nature*. (Cambridge, MA: Harvard University Press, 1979).

18. Thomas M. Achenbach, *Integrative Guide for the 1991 CBCL/4-18, YSR, and TRF Profiles*. (Burlington, VT: University of Vermont, Department of Psychiatry, 1991).

19. Pamela Wright and Pete Wright, *Wrightslaw: From Emotions to Advocacy— The Special Education Survival Guide*. (Hartfield, VA: Harbor House Law Press, 2006).

20. National Center for Learning Disabilities, "IDEA Parent Guide," (2004) accessed July 1, 2014, http://www.ncld.org/learning-disability-resources/ebooks-guides-toolkits/idea-parent-guide.

21. Family Educational Rights and Privacy Act (FERPA), http://www2.ed.gov/policy/gen/guid/fpco/ferpa/index.html.

22. Pamela Wright, "Advocating for your Child – Getting Started," WrightsLaw, accessed July 1, 2014, http://www.wrightslaw.com/advoc/articles/advocacy.intro.htm.

CHAPTER 18

1. Alan E. Kazdin, *The Kazdin Method for Parenting the Defiant Child: With No Pills, No Therapy, No Contest of Wills*, (Boston, MA: Houghton Mifflin Company, 2008); Dweck, *Self-Theories*, 1999.

2. Martin E.P. Seligman, with Karen Reivich, Lisa Jaycox and Jane Gillham, *The Optimistic Child* (New York: Houghton Mifflin, 2007).

3. Ibid.

4. Ibid.

5. Suniya S. Luthar, Dante Cicchetti and Bronwyn Becker, "The Construct of Resilience: A Critical Evaluation and Guidelines for Future Work," *Child Development* 71, no. 3 (2000): 543-562.

6. Donald Meichenbaum, "How Educators Can Nurture Resilience in High-Risk Children and Their Families," *The Melissa Institute for Violence Prevention* (2006) accessed July 1, 2014 from http://www.schoolviolenceprevention.org/Resilience.pdf.

7. Ibid.

8. Seligman et al, *The Optimistic Child*; Robert Brooks, "Fostering Motivation, Hope, and Resilience in Children with Learning Disorders," *Annals of Dyslexia* 51 (2001): 9-20.; Meichenbaum, "*How Educators Can Nurture Resilience.*"

9. "Protective Factors Framework," Child Welfare Information Gateway, accessed July 1, 2014, https://www.childwelfare.gov/can/factors/protective_factors.cfm.

10. Diana Baumrind, "Authoritative Parenting Revisited: History and Current Status," in *Authoritative Parenting: Synthesizing Nurturance and Discipline for Optimal Child Development*, edited by Robert E. Larzelere, Amanda Sheffield Morris and Amanda W. Harrist (Washington, DC: American Psychological Association, 2013): 11-34.

11. Ibid.

12. John Gottman and Joan DeClaire, *Raising an Emotionally Intelligent Child: The Heart of Parenting*, (New York: Simon and Schuster, 1997).

13. Ibid.

14. Ibid.

15. Kazdin, *The Kazdin Method.*

16. Diana Baumrind, "Authoritative Parenting Revisited: History and Current Status," in *Authoritative Parenting: Synthesizing Nurturance and Discipline for Optimal Child Development*, edited by Robert E. Larzelere, Amanda Sheffield Morris and Amanda W. Harrist (Washington, DC: American Psychological Association, 2013): 11-34.; Gottman and DeClaire, *Raising an Emotionally Intelligent Child.*

17. Alan Kazdin & Rotella (2013). *The Everyday Parenting Toolkit: The KAZDIN METHOD for Easy, Step-by-Step, Lasting Change for You and Your Child* (New York: Houghton Mifflin Co., 2013).

CHAPTER 19

1. Betsy Smith, Janet Surrey and Mary Watkins, "'Real' Mothers: Adoptive Mothers Resisting Marginalization and Recreating Motherhood," in *Adoptive Families in a Diverse Society*, edited by Katarina Wegar, (Piscataway, NJ: Rutgers University Press, 2006), 156.

2. Ibid.

3. Flynn, Welch and Paget, "Field Initiated Research"; Pamela Clark, Sally Thigpen and Amy Moeller Yates, "Integrating the Older/Special Needs Adoptive Child into the Family," *Journal of Marital and Family Therapy* 32, no. 2 (2006): 181-94.

4. Jocelyn Johnstone and Anita Gibbs, "'Love Them to Bits; Spend Time with Them; Have Fun with Them': New Zealand Parents' Views of Building Attachments with their Newly Adopted Russian Children." Small sample study in *Journal of Social Work* 12, no. 3 (2012): 225-45.
5. Clark, Thigpen and Moeller, "Integrating the Older/Special Needs Adoptive Child." Small sample study.
6. Jocelyn Johnstone and Anita Gibbs, "'Love Them to Bits." Small sample study.

CHAPTER 20

1. Karne Benzies and Richelle Mychasiuk, "Fostering Family Resiliency: A Review of the Key Protective Factors," *Child & Family Social Work*, 14, no. 1 (2009): 103-114.
2. James Garbarino, "Social Support Networks: Rx for the Helping Professions," in *Support Networks: Informal Helping in the Human Services*, edited by James Whittaker and James Garbarino (New York: Aldine de Gruyter, 1983), 3-28; Elizabeth M. Tracy and James Whittaker, "The Social Network Map: Assessing Social Support in Clinical Practice," *Families in Society*, 7, no. 8 (1990): 461-470.
3. Benjamin H. Gottlieb, "Marshalling Social Support: The State of the Art in Research and Practice," in *Marshalling Social Support: Format, Processes and Effects*, edited by Benjamin H. Gottlieb (San Francisco, CA:Sage, 1988), 11-51.
4. Gerald Caplan, *Support Systems and Community Mental Health: Lectures on Concept Development* (New York: Behavioral Publications, 1974); Lambert Maguire, *Social Support Systems in Practice* (Silver Springs, MD: National Association of Social Workers Press, 1991); Monrief Cochran and Jane Anthony Brassard, "Child Development and Personal Social Networks." *Child Development* 50, no. 3 (1979): 601-616.
5. Cochran and Brassard, "Child Development."
6. Victor Groza, *Successful Adoptive Families: A Longitudinal Study of Special Needs Adoption* (New York: Praeger, 1996).
7. Richard Louv, "Why Parents Need One Another," *Parents Magazine*, July (1993): 171-178.

CHAPTER 21

1. "You Don't Have to be Perfect to be a Perfect Parent," AdoptUSKids, accessed June 24, 2014, http://adoptuskids.org/for-the-media/help-raise -public-awareness.

CHAPTER 22

1. James, *Brothers and Sisters*.
2. Anda, "The Health and Social Impact."
3. Smith, "Keeping the Promise," http://adoptioninstitute.org/old/publications/ 2010_10_20_KeepingThePromise.pdf   http://adoptioninstitute.org/old/ publications/2010_10_20_KeepingThePromise.pdf.

CONCLUSION

1. North American Council on Adoptable Children, http://www.nacac.org/ parentgroups/value.html.